Vegas

and the

Chicago Outfit

Vegas and the Chicago Outfit

Copyright © 2022 Al W Moe

ISBN-13: ISBN: 9798353049210

BY AL W MOE

Vegas and the Mob

Nevada's Golden Age of Gambling

The Roots of Reno

Mob City: Reno

Stealing from Bandits

Getting Thin is Murder

Contents

Time Magazine / Public Domain

Time Magazine's March 1930 issue took Al Capone to new heights of notoriety for a voracious reading world to see.

Introduction

Chicago and The Outfit were late for the party in Las Vegas. Why bother with a town built on sand when you've got a stranglehold on the Windy City's politics and populace?

Al Capone was born in Brooklyn, New York, and only came to Chicago in 1919 to help Johnny Torrio, but Scarface was worth $100 million by 1927 as Organized Crime's first Rock Star. Newspapers dubbed him "Public Enemy No. 1."

His fall happened not because of the FBI (the Bureau of Investigation until 1935) but because federal authorities finally got angry and jealous enough of him to charge him with 22 counts of tax evasion. He was convicted of five counts in 1931.

As for the man entrusted to guard our country against the Mob, J. Edgar Hoover denied that the Mafia existed. He had plenty of good reasons for his ruse, including the facts that he couldn't beat the Mafia and that if he admitted there was such a group of coordinated gangsters who shared info, hitters, and money across state lines, he'd never get a wink of sleep. But there was more.

Hoover was an intelligent man, deeply flawed with self-image issues and self-protection needs, but smart. He knew if he took on a group of morally bankrupt, perversely crooked businessmen (like himself), then his agents would all get bribed.

What would keep a crook making $10,000 a week from slipping an agent (making $3,000 a year) a few Benji's to look the other way? And what would keep his agents from taking the cash?

Nothing, absolutely nothing. It worked with politicians, it worked with local police and sheriffs, and it worked with many reporters.

J. Edgar and the FBI were screwed, and that's the way the Mafia and the Chicago Outfit liked it.

FBI/United States Bureau of Prisons circa 1932 {{PD-USGov-FBI}}

Just two years later, Al Capone's record from the U.S. Federal Penitentiary in Atlanta, Georgia told a different story than Time Magazine's cover photo. Capone was sent to Alcatraz Federal Penitentiary in 1934 before being released in 1939. He died in 1946.

Chapter One

Early Chicago

Any way you look, Chicago was a tough go in the early 1900s. It was a mid-west metropolis, where tourists flocked in the summer to see twenty-story skyscrapers lording over blustery streets where the temperature could drop like a stone in minutes. Visitors were told in the Chicago and the Tourist handbook to "always bring a topcoat or a light wrap with him or her to Chicago, even in midsummer."

The city runs from the Indiana border at Hammond halfway across the state towards Wisconsin, never leaving the edge of Lake Michigan, a 345-mile-long delusion of splendor from an inland ocean that offers cooling breezes during the short summer and hammers the city incessantly with arctic thermals during the winter.

Calling Chicago, Illinois, the Windy City was a compliment for those living on beautiful Lake Shore Drive, but not for the downtrodden poor turning a sleet-wet collar to the ice crystals that blew through the dirty, crime-infested streets of the South Side's Little Hell.

Built on grit and ash, the city was leveled by the Great Chicago Fire of 1871 when flames jumped like fiery red devils in the night from one tinderbox structure to the next. German immigrants worked hard to reshape the landscape, and the melting-pots' demographics changed quickly from one oppressed ethnic group to the next as waves of newcomers found refuge in unheated, rat-infested clapboard shacks.

By the time the Sicilians arrived, it was a jumble of tenements bounded by North Chicago Avenue and Sedgwick and Halsted Streets. There were no streetlights, no police protection, and no hope for the weary masses.

Divided by the Chicago River into north and south branches, local divisions split the city further into North, South, and West Sides. The

Southsiders grew up with poverty, the stench of the Union Stock Yards, and thunderstorms that drenched inhabitants at least weekly from May through September when the rainfall turned to bitter-cold snow.

The Sicilians found themselves confined to rundown and dangerous trappings, especially for outsiders from marginalized but fought-over boundaries. Hunger, disease, and gangs were plentiful.

Shootings were so common that today's neighborhoods at Oak Street and Cleveland Avenue were then known as Death's Corner. Situated in the middle of Little Hell District, it was controlled by the Black Hand Society, which protected the impoverished residents but at a cost that left most merchants destitute.

"La Mano Nera," or The Black Hand, came from the old country, Italy, traced back to the 1750s and the Kingdom of Naples.

A simple drawing or black-ink smudge of a hand was all it took to get immigrants to pay off extortion demands. By the 1900s, the Black Hand was firmly entrenched in cities from New York and Philadelphia to New Orleans, San Francisco, Detroit, and Chicago. They distributed a plague of death over the nation's most vulnerable people.

Most practitioners were Sicilians, but Italian-Americans swore there was no connection to their families or heritage. Still, many of those same Italian Americans were victims, from demands for a few dollars each week from push-cart merchant earnings to thousands from successful businesspeople.

Those people received a letter demanding a specific dollar amount and a threat of violence, kidnapping, or even arson if a cash payment didn't follow the warning.

Often, the demands were met. When they weren't, victims were beaten, pets killed, and homes burned. City newspapers began using the term "Black Hand Letters" to amplify the violence perpetrated and generalized the idea of an organized criminal element in the US. Law enforcement, including (later) the FBI, refused for years to admit there was any such thing.

Renowned tenor Enrico Caruso was too frightened to ignore one such letter and paid a $2,000 extortion threat. After he admitted his deed, he got dozens more. One was suspiciously similar, asking this time for $15,000. Caruso reported the episode to the police and agreed to pay the cash at a predetermined drop.

This time, the perpetrators were taken down by several large policemen with guns and beaten with wooden batons. The false drop worked perfectly. Shortly after that, Big Jim Colosimo, a former Black Hander himself, was threatened with arson at his brothels if he didn't pay $10,000 immediately.

Born Vincenzo Colosimo (February 16, 1878 – May 11, 1920) in Palermo, Sicily, the boy moved with his parents to the Windy City. He ingratiated himself with the local alderman of the First Ward as a hard-working bootblack. The businessmen, "Hinky Dink" Michael Kenna and "Bathhouse" John Coughlin, took a shine to the kid and got him a job as a street sweeper. Colosimo cleaned up!

Within a few years, he owned a dozen brothels, one where his wife was the madam. By 1905 he was a big part of the nation's brothel capital with 50 houses of ill-repute. The fix was in, and so was Colosimo.

Working with Kenna and Coughlin, the young man learned how to dip his beak into the flow of cash the vice businesses in the Levee provided – any government license, permit, or utility the alderpersons could arrange for a fee.

By 1909, Colosimo had nearly 100 brothels, often stocked with white-slavery teenage girls lured to the Big City by promises of high-paying jobs and easy money. They were beaten, raped, and regularly drugged until their services were no longer needed if they lasted that long without dying of disease, being murdered, or taking their own life.

Many young ladies took to opium and laudanum, an alcohol and opium mixture sold at local pharmacies to treat headaches and menstrual cramps, or to overdose when the pressure, corruption, and heartbreak of their very existence became too much to endure for even one more breath. City managers and the police rarely noticed.

When Colosimo didn't pay the Black Hand letter carriers their $10,000 demand, they attacked him outside his home and gave him one last chance. The gun in his ear might have convinced him as he agreed to the payment a week later. Surprisingly, his wife Victoria offered another solution – her cousin, Johnny Torrio.

Torrio was born in southern Italy about the same time as Colosimo and was known to do a little Black Hand of his own. He then lived in Brooklyn, New York, and ran a bar called the Harvard Inn in Coney Island with fellow gangster Frankie Yale. The partners filled their pockets with extortion and graft cash, but he came to Chicago quickly by train after selling his saloon interest to Yale.

Torrio left the gang wars of New York for more of the same in Chicago, starting with Colosimo's little problem that he fixed by taking two shooters to meet the Black Handers in the Archer Avenue subway below the Rock Island tracks between Clark and LaSalle Streets. They hid in the shadows and ambushed the blackmailers with shotgun blasts that left two dead on the dirty concrete and one mortally wounded. You could say Torrio was a hit right off.

The wounded man was taken to a nearby hospital, where he regained consciousness and asked to see Jim Colosimo. Big Jim was summoned, arrived, and the dying man opened his eyes and sputtered, "Jim Colosimo, traitor, traitor," in Italian, and then faded quickly and died.

Torrio personally killed a dozen Black Handers during his first month in Chicago, but by then, the gangsters were buzzing around the city like flies at the stockyard. There were so many that he couldn't keep up.

The police finally got onboard and arrested more than 200 known Italian Black Hand extortionists, but no one was convicted, and they were all released back to the streets.

They did have some leaders, including Filippo Catalano, another southern Italian immigrant who spent most of his time drinking wine and extorting the masses. He moved with select business owners and city employees if they were powerful enough, but greed was his gift and his downfall.

His name was whispered among the locals, but none would have ever identified him. Not even John Jocko, who Catalano boldly shot outside a grocery and delicatessen at 1821 South State Street when the poor shopkeeper refused to hand over a $50-weekly "gift" from his shop that barely kept his family in rags.

Catalano was identified, and the victim miraculously survived, but he refused to finger his assailant as the shooter for prosecution. That seemed to gall Torrio more than the Black Hand tactics, and he disliked Filippo because of his seemingly invincible air and an increasingly large band of cohorts.

Something had to be done to turn the tide in Chicago for Colosimo, even as Torrio was shoring up the problems around the dirty, grimy streets. But was Big Jim severe enough to go all the way?

State Street, Chicago.

State Street Chicago circa 1910 – Public Domain

Chapter Two

No Booze - No Problem

Big Jim Colosimo was arguably the most successful brothel owner in the Windy City, but even he didn't scare the Black Handers. The ruthless blackmailers were often known to the police, but there were so many it seemed an entire squad of police or hitters from Big Jim's stables couldn't make an inroad to stop them. But Torrio kept trying.

On June 5, 1910, as Catalano strolled from the Vesuvius restaurant with his lawyer, Edgar K. Accetta, one of Torrio's hitters, Eugeno Monaco, drew a gun and shot Catalano five times. The lawyer's life was spared. He understood why and carefully told the police he didn't see the shooter's face. Life, and death, went on.

The Black Hand society was seemingly invincible, and victims paid a heavy price. In the first three months of 1911, thirty-eight people who refused or could not pay a demand for cash were killed by Black Hand assassins. Torrio kept his troops fighting back, but it was like shoveling

13

against Lake Michigan's tide.

At least one Chicago police officer was killed, and New Orleans lost Police Chief David Hennessy to the extortionists. In Little Italy, between Chicago's Oak Street and Milton Street, dozens of victims were killed by an unknown assassin with a dark, hooded face that neighborhood dwellers called Shotgun Man.

Still, in recognition of Torrio's hard work, Big Jim Colosimo finagled a low-ball purchase price for a four-story building at 2222 S. Wabash Avenue as the new headquarters for his right-hand man.

Torrio set up shop with a fancy saloon he dubbed the Four Deuces. Upstairs were offices, a not-so-fancy gambling joint, and the obligatory brothel where a twenty-minute ride with a lady of the evening ran two silver dollars.

Colosimo made a gift of the building after realizing that Torrio was invaluable to him. His murderous, cunning partner, John Donato Torrio, was born Donato Torrio (January 20, 1882 – April 16, 1957) in Basilicata, Southern Italy.

After his father was killed in a railway work accident, his mother packed up their meager belongings and caught a freighter to America. They settled into a one-bedroom apartment on James Street on the Lower East side of New York City, and his mother found work as a seamstress.

Torrio was slightly more refined than his classmates, but he listened in class and was quickly ahead of the children around him. His teachers considered him bright but quiet. His friends questioned his toughness until many older kids attacked them from across town. Although they were outnumbered and Torrio took a savage beating, he never stood down or ran from the fight, still wrestling with a much larger thumper when a pair of police officers started beating the boys with wooden batons to get them to stop.

A week later, he and his friend Robert Vanella joined a rival gang and quickly ascended to their leaders after several skirmishes to take back their tiny block of safe city ground. He and Vanella soon took jobs as bouncers in Manhattan saloons, and as soon as they had rolled enough drunks, they opened a pool joint with a small handbook in the back, taking bets on sporting events.

The gang members kept the place safe, and the boys loaned out cash at the going rate of 5% a week. A ten-dollar loan returned 50 cents a week in interest. Hundred-dollar loans got a lower rate but much heavier pressure from the gang members.

Instead of continuing with his gangland style, Torrio learned to finesse his growing group of business associates, able to establish an increasing cash flow from partnerships with nearly legal businessmen, one of whom was Paul Kelly, high-up in the Five Points Gang.

He brought Torrio into the fold to handle the gang's legitimate businesses. He was so impressed that Torrio was soon handling most of the shady stuff with his natural acumen for the numbers game, bookmaking, and loan sharking.

Turf wars were common, as were beatings for being in the wrong place at the wrong time. Members never traveled anywhere in the city alone. Safety was only available in numbers.

When Johnny's aunt Victoria contacted him from Chicago, he was ready to leave the fighting of New York and help his Uncle Jim with the Black Hand.

Eventually, the tide turned in Torrio's favor with the Black Hand Society as Colosimo's empire and police protection expanded across the city. Once they lost their preeminence and openness, their threats carried less weight.

Colosimo and Torrio blended a new Mafia-style way of doing

business. It was organized, it was vicious, and it was successful.

They considered it an insurance policy—a protection racket for people who couldn't go to the police. Gangsters, racketeers, burglars, and thieves had protection from outside gangs as long as they paid their insurance quota to Colosimo.

At first blush, ten percent of the take, or ten percent of your little restaurant's profit, seemed steep, but after having your plate glass windows smashed several times, the price was more palatable. You went along to get along.

Still, Colosimo was a champion of labor, so when the archenemy of unions, "Mossy" Enright was killed, Big Jim footed the bill for the four Italians rounded up and charged with his death. He even hired famed lawyer Clarence Darrow to represent them.

And then came Alphonse Capone, a tough as iron 19-year-old bouncer at a bar in New York. A bar in Coney Island, the Harvard Inn, where owner Frankie Yale kept in touch with Torrio for many years.

Alphonse Gabriel Capone (January 17, 1899 – January 25, 1947) joined the Five Points Gang in lower Manhattan and banged around the streets since he was six years old. After dozens of fistfights, he armed himself with a knife. Stabbed, sliced, and scarred, he had already killed two men when he was fingered for a bloody knifer and needed out of New York. Torrio told Yale he'd take care of him in Chicago.

Al Capone was 19 years old when he arrived in Chicago, but his new mentor, Johnny Torrio, had a job ready for the married Capone at a brothel.

Capone quit school at 14 after punching a female teacher in the face for demanding he stop talking. After working with Paul Kelly in the Five Points Gang, the athletic Capone played semi-pro baseball from 1916 to 1918. He went to work at Frankie Yale's bar in Coney Island after the 1918 season and married his girlfriend, Mae Josephine

Coughlin, in December, a month after they became parents of Sonny Capone (1918-2004).

Called "Snorky" by his friends because he was a snappy dresser, Capone was at work one night when he insulted a woman in the bar. Her brother, Frank Galluccio, pulled a knife and slashed Capone across the left side of his face three times.

His fellow bar mate stanched the bleeding with several bar rags, and a friend got Capone to the hospital, where it took dozens of stitches to close the wounds. The incident changed the happy "Snorky" nickname to "Scarface," a name Capone loathed with a passion.

After another fight where Capone was the aggressor with a knife, he and his wife moved to Chicago to work with Johnny Torrio. They were fast friends, with Johnny trusting Capone with bigger, better-paying jobs.

That didn't keep Capone out of the brothels, where he contracted syphilis. What kept Capone from being treated with Arsphenamine for his condition isn't known, but he may have ignored the first stages of itchy palms and rashes and moved quickly to a latent period and hoped he wasn't infected with the disease. Later diagnosis presented no chance for treatment.

Capone took to the power of his new position quickly. Still, the scars of knife fights and disease contributed to a menacing, despicable nature that took him through new phases in business, including bootlegging.

On December 18, 1917, the U.S. Senate proposed the Eighteenth Amendment to the Constitution of the United States – a National Prohibition Act that would ban the sale of alcohol. A year later, a temporary Wartime Prohibition Act was enacted and took effect on June 30, 1919. The effect was swift and sure. Alcoholic drinks with more than 1.28% alcohol content were a thing of the past, at least in a decent society.

Gangsters across the country saw a new way to make money with moonshine. After passing the Volstead Act, the U.S. government went even further on January 17, 1920, prohibiting all forms of alcohol. The country went dry. Bars went broke, and customers went crazy. Gangsters went to work.

Under Johnny Torrio's tutelage, Al Capone learned about the profits of running a speakeasy, where customers used passwords, connections, and cash to get served previously stored liquor and newly imported Canadian whisky.

Although Big Jim Colosimo was pragmatic about the effects of prohibition on his Chicago businesses, he was consumed with his marriage to his second wife, the beautiful and younger Dale Winter, who had come to Colosimo's Restaurant for a $40 a week engagement two years earlier and been swept-up by Big Jim's growing charm.

They eloped to West Baden Springs in French Lick, Indiana, just a few weeks after his uncontested divorce became final. When they returned, the heavily smitten Colosimo bought his new bride a home worth over $25,000 at 3152 Vernon Avenue.

He had worked hard to build an organized and financially secure business with plenty of political allies who happily took his weekly payoffs. That network of police and politicians gave Colosimo a false sense of security as he rebuffed Torrio's suggestions that by enacting the Volstead Act, the government was handing the Chicago Outfit the perfect business to get rich with – even better than the brothels, the gambling, and the loansharking.

At Torrio's suggestion, Colosimo spent nearly $34,000 updating and remanufacturing a brewery owned by Jake "Greasy Thumb" Guzik but chaffed at the idea of pushing so much booze that federal law enforcement might take action.

Torrio countered that the federal Prohibition agents, or Pro-highs, would be low-paid and easily influenced with a bit of cash. Colosimo and Torrio were at an impasse.

The big bosses, the Dons, needed strong underbosses and consigliere, but a history of those bosses becoming too powerful was dawning in Chicago.

Big Jim Colosimo circa 1920 – Public Domain

Chapter Three

Booze Wars in Chicago

Johnny Torrio called Big Jim Colosimo on May 11, 1920, about a special liquor shipment arriving at his restaurant. Hence, Colosimo got his hat and coat, told his new wife that he would see her later for dinner, and headed out.

Woolfson, his chauffeur, drove him downtown in his beautiful, highly polished Pierce-Arrow and waited outside. Inside, Colosimo asked porter Joe Gabrela if a shipment had arrived or anyone was looking for him. Gabrela shook his head and went back to work.

Colosimo returned to the foyer and looked out the window at the street but saw no new vehicles. When he turned to go back through the restaurant's inner door, a shadowy figure stepped forward from the right, pressed a .38 snub-nose revolver into the base of his neck, and fired twice.

One bullet went through his neck, and in settled in a phone booth inside the restaurant. The second lodged in the base of his brain.

Colosimo slumped to the floor, dead but still bleeding profusely. The chauffeur saw nothing, but the porter thought he caught a glimpse of the man hanging around earlier. He was 25 to 30 years old, about five-foot-eight inches, fat-faced and dark complexioned, and wearing a black derby hat, overcoat, patent leather shoes, and a white standup collar. He could have been anyone.

Colosimo's bookkeeper, Frank Camilla, heard the shots and found the body of Big Jim. Gabrela was in the kitchen. A doctor was summoned, police arrived, and State's Attorney Hoyne left the courthouse and hurried by taxicab to the restaurant. They were too late to help, but early enough to get some free but questionable press.

Dr. Cunningham provided little for the police besides mentioning powder burns on Colosimo's neck. The killer had hidden in the darkened foyer and waited for Big Jim to enter the small room. Had he been dining? There was a single guest in the café earlier, and the dishes had yet to be cleared. A crème pitcher was still moist.

If the killer stepped over the body, there was a small door hidden by a radiator he could have used to descend a set of stairs to the basement and escape into the alley behind the lower portion of the restaurant.

Lt. James J. McMahon took charge of the shooting scene while many other officers and detectives arrived. The police spent months running down clues and suspects, from ex-wife Victoria Colosimo, who was in Los Angeles at the time of the murder, to Arturo Fabri, the orchestra leader who brought the beautiful Dale Winter with him to Chicago. He was found in New York and offered to help find the killer.

Also in New York was Frankie Yale, who had been in Chicago at the time of the killing. The poor porter Joe Gabrela left work thinking he had helped by picking out a man named Frankie Yale from a book of mug shots. When the police took Gabrela to New York for a physical lineup, the now-schooled Gabrela said, "No, it's not him," and asked to be taken back to his home in Chicago.

When questioned, Colosimo's young bride said, "Big Jim had a heart of pure gold." The ladies of the evening he kept in veritable prison for years may have given him a more pungent description.

The police moved on but were perplexed by the ease with which his restaurant manager/partner Mike "The Greek" Potzin, handled his new responsibilities, even with a lack of cash on hand. Potzin told the police that he had seen Big Jim with stacks of $1,000 bills a week before. Where had they gone?

Although Colosimo had parted with $35,000 worth of jewelry when he divorced his wife and paid cash for his new wife's home, the only other assets the police found were inside his safety deposit boxes at two downtown banks.

When bank officers opened the boxes for the fluttering hearts of police and Rocco Steffano, Big Jim's longtime friend and attorney, they found hundreds of small IOUs from business patrons and $28,000 in Liberty bonds.

Everything else was in the hands of Torrio and Capone – a building, a gang of well-trained and motivated thugs, and the keys to dozens of brothels, bookie joints, and gambling halls. Little changed with Big Jim's political connections and the smoothly sanded weekly payoff system still intact. The new bosses of The Outfit had the keys to the city.

But first, a big blowout ceremony had to be thrown for Big Jim. One that included judges, alderman, members of Congress, and state legislators at Colosimo's home. Torrio paid all the expenses.

Later, hundreds of well-wishers followed Big Jim's hearse to Oakwood cemetery and watched as the custom-made $10,000 silver and mahogany casket was taken away.

Torrio moved easily into Colosimo's spot as the head of a growing and powerful business with honest and not-so-honest businesses making The Outfit the first actual crime organization.

They worked closely with everyone with money and connections, from "Jew Kid" Grabiner, brother of Chicago White Sox baseball executive Harry Grabiner, to Dennis Cooney.

Capone was given Torrio's old spot as second lieutenant and underboss. He reveled in his new position, always ready to butt heads with encroaching gangs. He personally saw to the death of any interlopers even as Torrio tried to negotiate pacts along the way.

By the end of summer, Chicago had hundreds of beer joints and speakeasies filled with enthusiastic, thirsty patrons 24 hours a day. The money coming in was phenomenal. As the liquor stored away began to dwindle, Jake Guzik's factory took up some of the slack, and Torrio and Capone worked daily with suppliers in Ohio and Detroit. Any places along the Great Lakes waterway and the canals had safe delivery steps ahead of the Pro-highs.

Capone spent his cash on a home at 7244 South Prairie Avenue in the Park Manor neighborhood - $5,500, when you could buy a new Ford for $500 – and touted himself as a boxing promoter, which he was, briefly in 1923, trying to shield himself from his various crimes.

Vegas and the Chicago Outfit

In May, new Chicago Police Chief Morgan Collins said he would smash vice, reduce crime, and abolish gambling. He sent his officers into the streets with orders to "arrest the vermin who are plaguing our city." 900 arrests were made in the last week of April and another 600 on the 6th of May.

The next day, Capone had competitor Joe Howard killed after he tried to hijack a load of Torrio-Capone bootleg beer. Police presence or not, it was no time for accommodation or weakness.

The Torrio-Capone syndicate was a two-headed snake brewing beer, importing whiskey, imprisoning young girls in brothels, breaking the arms of slow-paying loan shark borrowers, and killing anyone who tried to interrupt their happy clan of mostly Italian mobsters.

The Opposing Gangs

On the far side of town, the North Side Gang of more mixed ethnicity (although heavily Irish) was getting pushed around by the Genna brothers. The NSG's leader, Dean (Dion) O'Banion, knew the Genna's were allied with Torrio and fought hard to keep what they had worked, sweated, and killed for.

O'Banion could often be found at his flower shop at 738 North State Street across from the Holy Name Cathedral, up to his lapels in floral arrangements. Local wartime revenues were substantial, and his shop quickly did $1,000 in flower sales the day of a funeral, and there were dozens of funerals of wise and not so wise guys in Chicago every month.

Mourners on funeral day expressed their grief with bouquets. Later, they expressed their grief with bullets, but that was Chicago.

O'Banion and Torrio owned the city's largest brewery together, and one night a couple of flatfoots came asking for cash. It was a setup, with a tapped phone at O'Banion's home connected to police headquarters. When the brewery manager told O'Banion the officers wanted $300 to go away, O'Banion said, "Three hundred dollars, to them bums? What say I pay half that to have them bumped off?" and hung up.

The police, knowing O'Banion could quickly get $300 into action and have the officers killed, sent in another squad to save them. But in the meantime, from the same tapped phone, the brewery manager called Torrio, who said, "Oh, we don't want any trouble; give them the $300."

O'Banion wasn't happy with that arrangement and decided to sell his share of the Sieben brewery to Torrio. They arrived at a $500,000 price, Torrio paid, and on the last day of their deal, a police raid took everyone on the premises to jail, including O'Banion and Torrio.

O'Banion had no prohibition convictions and was released. Torrio did have convictions and was held and tried. He was frustrated until he got the truth – O'Banion knew the raid was coming. Then Torrio was livid.

O'Banion refused to give Torrio his $500,000, and Torrio looked the other way as the Gennas moved into the North Side Gang's territory.

At his flower shop on November 10, 1924, O'Banion greeted what he thought were three friendly flower buyers - Frankie Yale, John Scalise, and Albert Anselmi. When O'Banion shook Yale's hand, the New Yorker grabbed his wrist with his left hand, and Anselmi and Scalise stepped forward and fired five shots. Two in the chest, three in the neck and cheek. Anselmi then leaned forward to the prostate O'Banion and fired a final shot into his other cheek to be sure.

O'Banion got the finest funeral the city had ever seen, with ten times the flowers, pomp, and circumstance Colosimo had received. The townsfolk grieved, although nobody was sure just why.

Torrio left Capone in charge and went on the lam. O'Banion's loyal henchmen found him in Hot Springs, Arkansas, but he was safely guarded, so they waited.

His next stop was Havana, Cuba, and finally, St. Petersburg, Florida. When he returned to Chicago, Capone told him there had been six ambushes and at least twenty of their and the North Side Gang's members hit by gunfire. Several were dead. Otherwise, everything was fine, and business was booming. Christmas passed without incident.

But O'Banion's killing kept coming up in Hymie Weiss's throat like bitter bile consumed him. He sent men to watch Capone, but he was securely secluded in hotel rooms with bodyguards loaded for an ambush in the rooms beside him.

Finally, just after the new year, Weiss had a chance to take out Capone, and he was attacked with gunfire but left unhurt, so Weiss turned his attention back to Torrio and waited and waited.

And then Torrio took a breath. With his bodyguards at bay, he walked towards his doorstep from his chauffeured car on January 24th and was met with a fusillade of bullets that left him gasping for breath before the shooters scattered into the wind.

Years later, there was scuttlebutt that the hit came from inside – from Capone – employing some of the 42 gang (the 42s were from the Patch and worked with Esposito) members that might have included Sam "Mooney" Giancana and Leonard "Needles" Gianola. True or not, the guard was changing.

The hit on Chicago's richest and most powerful vice purveyor was not surprising, but it was still shocking. And through it, all: a shattered jaw, decimated collar bone, punctured lung, and clipped ear, Torrio was lucid and demanding at the hospital.

He hissed through a bloodied mouth missing bone, muscle, and teeth that he wanted his wounds cauterized because the bullets used were most certainly boiled in poison to cause death or at least gangrene.

He lived, but only because his hospital room was never without bodyguards, and Torrio immediately agreed to have his previous sentence for bootlegging started. Assistant state's attorney John Sbarboro asked Torrio if he knew who had shot him. His response was, "Yes, and it's my business. I'll tell you later."

Sbarboro turned to Torrio's wife, Anna, and asked her the same question. She responded, "Yes, but I'm not going to help you. What good would that do?"

Capone, who wasn't present, and the chauffeur, who took a bullet through the knee, also kept quiet. The only witness to talk was a 17-year-old neighbor, Peter Veesaert, who gave a statement and fingered George "Bugs" Moran from a line-up.

"Bugs" was held for a day before Judge William J. Lindsay slapped him gently with a $5,000 bond, and he skipped away, never bothered by the police again.

In February, Torrio was taken to jail in Waukegan, where his caretakers furnished his cell with a thick rug, new bed, a rocker, bulletproof shading over the windows, and employed two extra deputy sheriffs in the hallway.

When Torrio's time as a jailbird ended, so did his direct connection to Chicago's beer wars. He was in the wind for years, leaving Capone fully entrenched with the gangland style of business that Chicago was now known for.

The Chicago Daily News said Torrio was allied to one Joseph Stenson, who bankrolled his breweries and provided "the silk hat to the crowd and the avenues into the federal building." It also estimated that Torrio's gang of hitmen, drivers, brewers, truckers, and salesmen took a $25,000 weekly payroll from a $50 million business split several ways.

From 1922 to 1926, Chicago gangland killings reached 215 dead.

During the same period, Chicago police gunned down another 160 "known" gang members. The fun was starting!

Downtown Chicago during Prohibition circa 1920s – Public Domain

Chapter Four

Al Capone Takes Control

While Capone started as a brothel manager, so had Harry Guzik (Jake "Greasy Thumb's" brother). Harry and his wife Alma ran a 30-girl dive called the Roamer Inn in Posen, Cook County. They were expected to produce a $9,000 monthly profit and share at least half with Johnny Torrio.

They were convicted in 1921 of white slavery for running ads for maids and putting country girls to work as prostitutes. In 1923, Governor Len Small pardoned them before their sentence started, and they returned to work as pimps.

They moved next to a new bawdy house in Cicero, where Capone was running a brewery. That and dozens of bars, saloons, brothels, and gambling houses. Even the bars and roadhouses had slot machines from local Chicago manufacturers like Watling, and nobody cared.

The police tried to make a dent, but the Capone and Weiss outfits were like steel.

Hymie Weiss - shortened from Waiceichowski - helped boozedom to the day when it ran distilleries and ships instead of risking life and limb on warehouse robberies searching for booze. And he enriched himself and his North Side Gang members with extortion, numbers, prostitution, and gambling.

Newspapers reported that he was ugly, especially when he threatened to kill photographers for taking his picture. Still, he carried a gun he could wave as he wanted since he had been deputized as a sheriff. He once pointed a shotgun at a US Marshall serving a warrant to search his apartment for violation of the Mann Act – white slave kidnapping, but the Marshall had backup, and Weiss relented. His flat yielded knockout drops, booze, handcuffs, sawed-off shotguns, and revolvers. Instead of being embarrassed, Weiss sued the state for the loss of his silk shirts and socks that were never returned.

Weiss and Moran were certain Torrio and Capone authorized the killing of O'Banion, so they tried to kill both Capone and Torrio. In retaliation, Capone sent hitters to the Standard Oil Building on Michigan Avenue and 9th Street on August 26th to knockout Vincent Drucci. Just as Weiss had missed Capone, his men missed Drucci.

Weiss and Drucci responded on September 26 with another try at Capone with machine guns from moving automobiles which swept in front of the Hawthorne Hotel where Capone kept council – behind steel-shuttered windows – and blasted more than 1,000 shells into the building. Capone was unhurt.

The police tried to take charge of the streets, and in June of 1925, there were 50 raids and 320 suspects arrested. Suspects were beaten, cuffed, and taken away in paddy wagons. It took specially-enforced trucks to carry away the shotguns, rifles, and knives impounded, not to mention the more than 10,000 gallons of alcohol. The Genna brothers were in business with Capone by then, importing hundreds of Italians like so many cans of olive oil to operate their businesses.

So, Weiss took to the streets again, and the North Side Gang turned their murderous vengeance on the Genna brothers – a clan of six siblings whom Weiss knew had planned the killing of O'Banion for their attack on Genna's bootlegging operation. After waiting in the early dawn and late night for two days, "Bugs," Moran chased Angelo Genna in a high-speed car race through the streets of Chicago and shot him to death. In June, Mike Genna was gunned down by police after they joined a gun battle with the North Siders. The following month, Antonio Genna took a dozen bullets in another gun battle. Brothers Jim, Pete, and Sam took the heavy hint and skipped town.

Of course, things were tough all over. Even politicians and their friends were targets. Diamond Jim Esposito dabbled in the rackets and later, with bootleggers, had a spot on Senator Deneen's platform as a ward committeeman. He was threatened by both racketeers and reformers while a proponent of the Genna brother's murderous siege.

Alderman Joe Powers had a bomb thrown into his home. Two days later, court bailiff Paul Labriola was shot and killed, as was Harry Raimondi – both lieutenants of Alderman Powers. Later, another ward leader, Anthony D'Andrea, was killed, as was Joseph Laspisa. Diamond Jim attended both funerals of D'Andrea and Laspisa, but that didn't soothe the hurt felt by bootleggers angry with him for not convincing his boss, senator Deneen, to stop trying to shut down the bootleggers.

So, Capone sent a few hitters to give Esposito "the talk." While walking down the street with his two bodyguards (Ralph and Joseph Varchetto) at his side, three killers pumped 50 shotgun pellets into his body, including a final double-barreled blast as he lay face down on the sidewalk. His bodyguards did not return any gunfire and were unhurt by the multiple blasts. They were also unable to identify the shooters. Capone was too strong. No sense getting dead over a fight with the king.

As Al Capone was cementing his legacy as the most powerful man in Chicago, he organized what John Torrio had left him into squads with lieutenants in charge of specific boroughs and districts. Income from all racketeering operations funneled through a group of captains, and the money made its way to businesses owned by even more businesses Capone controlled but never touched.

State Attorney Crowe and Chief of Police Collins revved up their engines after killing four police officers in one week, including Harold Olson and Charles B. Walsh, on Saturday when Mike Genna was killed.

The State Attorney's office sent 20 squads out to raid roadhouses in Cicero, and still, they couldn't stop Capone. They had little success with his underlings, but some charges were eventually filed, and Scalize and Ansellmo got indicted for the murder of two police detectives. The first trial was scuttled. A second trial ended in acquittal for "defending themselves against police aggression."

Before the third trial, a witness, Officer Sweeny, was threatened by phone. Later his home was bombed. Crowe's office had shots fired into it after Crowe told the press he believed Scalize and Ansellmo were also O'Banion's killers.

A vast defense fund was collected by friends of the defendants (Capone gang members) – with threats of violence if one did not contribute. Violence was no exaggeration, and eight people connected to the collections (contributors and refusers) were killed. The irony fell on blind eyes and deaf ears.

Franis Zolfano, a bookkeeper for Genna's gang, was subpoenaed, and, in his deposition, he stated the brothers paid $48,000 each month for police protection. The statement made the papers.

Vegas and the Chicago Outfit

On March 10th, two witnesses swore Mike Genna fired on officers Olsen and Walsh first before Scalize and Ansellmo fired on the officers, killing them both. Still, they were acquitted. Some lives went on, and others ended.

At 4 o'clock on October 11, '26, five men emerged from an automobile on Superior Street – Hymie Weiss, Patrick Murray, W. W. O'Brian, Patrick H. O'Donnell, and Sam Peller. Weiss was hit with ten bullets, Murray seven. They both died on the spot. The others were injured but escaped eight doors down to a doctor's office. Terrified passersby continued on their way, seeing nothing they would ever admit to a coroner's inquest.

Officers found a crow's nest above the North Side Gang's hideout. Inside they found Thompson machine guns (Tommy guns) and dozens of empty .45 caliber shells mixed with hundreds of cigarette butts. The shooters had long waited for their quarry in that apartment above Weiss's lair – the same place O'Banion took his music.

On Weiss's body was found $5,300 and a list of all the men recently called for jury service in the trial of Joe Saltis, charged with killing "Mitters" Foley, a Capone crew member. Found in the Weiss safe was a list of all state witnesses set to testify against Saltis. The corruption and hypocrisy ran deep as a well. Saltis was later found not guilty.

At the inquest, Weiss's brother said of the crumpled body, "sure, it's him, but I ain't seen him but twice in 20 years, and the last time was six years ago when he shot me." Only "Bugs" Moran missed Weiss.

St. Valentine's Day Massacre

On February 14, 1929, Chicago was the site of an even more appalling, lurid display of murder than it had become accustomed to seeing. On an otherwise calm day involving what appeared to be several relaxed and serene police officers on casual duty, seven men were lined up and shot.

The newspapers reported that all seven victims were facing an interior garage wall of the S. M. C. Cartage Company at 2122 N. Clark Street on the Northside. Four were standing; three were seated. The situation suggests that there was some relaxation by those murdered and that perhaps they had assumed some interrogation would transpire – perhaps it did.

Either the assailants (Police or posing as police) had asked questions and gotten what they wanted or didn't. Either way, they opened up with machine guns and shotguns, filling the garage with hot lead and smoke and sending shattered bones, clothing, and concrete into the air and surrounding the now-slumping bodies.

Six members of "Bugs" Moran's gang were killed—most of his domain's upper echelon – and just a tiny part of what was once Hymie Weiss and previously Dean O'Banion's mob. Also killed were Moran's brother-in-law, James Clark, and a doctor friend of the mob, R. H. Schwimmer.

The papers predicted that the hit was retaliation for a series of liquor heists pulled by the group against Detroit's Purple Gang. That was an interesting tact since the truth was that the gang had hijacked several liquor trucks from the Detroit area, but those trucks were filled with Capone's liquor and heading to Detroit, not the other way around.

Later it was learned that Moran had a phone call the day before, offering a newly hijacked truck for purchase. A price was met, and the truck was due to arrive at 10:30 am.

Instead, those arriving were killers from Capone's crew, but they were there for retaliation – the latest move by Weiss against Capone – and they assumed Moran would be at the garage. It appears North Sider Al Weinshank was misidentified as Moran before the killing started.

Frank "Goosey" Gusenberg survived the shooting and was taken to the hospital, wherein true gangster fashion, he refused to identify the shooters who became killers minutes later when he died. "Bugs" Moran famously missed the massacre, having slept in due to a cold.

Al Capone got questioned, but he had been in Florida the day of the hit. No one was ever convicted of the crime.

Moran held on to his diminishing gang for a few more years before retiring from the area. He was later convicted of conspiracy to cash $62,000 worth of American Express checks – nearly broke after being one of Chicagoland's richest gangsters.

He was jailed for two years in 1944, released, and jailed again until 1956. Upon release, he was jailed a third time for bank robbery and died of lung cancer in 1957 while serving his sentence in Leavenworth Federal Penitentiary in Kansas.]

The decade of Capone and the '20s ended with more murders and sensational trials. The Capone kingdom took a severe hit when their headquarters at 2446 South Michigan Avenue was raided. Loose-leaf ledgers showed profits and cost systems for bawdy houses in Burnham and elsewhere, connections for booze from Rum Row of New York harbor to Miami, Florida, and dents and indentations of sales and purchases in Cleveland, Cincinnati, Steubenville, Covington, and Detroit.

Johnny Patton, a higher-up on the headquarters list of accountants, offered Police Sergeant Edward Birmingham $5,000 to forget the bookkeeping system. He declined.

As the new decade emerged, Al Capone spent time at his villa on the water in Florida. His days as a free man were numbered, but his bravado and bluster may have deceived everyone, including himself.

Still, he knew his organization was bleeding cash as the Great Depression started to take hold. Any downturn hurts when you've got a weekly payroll of $25,000 and a monthly graft payment budget of twice that going out the door. A fifty-percent drop in revenue is an enterprise crusher, and Capone was getting crushed. He took his frustrations out on his competition.

Giuseppe "Joey" Aiello and his brothers Salvatore "Sam" and Pietro "Peter" pushed their way into the booze-induced frenzy of brewing, shipping, and money-grubbing that came with the rackets by declaring themselves bosses of the old Genna brother's brewery distributors.

Joey was in charge, and as his kingdom grew on the North Side, he pushed across Madison Street into Capone territory and forced saloons and shops to carry his beer with threats – and actual instances – of beatings and bombings. When his movement into the wrong territory reached Al Capone's ears, he sent gunners to set a trap for him.

When Joey left a known hideout on October 24, 1930, two sets of machine gunners caught him in a crossfire. More than 30 bullets entered his back, one went through his left eye, and another shot a right toe away. According to the deputy coroner, his right leg was broken in two places from the bullets – 62 in the dead gangster's body.

Perhaps Capone was cranky because he was then involved in an actual court proceeding after having a series of "snot-nosed college boys" dig into his business records that were confiscated in a raid, or because his brother, Ralph "Bottles" Capone, was serving a three-year sentence for income tax evasion. Hmmm.

Much of his court proceedings were based on a 1927 Supreme Court ruling in the United States v. Sullivan that illegally earned income was subject to income tax.

Afterward, the Treasury and Justice Departments made plans for income tax prosecutions against Chicago gangsters. An elite crew of Prohibition Bureau agents, including Eliot Ness, headed to the Windy City. In writing for the *Chicago Daily News*, Charles Schwarz called the Untouchables.

Al Capone was first arrested on March 27, 1929, by Bureau of

Investigation agents. Things spiraled out of control afterward as his regular use of graft and bribes brought only more indictments.

Eventually, on the lucky 13th of June 1931, a Federal Grand Jury indicted 67 known Capone operatives for violating liquor laws. Capone also drew contempt of court charges and an IRS summons for more than $200,000 in taxes he tried to evade.

In producing an unbeatable series of raps, the jury leveled 19 separate overt acts. The purchase of his beer trucks was even traced to Betz Motors in Hammond, Indiana – and the money used was traced to money deposited in accounts his company controlled from buyers his company also controlled.

Three days later, Capone pleaded guilty to income tax evasion and 5,000 violations of the Volstead Act. It was part of a 2.5-year prison sentence plea bargain, but Judge James Herbert Wilkerson rejected the plea deal, and a trial for income tax evasion began.

He was convicted on five counts (five years' worth of tax records) of income tax evasion at age 33. He entered the Atlanta U.S. Penitentiary in May of 1932. He was transferred to Alcatraz Federal Penitentiary, better known as The Rock, since it sat alone in the middle of San Francisco Bay and had never had a successful escape in 1934.

His business and organizational skills were of no use to him in prison, but he left Chicago's crime scene to his second underboss, Paul "The Waiter" Ricca, for six months.

Underboss Frank Nitti also drew a prison sentence for tax evasion. When his 18 months were up at Leavenworth in March of 1932, Nitti took control of The Outfit and began moving muscle from prostitution and gambling into unions and extortion via the unions.

Ricca continued to command respect and worked as an emissary to other mob groups, including Lucky Luciano's Five Families in New York.

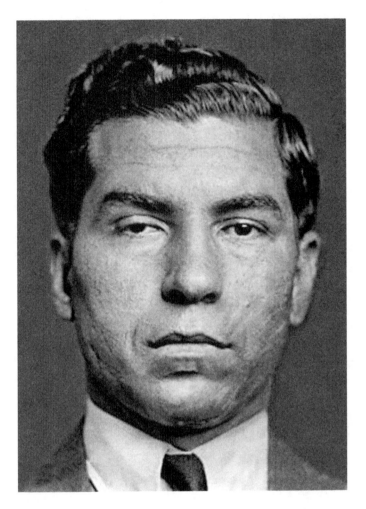

Charles "Lucky" Luciano circa 1936 - New York Police Department / Public Domain

Chapter Five

Chicago's Hot - Lucky Luciano Takes New York

Salvatore Lucania was born in Lercara Friddi, Sicily, Italy.

Vegas and the Chicago Outfit

(November 24, 1897 – January 26, 1962) He moved to the United States with his parents, three brothers, and a sister in 1906. Like gang member Al Capone, he dropped out of school at 14 to earn a living, and like Capone, he had a low-paying job but happily quit to scarf up the money to be made in the underworld.

He was soon known as "Lucky" Luciano because the press got his name wrong, and he joined the Five Points gang with later gangland stars Johnny Torrio, Al Capone, Meyer Lansky, and Benjamin Siegel.

According to legend, Lucky met Lansky as the boy walked home from school. He offered to protect him, as he did for dozens of other Jewish kids, for 10 cents a week. Lansky offered to kick his ass for free, and the two became lifelong friends.

While Johnny Torrio was running the booze and broads in Chicago's South Side in the early '20s, Luciano was doing the same in Lower Manhattan. When push came to shove, as it always does in the underworld, Lansky hired dozens of hitters like Siegel, Lansky, and Joey Adonis to give him that added push when needed.

Siegel and Lansky were already running booze in Brooklyn and took sides early with Luciano to solidify their territory. "Lucky" may have gotten his nickname for being arrested 20 times between 1916 and 1928 and never spending time in jail.

The start of Prohibition gave New York's gangs (as well as those in all other major US cities) the perfect leverage to take a few dollars and some sugar, add heat, and deliver dollars to police and politicians and booze to happy customers for more than a decade. The money made was otherworldly. The gang said you could throw silver dollars into the East River until all of Brooklyn flooded, and it still wouldn't be as much silver as they were making every week. I believe it.

In 1925, when former Coney Island bar owner Johnny Torrio quit the Chicago beer wars and left for Europe, he left The Outfit, which was grossing $50,000,000 a year. That's about a billion dollars in today's money.

Torrio got pressure in Italy when Benito Mussolini pushed the Italian Mafia for cash. He returned to a relatively safe New York, met with old friends Yale and Lucky Luciano, and convinced them to ally with Longy Zwillman, Joey Adonis, Meyer Lansky, Bugsy Siegel, and Frank Costello to coordinate their nefarious businesses.

Luciano was already leaning in that direction, having learned business systems from heavy-hitter Arnold Rothstein and getting a toehold in high society. Rothstein bankrolled Luciano in an early bootlegging operation for half the profit. Luciano chose Frank Costello and Vito Genovese as his partners.

In May 1929, Luciano and Torrio met with the heads of several families in Atlantic City. Those in attendance included New York associates Bugsy" Siegel, Frank Costello, Joe Adonis, Albert Anastasia, Frank Scalise, Louis Buchalter, and Dutch Schultz; Gambino crime family boss Vincent Mangano; Chicago boss Al Capone; Atlantic City bosses Nucky Johnson and Abner Zwillman; and Rothstein associate bookmaker Frank Erickson.

They agreed that an interconnected national association sharing products, information, and hitters would be good. After all, business was booming, and although Luciano was grossing more than $12 million per year and taking home a third of that, he still needed to be part of a larger mob to stay in business.

At the time, Luciano was a significant producer for his boss, Giuseppe "Joe the Boss" Masseria (January 17, 1886 – April 15, 1931), who was making millions in bootlegging, extortion, and loansharking throughout New York. Joe the Boss operated with impunity but kept smart and dangerous underlings like Frank Costello and Lucky Luciano around to keep him safe. Joey Adonis and Albert Anastasia were also on the payroll to keep the Salvatore Maranzano and Joseph Bonanno group at bay. In that sense, no one was in charge, and no one was safe. Luciano had plans.

Those plans got a jump-start when a load of Masseria's bootleg liquor got hijacked by the Castellamarreses, a well-organized group with many allies. When Maranzano took over the family, they were allied with Buffalo (Boss Stefano Magaddino), Detroit (Boss Gaspar Milazzo), Philadelphia (Boss Salvatore Sabella), and the Bronx (Boss Gaetano Reina).

Maranzano also wanted to take control of New York's families and hated Masseria's demands for tributes from the local groups. When Gaspar Milazzo in Detroit and Gaetano Reina in the Bronx were murdered, all roads led to Masseria's doorstep. The Castellamarreses War had begun.

As both sides took to the mattresses and waited to pounce, gangsters continued to die. Alberta Anastasia, Joey Adonis, and Lucky Luciano agreed to turn their alliance to Masseria to end the bloodshed and perhaps more. Bugsy Siegel was on board too.

On Tax Day, April 15, 1931, Joe the Boss Masseria sat playing cards at Nuova Villa Tammaro on Coney Island with Lucky Luciano. When Luciano went to the can, Adonis, Vito Genovese, Anastasia, and Siegel entered the restaurant and emptied their guns on the surprised and soon very dead Masseria.

Anastasia flopped a coat over a chair and joined the others in the getaway car parked at the curb with Ciro "The Artichoke King" Terranova at the wheel. Still, nothing happened. Terranova was momentarily frozen, so Siegel pushed him aside and drove the shooters to a safe house.

Although Luciano was picked up for questioning, the police were also looking for John "Silk Stockings" Giustra, whose coat was found at the murder scene. Luciano walked. Giustra was found dead a month later, and the case was dropped.

In the meantime, Maranzano declared himself capo di tutti capi, the boss of all bosses, and organized the Italian American gangs into Five Families. Their boundaries and business interests were rearranged to favor himself heavily.

The new families were headed by himself Vincent Mangano, Lucky Luciano, Tommy Gagliano, and Joseph Profaci. Instead of being organized, the families were just shackled by Maranzano into easily controlled groups. None of the bosses were happy, and Maranzano knew it. He also knew Luciano was the smartest and decided to take him out and appoint an ally to his family group.

The Gagliano family's underboss, Thomas Gaetano Lucchese, heard Vincent "Mad Dog" Coll had been ordered to kill Luciano and, as a friend, alerted him. When Maranzano ordered Costello, Genovese, and Luciano to come to his office at 230 Park Avenue in Manhattan, Lucchese arrived with four unknown Jewish gangsters provided by Bugsy Siegel.

The first two gangsters identified themselves and took Maranzano's bodyguard's guns, then the other two stepped forward and stabbed the boss repeatedly. Then the bodyguard's guns were used to shoot Maranzano to prove a point.

Days later, other Luciano's hitters served notice on Samuel Monaco and Louis Russo that their boss was dead. They were tortured for information on other Manzano allies before their bodies were thrown into Newark Bay. At the same time, Joseph Siragusa, the Boss of the Pittsburg crime family, was killed in his kitchen.

Luciano called a truce with the other New York families, and his agents arranged a Chicago meeting with bosses from across the country, where he initiated the idea of a supreme Commission to rule what would become organized crime – calling for peace, cooperation, and shared resources.

Vegas and the Chicago Outfit

The Five Families of New York representative may have held slightly more power initially, but Luciano was accepted as the Commission's boss. Also included were families from Buffalo, Philadelphia, Detroit, and the Chicago Outfit.

No family was left out if they wanted in, but those with less muscle were grouped under existing families. Virtually all were run by Italian American bosses, although Lansky first represented a New York Jewish criminal organization group that splintered into several smaller factions as the years passed.

Luciano maintained several essential Italian imports, most notably the law of omerta, to keep the families from being apprehended by the police or prosecuted for their crimes. He also insisted with friend Vito Genovese that only Italians with a bloodline (and a family line to the old country) could be "made men."

Genovese was certain that obedience was easier to obtain when their Young Turks had rituals to adhere to and goals to obtain. It worked.

Young enforcers were paid $50 a week, while a common laborer was paid 40 cents an hour. That common laborer made do with $16 bucks a week and bought milk for 50 cents a gallon, eggs for 45 cents a dozen, and sugar for 6 cents a pound if he could find it. The damn bootleggers were buying it up at any cost to make booze.

On the other hand, the enforcers had the money for steak dinners that cost less than a buck and cigars that were still a nickel. If they did a good job and were part of a crew, their salary rose as high as sixty to ninety dollars a week. If they were doing heavy work, dishing out beating, and an occasional killing, their stipend was raised as high as $125 weekly, about 25% of what the average American was making in a year.

And what would they be doing? Anything the bosses asked, like getting rid of Mad Dog Coll, whom Maranzano paid $25,000 to kill Lucky

Luciano. He was supposed to hit Tommy Luchesse first, but he showed up late to his meeting with Maranzano, only arriving after the boss was killed. Dutch Schultz was so incensed that he and Owney Madden offered a $50,000 contract for Coll's head.

When four hitters arrived at Coll's Bronx apartment, gunshots filled the air, but only Coll gangsters Emily Tanzillo, Fiorio Basile, and Patsy Del Greco were killed. Three others were wounded, but once again, the target didn't show up until later, after the ambush.

Coll was lucky, but $50,000 was a lot of incentive. A week later, two shooters caught up with Coll in a drug store at Eighth Avenue and 23rd Street in Manhattan. They found their quarry in a phone booth.

One man stayed in the getaway vehicle while the other two entered the drug store. Seeing Coll was on the phone, one stepped out to the street while "Tough" Tommy Protheroe told the cashier to "Keep cool, now" and pulled his Tommy gun from inside his overcoat and opened fire.

Coll's body was taken to the coroner, who said he found two dozen bullets in the outlaw. Dutch Schulz sent a final farewell to Coll's funeral with a floral wreath bearing a big yellow banner that read "From the Boys."

For his trouble, Dutch Schultz, who started life as Arthur Simon Flegenheimer (August 6, 1901 – October 24, 1935), was given more leeway and a special place on the Commission. At least, that's what he thought.

Unfortunately for Schultz, his future was going to be tied up with court dates and publicity as law enforcement agencies (including the revenue department) fought over who would reign supreme in bringing him down. Special Prosecutor appointed by New York City Mayor Fiorello LaGuardia had an inside track, but the first trial ended in a deadlock.

Vegas and the Chicago Outfit

Schultz's lawyers had the second trial venue move to tiny Malone, New York, where Schultz promptly moved. Then, Dutch spent so much money on charitable causes in the town that everyone loved him when it came time for trial. He was acquitted.

Mayor LaGuardia and Dewey told Schultz he would be arrested again for additional charges, so Dutch asked for a meeting with the Commission. At the conference, Schultz insisted that he be allowed to kill Dewey, taking it under advisement.

After deliberation, the Commission noted that the assassination would bring an unprecedented crackdown on all their businesses and voted unanimously against Schultz. Dutch took the news as well as a crazed killer could: he said he would kill Dewy anyway.

Schultz mulled over his options, finally deciding that his best chance was to have Albert Anastasia keyhole Dewey's apartment building on Fifth Avenue and keep track of when he arrived home at night. Schultz wasn't as brilliant as he was deranged, and Anastasia passed the plan on to Luciano.

A new meeting of the Commission was convened, and everyone agreed that Dutch Schultz had to go. Louis Buchalter was told to get rid of the Dutchman.

On October 23, 1935, Schultz went to a meeting with his accountant and two bodyguards at the Palace Chophouse at 12 East Park Street in Newark, New Jersey. It was a quiet place with good veal chops. After lying low for months and staying out of the papers, Dutch was happy to be out.

When dinner was finished, Schultz hit the restroom, and Charles Workman hit him with a gunshot to the chest. The Dutchman went down immediately. Two other shots missed him, but Workman was a thinking killer and had soaked his bullets in water for days, making them rusty, so even if the bullets didn't kill Shultz, he would develop peritonitis. Workman moved out of the bathroom and into the restaurant, where he joined his partner, Emanuel Weiss, who was unloading his shotgun at the rest of Schultz's party.

All three men, Otto Berman (no relation to Dave Berman), Abe Landau, and Bernard Rosencrantz, were hit with lead buckshot; Landau also caught a bullet through the aorta from Workman's gun. Landau and Rosencrantz crumpled to the ground but returned fire, and Workman and Weiss high-tailed it for the door. Landau grunted, got to his feet, and followed them outside, emptying his gun before collapsing against a trash can.

Back inside, Rosencrantz staggered to the bar and demanded nickels for the pay phone. The bartender stood reluctantly from behind the bar, snapped open the cash register, and spilled a handful of nickels on the bar. Rosencrantz struggled to the phone booth, got the operator, and ordered an ambulance before staring at his shoes, filled with his blood. He then collapsed inside the booth.

Outside, an ambulance siren shrilled from far away. When the medics arrived, they assumed Rosencrantz was dead from his slumped position with his head down and nearly touching the floor, but he spoke two words, "Lotta blood." He and Landau were whisked to the nearest hospital because they were in the worst shape. Police refused to let either man go into surgery before spilling the details of the shootout, but neither man spoke. Eventually, the doctors prevailed, and the men went under the knife.

Berman and Schultz were in desperate shape when the second ambulance arrived. The Dutchman, refusing to die in the john, crawled twenty feet into the restaurant and propped himself up against a booth. He was still lucid when the new medics attended to him, and he thrust a stack of $100 bills at them, "To make the trip fast and fruitful," he said. The ride was quick, the surgery long, but ultimately it was unsuccessful. Dutch Schultz died the following afternoon.

Vegas and the Chicago Outfit

Downtown Las Vegas circa 1940 – Public Domain

Chapter Six

Las Vegas Beckons

Although Luciano successfully brought together a commission of mob families to discuss problems and solutions, each family had its local issues. And, they met their challenges before considering anything or anyone else. Their businesses weren't a game or a part-time industry. It was all day, every day. Gun molls and wives weren't married to 9 to 5 guys; they were married to robbing, thieving, murdering gangsters.

Chicago and The Outfit had a series of bosses who molded their territory and syndicate in their image. The more organized the previous boss and underbosses were, the better the next ones did.

Al Capone wanted all the information from more than 100 brothels, dozens of restaurants, casinos, breweries, truck shops, roadhouses, and bookie joints at his fingertips. The compiled ledgers led to his downfall: that and the foggy-bottom memory of syphilis.

In the late 1920s, Frank Nitti ran Capone's import and distribution of liquor through speakeasies in Chicago and Cicero. Canadian whiskey often flowed from Canada through Detroit, Indiana, or Ohio and into Chicago. In return, Chicago beer often followed the path back to Detroit, and both towns' gangs prospered enormously.

With Capone in jail, Nitti was the head of his three big hitters: Jack "Greasy Thumb" Guzik and Tony "Joe Batters" Accardo. Nitti was one of Capone's closest bodyguards, but he had a natural acumen for business and structure, so that's where he put his emphasis.

Never again would the mob have detailed books and ledgers that could lead to prosecution. They evolved, grew into the control of labor unions, and considered the money spent supporting them would pay off well when they needed to squeeze a business through a work stoppage.

Nitti and his captains knew their associates were taking a little skim from the top of the profits. It was expected. A man had to provide well for his family. If he didn't take a little something to buy his wife jewelry or a lovely house, he was looked down on instead of up to.

The opening of legalized gambling in Nevada arrived on March 19, 1931 and didn't go unnoticed in Chicago. The idea of having a casino above board and legal was enticing, but Reno was still home to James McKay and Bill Graham, whose political connections and illegal clubs had paid the way for the new laws.

And they ran a tight ship where Chicago gangsters could go on the lam or get their kidnapping boodle laundered, but Jake "Greasy Thumb" Guzik (March 20, 1886 – February 21, 1956) didn't see much sense in joining that gang of casinos and paying a fee to the Reno boys for the privilege.

Guzik was the financial wizard for The Outfit, even more, hands-on than Meyer Lansky was for Luciano's Mob. Still, he was conservative, unlike Lansky, and even reticent to exert his power over others.

Instead, Guzik stayed with his tried-and-true system of keeping the wheels greased – heavily greased at times, so the politicians and police always knew they had a friend in Capone – a financial friend.

When both Capone and Nitti were in jail, Guzik ensured their wives had cash for expenses and that Tony Accardo, The Outfit's enforcer, kept his boys around their houses so they were safe. Perhaps safer than when their men were at home. Paul, "The Waiter" Ricci, handled everything else.

Most of the Chicago Outfit's top officers were in their thirties and forties. They had wives, families, and children, and their path to the future was never known since death was a constant visitor to their homes.

As for Nevada, Guzik watched Las Vegas, an old west town with thousands of Boulder Dam workers spending their money like the drunken damn workers they were. And it was close to the wide-open town of Los Angeles, where Hollywood and its excess were waiting like a plum to be picked clean.

At the same time in Chicago, 17-year-old Virginia Hill (born 26 August 1916) took a waitress job at the San Carlo Italian Village, a popular spot with the Capone gang. She was a terrible waitress, but oh, the legs she had! Joey Epstein, the accountant for Jake "Greasy Thumb" Guzik, took a shine to the fresh-faced kid. He told her boss to find another dame, and off they went to the track, where he used her as a front to bet a few steamers (winning horses in rigged fields).

Later, he introduced her to Major Arterburn Riddle, a local trucking company tycoon the Chicago Outfit kept happy so he would front for them in various enterprises. Riddle fell immediately in lust with Hill and bought her a mink coat and a diamond necklace. She could be had regularly, but she couldn't be bought and owned.

Vegas and the Chicago Outfit

When she gained Epstein's trust, Hill worked as a money handler, transporting suitcases of cash from one enterprise to another and from illegal enterprises to legal ones to be laundered. Virginia also became a plaything for the bosses, livening up the Fischetti Christmas party and passing around the table like hard candy; she performed fellatio on every boss in the room after wishing them a Merry Christmas. What-a-gal.

Meanwhile, Prohibition, seen as cleansing the United States' soul, was a complete bust. People were killed, the government went bankrupt with lost tax income from liquor sales while gangsters got rich and powerful – and still, people drank.

As the Great Depression stumbled on, there were more and more rumblings that the legalization of alcohol might be just around the corner. The Outfit needed to brace itself for such a possibility since bootlegging was their primary source of income.

Nitti was in regular conference with his top men. Their conversations ranged from Vegas to Phoenix and local issues and politics. That, and the situation in Los Angeles.

Although the Mafia (with Luciano as Boss) was relatively new and idealized the spread of their organization across the states, there wasn't exactly a specific plan or messaging system in place. Still, things were happening.

Tommy Lucchese from New York was working with Jack Dragna in Los Angeles, and Johnny Roselli, who worked in The Outfit but had moved to Los Angeles, was also working with Dragna. It seemed more prudent that the underboss to L.A.'s crime boss, Joseph Ardizzone, might be a better fit for the modern world.

About that time, "Bugsy" Siegel took a train trip from New York to Chicago. Then he visited California, and just about that time, Ardizzone disappeared on the way to his cousin's house with his .41 Colt revolver at his side. Jack Dragna took his place as L.A.'s Boss. No one complained.

"Bugsy" took a train to Las Vegas, then returned to Chicago and New York. Nobody complained there, either. However, Chicago Mayor Anton Cermak was frustrated with how the Chicago Outfit was branching out into more lucrative endeavors. Especially since he was on the payroll of another gangland group, he hatched a plan.

On December 19, 1932, Detective Sergeants Harry Lang and Harry Miller led a squad of officers to 221 N. LaSalle Street in Chicago, barged into Room 554, and started shooting. Nitti took three bullets in the back and neck. Sergeant Lang then shot himself so he could claim Nitti had opened fire.

Against all odds, Nitti survived and was acquitted of the charge of attempted murder of Police Sergeant Lang, whose self-inflicted flesh wound had been suspected anyway.

Miller turned on Lang, admitting that Lang had gotten $15,000 to kill Nitti and that Nitti was unarmed when they entered his office.

The new information didn't help Miller, as both he and Lang were discharged from their duties and fired from the force. But the charge for shooting Nitti? A hundred bucks for simple assault.

Ironically, Mayor Cermak was accidentally shot and killed two months later while talking to President-elect Franklin D. Roosevelt. Giuseppe Zangara, the shooter, said he was aiming for Roosevelt and got nervous. Bummer.

With the loss of the unbelievable money that bootlegging brought in, Ricca expanded The Outfit's labor sources and strengthened his ties with Moe Dalitz and the Mayfield Road Gang in Cleveland and back down to Texas, where booze came years earlier through Galveston.

Dalitz had casinos in Steubenville and Cleveland, plus Covington, Kentucky. And he was a man who never minded doing a favor for a friend, as long as it didn't cost him a piece of his political clout.

Vegas and the Chicago Outfit

Ricca never moved into Ohio, Dalitz was too powerful, and Luciano kept tabs on the Big Bosses. In 1931, when Luciano consolidated New York's five families and pressed for a national cooperative of crooks, he designated Vito Genovese underboss and Frank Costello as his consigliere.

But Costello was more than an adviser. He controlled the families' bookmaking operations and spread slot machines throughout New York and New Jersey, using Philip Kastel as an enforcer to get tens of thousands of slots into bars and restaurants.

When he got push-back from Mayor Fiorello L Guardia (who confiscated gaming devices and dumped them into the East River), Costello allied himself with Louisiana governor Huey Long.

Long had help from New York and Chicago to get elected and shared his state's slot win with both families at a 10% clip. Kastel's direct partner in Louisiana was New Orleans boss Carlos "Little Man" Marcello, who took his share and opened up the French Quarter to bookmaking and its twisted sister, loansharking.

Genovese was charged with a 1934 murder in 1937 and skipped the states for Italy. Although the charges were thin at best, Luciano was convicted of pandering – running hookers. He was sentenced to a minimum of 30 years in the state pen and skipped to Italy. Costello took the reins, with Luciano still calling the shots for years to come.

Unlike keeping the peace in Cleveland and the rest of Ohio, The Outfit had no problem expanding their gambling and loan sharking business into Milwaukee. Over the next decade, The Outfit moved into labor racketeering, gambling, and loan sharking. Geographically, this was the period when Outfit muscle extended to Milwaukee and Madison, Wisconsin. Kansas City, Missouri, was another cheap but lucrative plum, and Los Angeles was too big not to take a bite out of for Ricca.

In 1931, connected rumrunner Tony "The Hat" Cornero and his

brother opened the Meadows casino and motel on Highway 91, just a short drive along Fremont Street from the Downtown casinos.

Since Tony was a jailbird (convicted bootlegger), the license for the Meadows Club was in his brothers Frank and Louis's names. That little ploy didn't fool Lucky Luciano, who sent Meyer Lansky to scope out the operation.

After the May 2, 1931 opening, he found a well-financed joint with three dozen motel rooms, a fancy restaurant, bar, and small casino where the Meadow Larks band played.

Lansky liked the place and told The Hat that if he wanted to stay connected to his friends like Luciano, who, along with other Mob families, had helped bankroll his bootlegging and bought millions of gallons of whiskey, he should share the wealth. A number of around 25% sounded right to Meyer.

Tony declined the veiled threat but took Meyer's visit seriously enough to "sell" his club and get a frontman to run the joint. Again, Luciano was neither fooled nor happy, and that's why the club went off like a Roman candle one night in September. Then, for some reason, the Las Vegas city fire department refused to stop the inferno. By morning there was nothing left but smoldering ash.

The Chicago Outfit's muscle was strong, so when they pushed into the sawdust joints of Downtown Las Vegas, there was little squabbling. Then, they bled the current frontmen (and actual owners) dry with packages of services from security to customer service – which meant hookers, lots of hookers. Vegas was an open city, Mob-wise, so whoever got there first got the best deals.

The Apache Club on Fremont Street had many "owners" over the years, as did the Boulder Club. When Bugsy Siegel put his offices in the Las Vegas Club, the FBI listened secretly to every phone call he made. Still, they didn't do anything – because J Edgar Hoover insisted there was no organized crime in America. That's good to know.

From 1935 to 1940, Vegas was a small but profitable waystation for travelers by train and automobile. The Chicago group got easy cash weekly coming home via the same train that sat puffing smoke at the Union Plaza stop on Fremont Street. But Bugsy Siegel and his Hollywood connections brought in the most money and trouble behind it.

Like Las Vegas years later, Chicago learned there was tons of money to be made from the masses, even if it came in just a few coins at a time. Slot machines in bus stations, gas stations, and roadhouses propelled The Outfit to new highs in political chicanery, opulence, and corruption.

And pushing the newfound love of unions onto every corner of the working world produced the same flow of coins and bills that fed the syndicate's insatiable hunger. Do you know what it costs to run an operation with big bosses, dozens of trusted lieutenants, and hundreds of soldiers on the streets? Murray "The Hump" Humphreys did. So did Nitti.

When Paul Ricca (Felice De Lucia, November 14, 1897, Naples, Italy) met with Chicago politicians, it was always with the intent that his views were seen as serious; and that he was a generous man. When the men he met with weren't convinced, he sent "Fat Lennie" Leonard Caifano or "Mooney" Sam Giancana to convince them. They were ever so persuasive.

The sight of "Mad Sam" DeStefano or Giancana convinced most workers and owners to think union-first! If not, they were beaten until they got the message. When there were no unions for some businesses, Humphreys made one up. When any owners complained, they got wise after a mugging or a firebomb in their place of business.

The Camel (Humphreys) had an innate ability to work with the unions, infiltrating Chicago's south side dry cleaner's union and making it a model for later union takeovers. When you could threaten the workers with a management-imposed work stoppage and no benefits, you could demand higher union dues. And when you could threaten businesses with a strike, you could get your workers higher wages, and those same workers could pay higher dues. It was a no-lose hustle.

Murray took to his duties faithfully, loading a closet with fine suits and camel-hair jackets. He improved his manners, said thank-you when necessary, and with a fancy shave and manicured nails, his big ears and beady eyes were less noticed.

Moving in the polite company made Ricca and Humphreys a formidable pair. They spread the wealth for the common good of the family, and while Las Vegas was producing profits, the movie industry in Los Angeles had deeper pockets and more unions to exploit.

Bugsy Siegel was a confidant and extortionist/killer for the New York Mob and the Chicago Outfit. When he got too hot for either location, Los Angeles was as far away as he could get and still be the prime money-maker he'd always been. Fortunately for Siegel, his reputation preceded him.

Upon arrival in Hollywood, Siegel ingratiated himself with movie actors, directors, and producers. He bought a home, threw lavish parties, and spent money like it was going out of style.

After getting close to some of the world's best-known actors, he started taking loans from the likes of old friend George Raft, new friends Clark Gable and Cary Grant, studio heads like Jack L. Warner and Louis B. Mayer of MGM – Metro, Goldwin, Mayer.

Siegel never paid any of those loans back, which amounted to more than $500,000. Who would confront a known killer? Not the Hollywood elite. They liked movies with happy endings, and getting beaten or dead wasn't their idea of a happy ending.

Instead, while Siegel was also getting his bosses and himself rich with casinos on boats offshore Santa Monica pier, a new drug route through Mexico, and the Los Angeles numbers racket, he also helped hit the local unions. LA Boss Jack Dragna wasn't happy, but he was too small to fight NY and Chicago.

So, without a whisper to Dragna, Johnny Roselli, Willie Bioff, and Siegel pushed hard, extorting the movie studios for even more cash, usually through planned strikes of the Screen Extra's Guild and the Los Angeles Teamsters.

No Hollywood studio could stand the pressure and expense of a significant union stopping the production of a movie. Not with dozens of stars, producers, and directors drawing exorbitant salaries during a shutdown. So, they paid. And they paid for years.

It wasn't until 1943 that the Outfit was finally caught doing the dirty deed to the studios, and by that time, Siegel was safely at home in Las Vegas, skimming everything he could from the casinos and his race wire connections.

To avoid prosecution, Wille Bioff turned on the Outfit and defied the law of Omerta', which forbade the Mob's members from ratting on their friends. The bosses in Chicago were less than happy, both with Bioff and the man who had sent him – Frank Nitti.

In 1939, Sam Giancana caught a four-year term in Leavenworth Federal Prison for bootlegging. Just because Prohibition had been repealed didn't mean the Outfit would stop making booze.

They had plenty of distilleries and all the trucks and man force they needed to keep the illegally brewed alky going to their bars and casinos, so why stop producing?

Giancana was lucky and never indicted for tax evasion and extortion of the millions of dollars raked from RKO, MGM, 20th Century Fox, and other studios. And he got home just in time to sit at the big kid's table before the not-so-lucky were dealt with.

Ricca, Roselli, Philip D'Andrea, Charlie Gioe, Lou Kaufmann, and Frank Nitti were each given 10-year sentences after Bioff turned state's evidence to avoid prosecution. Most went to prison and did severe time. Two did not. Willie Bioff went into the witness protection system only to reappear in Arizona years later. And then there was Frank Nitti.

We don't know much about how Francesco Raffaele Nitto (nee: Nitti) entered the world, but we know how he went out. Each man prepared for his prison time in his way.

Testimony from Nitti's much younger wife Antoinette, three railroad workers, Conductor William F. Seebauer and his switchmen L.M. Barnett and E.H. Moran, and of course, the coroner's office, set things straight.

On March 19, 1943, Frank Nitti dragged himself out of a warm bed and into a cold house, putting on his long johns. He puttered around the house, took a call from his lawyer, A. Bradley Eben, who told him he was being indicted for extortion and mail fraud in New York and sent his wife to church, where he told her to "go to a novena at Our Lady of Sorrows."

Then Nitti quaffed several shots of expensive brandy, put his rosary in a small leather case in his vest pocket, and dropped $1.03 of change into his pocket. He slipped a 32 caliber Colt revolver into his suit. Then he headed out the door with his flowered necktie covered by his brown overcoat.

It was bitterly cold, but his brown fedora kept his head warm. He had been losing hair recently, and his ulcer was acting up. He was severely claustrophobic, and getting through his last prison sentence for tax evasion had been a harrowing 18 months.

As he walked, he felt the bulge of his billfold, the one with "Frank" spelled out in gold at his chest. On the other side were his cigarettes. He pulled one from the pack, turned against the wind, and scorched the end with a match. The booze was making him numb.

He stumbled slightly as he reached Cermak Road, his five-foot-five-inch body swayed by the crushing breeze. According to train Conductor Seebaur, Nitti stepped onto the tracks with his back to the train, which the crew was backing down the track heading south with the caboose in front.

The man stepped back off the track a moment later and walked towards a chain-link fence. As the distance between the train and the man closed, the Conductor said, "Hi there, buddy," but instead of a verbal response, there were two gunshots that reverberated back and forth between the railroad engine's steel sides, and the men ducked for cover as the train stopped.

The Conductor and switchmen jumped from the train, leaving through the side furthest from Nitti, and peered from underneath at the man once called The Enforcer. There was no enforcing that day; Nitti was shooting at himself, and he was a lousy shot.

He'd managed to shoot his hat off with the first bullet, the second broke his jaw, but for the Chicago Outfit's alleged head man, the third time was the charm. An instant later, the conductors saw Nitti blow a bullet into his skull behind his right ear and slump down against the fence that left him on his back with just what was left of his head propped up, looking out at the city he once ruled.

Ruled might be a stretch, but things got done between Paul "The Waiter" Ricca and Tony Accardo. If there's anything The Outfit learned from Al Capone, it was to put a little money into legit businesses so you didn't get pinched for tax evasion. There's nothing wrong with the papers naming your second-string quarterback as the boss. Nitti was a paper-pusher by then, even if he was great with finances.

In New York, Meyer Lansky was a god too, but still Jewish (as Chicago's Jake "Greasy Thumb" Guzik was), and never would he be trusted with every secret. He was the East Coast finance boss, happy to distribute the cash scammed from joint-family businesses. However, Lucky Luciano was still the boss of the east, whether he was in Italy, Miami Beach, or taking visitors in Cuba.

As for Nitti taking one for the team, no, he knew the confines of prison would be his death, either the claustrophobia or a prison-hit, with eight other defendants in the Hollywood studio extortion case bound for trial. He was the one who had hired Willie Bioff and placed him in charge of the Theatrical Stage Employees - a 46,000-strong union – the International Alliance. And then Bioff rolled over, sang a tune for the government, and went into witness protection. They were all going to prison for a long time.

Ironically, the last street Nitti crossed, Cermak Road, was named for crooked Chicago Mayor Anton Cermak, who crossed Nitti in 1932 by spending $15,000 hiring a killer police officer to shoot him. Nitti lived; Cermak, as mentioned earlier, was not so lucky.

What was not mentioned earlier was that perhaps Cermak's killer, Giuseppe Zangara, wasn't aiming for Roosevelt after all. Maybe he had hit the intended target as one of the Italian Army's best sharpshooters before coming to the United States. Dirty, double-cross deals make Chicago what it was – double trouble.

When you head out to kill, you've always got a backup plan with your emergency backup plan. Just ask Lee Harvey Oswald – or his killer – Jack Ruby. Ruby, by the way, was born Jacob Leon Rubenstein on March 25, 1911, in Chicago. He grew up with a temper, an inferiority complex, and a love for horse racing. Ruby sold horse-race tip sheets and steered passersby to Outfit bookie joints. Later, he worked with a local garbage collectors union that became part of the International Brotherhood of Teamsters at the direction of Murray Humphreys.

By the mid-1940s, Dallas was a tough go for gamblers (a euphemism for casino owners and bookies). The Chicago Outfit made massive money in the oil state with Benny Binion, the Boss of Dallas and a trusted friend and ally. But with the 1946 election of Dallas County Sheriff Steve Gutherie, Binion knew his time in town was ending.

Jack Ruby and his brothers were given the green light to open shop in Dallas once Binion was in Las Vegas, so they shortened their surnames from Rubenstein, took over sleazy strip clubs and bars, and managed prostitution and some gambling. Like Binion, Ruby ingratiated himself to the faithful Dallas Police officers who dropped by his clubs looking for free booze, free girls, and free cash.

Ruby wasn't paying the high prices for safe passage some other Chicago Outfit members were. His clubs were small by comparison. Still, the tentacles that stretched from Chicago to points east, west, and south were long and strong.

Tony Accardo circa 1960 – Associated Press / Public Domain

Chapter Seven

Tony Accardo Takes Charge of Chicago

When two-thirds of the Outfit's brains and balls headed to prison for the Hollywood union extortion capers, a younger and hungrier pack of wolves took charge of the rackets, Paul Ricca may have still held sway over the newbies. Still, somebody had to drive the bus while he was in school (prison).

Tony Accardo (Antonino Joseph Accardo April 28, 1906 – May 22, 1992, Chicago, IL) was the son of a shoemaker. Like many gang

61

members, Tony took to the streets at 14 after getting tossed out of school. He found the local pool halls more to his liking, and when he couldn't beat someone at pool for 50 cents, he beat them over the head with his pool cue.

He ran with a gang of toughs called the Circus Café Gang, rolling drunks, robbing apartments, extorting shop owners – the usual for inner-city youths in the Chicago area – until he impressed Machine Gun Jack McGurn about the same time McGurn was recruiting Sam Giancana.

Both men drove for McGurn and worked as lookouts, bodyguards, and killers. Although Accardo bragged years later (on FBI recording devices) about being in on the St. Valentine's Day Massacre, he may have just been a lookout for that massive hit.

On the other hand, he was a likely gunman when Northside gang leader Hymie Weiss took dozens of bullets in 1926. If you ever saw the Kevin Costner movie The Untouchables, there's a scene where Al Capone smacks a guy dead with a baseball bat. In reality, the guy with the bat was Tony Accardo.

Capone brought Accardo to a dinner where he planned to send a message to his lieutenants about loyalty while sending two men from his crews to the Promised Land.

After the cannoli hit the table, Accardo repeatedly hit the two thieves with a baseball bat. The cannoli were ruined. So were the men's suits, ties, and skulls. Capone was impressed, though, and said, "Boy, this kid's a real Joe Batters." The "Joe Batters" name stuck.

Accardo was awarded a crew of his own as a capo. He took his 5% street tax from the crew's profits as they terrorized union workers and officials, set up illegal gaming operations, and then loaned out 2% a-week vig cash to the gamblers they broke at often shady table games.

The Outfit's best weapon was to offer cheap gambling, cheap

booze, and cheap girls to men who were constantly short of cash – and then let them borrow whatever they needed to get through the week until their next paycheck. A paycheck that went first to the vigorish, $2 on every hundred borrowed. If they couldn't pay down the loan amount, which usually grew as the weeks went by, the effective interest rate was over 100% a year.

After Frank Nitti put a gun to his head (several times before getting it right), Paul Ricca was officially noted as the head of Chicago's Outfit. He named Accardo his underboss, and when Ricca went to prison in 1943, Accardo was acting boss.

When Ricca got paroled three years later, he was forbidden to have contact with his hoodlum friends, but the two men shared power for decades until Ricca's death in1972.

In 1943 there was still plenty of hungry talent in Chicago, and Accardo leaned heavily on Gus Alex, Joey Aiuppa, and Sam Giancana.

Giancana was a feared guy, even in his own family. His father beat him when he was younger, and Sam returned the favor when he got old enough. When his younger brother Chuck got out of line and disrespected him, Mooney followed him and his friend Joe Ingolia as they drove Joe's Model A to a cab stand where they shot the breeze with Tony Accardo's brother-in-law, "Queenie."

When the guys headed to an all-night diner and stood on the curb shooting craps, Mooney got out of his car. The boys ducked around the corner, but Giancana didn't care. He just went to his trunk and retrieved the gas can he had placed there earlier.

Then, Giancana doused the outside of the Model A with gas, put the can in the driver's side seat of the car, and struck a match. He yelled at his brother Chuck, "I know you're there, so watch closely."

A minute later, a whoosh of air sucked into the car as it burst into flame and shot the same air out into the cool morning air. Giancana walked calmly back to his car and drove away.

Later, when Chuck finally made it home, Mooney gave him a beating to ensure there was no misunderstanding. Over the years, the older Giancana took care of his brother with family-business jobs, but he never elevated him to a high-profile, high-paying job. Why is anybody's guess?

The Local Skim

Sometimes there's some confusion about how the Mob and, more importantly, The Outfit made their money. When you were in a gang, there was always a gang leader who masterminded jobs, set the parameters, and paid off his workers.

In the Mob, you became part of a crew as a soldier, and you got a weekly stipend to be on call for whatever came up. A big job might get you a bonus, but even a hit might just be part of the job. You didn't find an extra two-grand in your envelope for whacking a rival. It was expected. If you didn't take the job, you never get your stipend again.

When you move up in the ranks, you might get a little something for your efforts from your lieutenant for a job well done. That boss was likely taking a little something from their job, whether they were running an Outfit bar or a brothel. That was all right; a man's got to make a living. But he better not take too much. It was a tightrope.

The Capos got to engineer the best jobs, and they set a price for their direct underlings. And, if they were picking up the winnings from their neighborhood's casinos, they were responsible for the money. They, too, got a cut, but the top bosses set that. As Giancana said, "you gotta keep 'em guessing." And he lived that motto.

No underlings ever knew what they would get from their latest score or the weekly take. Still, when World War Two was taking men from the streets and raw materials from construction and the auto business, Giancana arranged to get his top producers the latest model cars. He wasn't cheap, but he wasn't easy with the cash.

As for the money collected by Giancana (and what made it to the financial bosses and Accardo), some of it was washed through a growing list of legitimate businesses like restaurants, bars, office buildings, and factories that Tony Accardo knew were going to be the backbone of his future.

The rest of the cash, from loansharking, gambling, and all those great cash businesses like vending machines and pinballs, went to the soldiers under the table and the bosses' vaults (and their wife's minks, cars, and diamonds).

Every business had a hook, a scam, and a way to improve profits. When hijackers took down trucks full of cigarettes, the cartons got torn open, and the packs fed into vending machines where the daily take was all profit. Jukeboxes made steady money from the coins dropped, but even more in backrooms where record producers and their artists paid to get their latest hits (or coming hits) included in the stacks of records the jukeboxes played. If your song wasn't in a single juke in the midwest, how would it be heard and sell copies at the record store?

And how about those new legitimate businesses that The Outfit was opening in small and big towns across America's Breadbasket? Well, plenty had great receipts when The Outfit was funneling cash through them every week, but somehow new owners who paid a high price for a thriving business just couldn't seem to make a go of them!

There were scams for scams, and cooperation between the families in Detroit, Los Angeles, Miami, and of course, New York. When Frank Costello designed a series of Midwest gem heists, Accardo and Giancana took the bulk of the jewelry and sent it to points west and south for distribution.

Even with each intermediary taking a little skim, the operation netted millions. Costello was happy and agreed to stay on the periphery of the growing racing wire business. Of course, his operations in New York would get special bulk pricing, but he wasn't taking a cut of the pie. At least that's what he said.

While the wire was making the owners rich, Bugsy Siegel took over more casinos in Nevada, where he placed the wire and took a big cut of the franchise fees. And Costello always got a piece of the pie from Nevada via Meyer Lansky.

He'd done the same in California, where there were hundreds of bookies to beat into submission, and his weekly income was over $25,000.

By then, Siegel was happily living in California, leaving his wife and children behind in New York. For several years he stayed married, even while living in LA with that chick with the long legs that Esposito used to have fun with Virginia Hill. When they went to casinos in Mexico, the dealers called her the Flamingo. Bugsy didn't mind, but you got a beating if you called him Bugsy.

Bugsy's investment in casinos in Los Angeles, San Diego, and Mexico paid well, more than what was getting skimmed from his three strong-armed takeovers of casinos in Las Vegas. In particular, the Agua Caliente was a bright spot, where he shared a cut with Chicago, New York, and Reno's boss, Bill Graham.

In return, Graham shared a cut with Chicago in three clubs, including the Golden Nugget, the highest-earning casino in Nevada. Moe Sedway kept watching over Bugsy's domain in Vegas, where the skim was set at 20% of what dropped in the slots and 60% of the win-at-the-table games.

In a shoe store, there's some accountability. You order shoes from the factory, you sell shoes, and you keep your ledgers to show a profit. You can still scam, but it's more challenging. In a casino, there's no retail inventory – your inventory is cash, and the state of Nevada had no regulations regarding who went to the count room and counted the coins from the slots or the cash from the table games. There were no cameras, so it was the greatest skim in the world! And a good thing since it was expensive to run a mob.

Bugsy had a gift for spending money, especially when he had to buy houses, politicians, police chiefs, sheriffs, and local council members. There were new cars, trips to Mexico, and a year-round suite at the St. Francis hotel on Union Square in San Francisco, where he regularly met with Reno casino owners.

Siegel also had partners, friends, and a Flamingo to feed. Only the bird, Anita Hill, could match his spending habits. Their lavish lifestyles would eventually bring down the greatest casino strongman and builder the West Coast had ever seen.

In the meantime, old friend and partner Meyer Lansky took the Mob's share of the profits to Miami, Chicago, Detroit, Philadelphia, Kansas City, and New York. He'd used Anita Hill as a bag woman before, but now Siegel felt uncomfortable with his girlfriend traveling across the country with satchels filled with cash.

In the early '40s, Siegel's contacts in Hollywood got a sigh of relief when Chicago's top hoodlums were indicted, and he backed away from extorting the unions in town. But he was still pushing buttons in town.

He and his brother-in-law, Whitey Krakower, went to see Harry "Big Greenie" Greenberg, who had helped with the Louis and Andy Frabazzo killing. They brought along Frankie Carbo and Allie "Tick Tock" Tannenbaum. They talked, smoking Lucky Strikes, and asked what "Big Greenie" had meant when he said he "knew too much to be ignored." Was he threatening to squeal? Because Bugsy hated squealers.

Greenberg wasn't the sharpest tool in the shed; instead of taking any chances, the boys whacked him. It was another day at the office, as slayings were becoming more common in L.A., with criminals taking advantage of narcotics, prostitution, bookmaking, and gambling to fill their coffers. With that many vices, some toes would get stepped on, and some heads, too.

Siegel fit right in, and he ensured everyone knew he was in charge. At a business meeting to discuss his terms (it's my way, all the way, and 25 percent), local loan shark and bookie Les Brunemann asked, "Are you fuckin' kiddin' me?" Bugsy wasn't. A month later, he was shot three times at the Roost Café in Redondo Beach, his turf. He recovered, but he wasn't any smarter than the last time he asked Bugsy a question. The next time he went to dinner in the same restaurant, he caught seven bullets. It was his last meal.

In between the shootings, Siegel's thugs, armed with pistols and tire chains, raided every bookie's joint they could find and took over the bookmaking in Redondo Beach. Then, they worked their way up and down the coast, forcing deals from backroom casinos, poker parlors, and even the local dog and horse tracks.

When Bugsy was strong enough in Southern California with a big enough gang, he met Tony Cornero and demanded a more significant cut of his profits with the SS REX. Why not? His gambling boat anchored strategically 3.1 miles off the coast of Santa Monica (three miles to international waters and no gambling ban at the time) was doing great. Little skip boats (water taxis) took players to the ship each night, and with all the money in Los Angeles, Cornero was getting rich. Bugsy got what he wanted. And then the sports wire business got weird.

Bugsy Siegel circa 1928 - New York PD / Public Domain

Chapter Eight

The Race Wire

Local Chicago businessman James Matthew Ragen, Sr. (August 9, 1880 – August 15, 1946) was an Irish businessman who began his career on the town streets with a gang of toughs called Ragen's Colts. After earning his bones in street fights and bootlegging, Ragen became a puncher (buy or get punched) for Moses Annenberg, who published the Daily Racing Form.

Ragen and others forced newspaper stands to sell his forum and the Chicago American newspapers in what was pleasantly called bootjacking. If you didn't carry the racing news, you got a boot in the ass or a blackjack to the head.

In the early 1930s, Ragen was inside the offices, selling and later operating the General News Service. That generic name became the Nationwide News Service, the country's only distributor for racetrack and sports results.

When Annenberg refused to sell the service to The Outfit, they sought the help of the Roosevelt administration, who charged Annenberg with anti-trust and income tax evasion. Before going to prison, Annenberg sold National to Ragen. The Outfit rejoiced. Their own race wire!

But no, Ragen was more stubborn and even dumber than Annenberg was, and Tony Accardo wasn't happy. You could make Jake Guzik mad or even Humphreys, but not Joe Batters.

Accardo made a deal with Western Union to transmit their race and sports results and started the Trans-American Publishing Company, which Bugsy Siegel pushed in California with the backing of Jack Dragna and the muscle of ex-boxer Mickey Cohen.

Cohen usually just had to show his face and explain the wire principles of buy or die. When the bookies resisted, Mickey went a few rounds with them if they lasted more than one vicious punch. Nobody refused twice.

At night, Cohen sometimes got lucky with the women rejected by the handsome and now polished Siegel, who only slept with the classy dames he met in bars. Mickey, not much of a talker and built like a fireplug, needed all the help he could get.

In Nevada, every club in Las Vegas that had a sportsbook caved to Siegel at as much as $100 per day – even if they already had a deal with Nationwide. The competition and threats unnerved Ragen, but he refused to sell his service, so Accardo put a contract on him.

Thinking he needed protection, Ragen contacted columnist Drew Pearson, who took some notes about Ragen, Accardo, Guzik, Annenberg, Giancana, Henry Crown, and others. Then Pearson took his inside information to U.S. Attorney General Tom C. Clark.

Clark said he had no federal jurisdiction to prosecute the suspects but turned the information over to the FBI, who interviewed Ragen several times and gave him six agents to watch over him.

J. Edgar Hoover said the names obtained from Ragen reached the highest levels. The FBI thanked Ragen after their last meeting and said goodbye. Then they removed his protection.

Weeks later, Ragen was met with a shotgun blast as he drove down State Street. He was taken to a nearby hospital and signed an affidavit identifying his assailant on June 24, 1946. But he never left the hospital.

After surgery, the prognosis was good, but he relapsed every time he seemed to get better. He lingered for three weeks, regularly visited by a few friends, one of whom kindly brought him a daily Coca-Cola.

Ragen seemed to be improving for a while but passed on August 15th. An autopsy showed he died of mercury poisoning, likely administered daily in a bottle of Coke by an old friend. It's the real thing!

After his death, State Attorney William Touhy could not prosecute his shooter or any of the people Ragen had named since the original affidavit mysteriously vanished. Those Chicago winds could be powerful!

Back in Las Vegas, the two casinos built on what became known as the Las Vegas Strip weren't doing any more business than those downtown. Even when they had a racebook going.

The El Rancho opened on April 3, 1941, at 2500 Las Vegas

Boulevard, with 63 rooms. Built on 33 acres of sand Thomas Hull and James Cashman had paid $150 an acre for, the club drew weary, sweat-soaked drivers, happy to pay $4 a night for a room, especially since the resort pumped extra water into the property to fill a large swimming pool and keep the grass green.

In the casino, they fund men from Steubenville, Ohio, Covington, Kentucky, and Chicago. Thomas Hull wasn't a casino operator, but luckily there were a few men in town ready to run the slots and table games for him.

There were only two 21 tables when the club opened, along with a roulette game, craps, and 70 slot machines. And they didn't seem to do much business even though they were busy. Hull didn't care, he leased out the casino, and nobody bitched. Especially not the Cleveland, New York, or Chicago groups who sent their boys to run the place. Skim was set at 75% of the gross win.

Shortly afterward, the El Rancho opened, and Siegel was arrested in Los Angeles by the FBI for harboring fugitive Louie Buchalter. That happened after Abe Reles dropped a dime and told the feds that Buchalter called the shots on the Greenberg hit and others. The FBI said they'd have Bugsy, Buchalter, and Frankie Carbo cold for 14 Mob hits when Abe sang in court.

Reles was moved from town to town for months, keeping him on ice until the trial, but the Mob had too many informants and too much money.

Even though Reles was held under guard, he somehow managed to slip and fall up and out of the fifth-floor window of his room at the Half Moon Hotel. Yeah, he made a splash in Coney Island.

The door was locked and guarded by a local officer. Without a witness, the FBI's case dissolved.

In Vegas, life went on, and the second hotel-casino on the Los

Angeles Highway opened just up the street from the El Rancho. Retired Los Angeles Police Captain (oh, how much money the Vice Squad can make you!) Guy McAfee had been running a club called the Pair-O-Dice where the Last Frontier came to being but sold out for $35,000 to R.E. Griffith. Griffith was connected to the El Rancho Hotel group, owned the property in Gallup, New Mexico, and wanted nothing more than to upstage the El Rancho with a superior property, but he was delusional. His property didn't turn out any different at all.

It was a cowboy town setting in a second-rate town in the middle of nowhere. It was the freaking desert, it was hot, it was Las Vegas, and it was tough to get built with the Second World War raging on and restrictions on electrical wiring, metal tubing, wood, and cement. "It's the desert, for Christ's sake," Griffith said, "Get me some concrete!" But it wasn't that easy.

Obtaining materials was an adventure in patience, persistence, and ingenuity. Bribe money helped too, but the contractors had to be resourceful. They went out and bought old mines in Northern Nevada so they could strip the materials and reuse them. They bought farmland to grow crops to feed the new guests coming to town. And last but not least, they found someone to run the casino. And who could that be?

Why the boys from New York and Cleveland, of course! After six months of pressure, Thomas Hull sold his points in the El Rancho to Moe Dalitz and Meyer Lansky. The new owners of record for the Clark County gaming license, Hilton-Brown, worked fine as a front for a while, but they kept wanting to be in the count room when the gaming table drop boxes were opened, and the money was counted. The nerve of some guys. The Mob needed a guy who knew the score, a guy with more ego and less greed, and that man was Wilbur Clark.

Wilbur was an old hand at casinos, especially after taking a piece of the Rex floating casino off the coast of California and later fronting for Bugsy in a bar and casino in San Diego. When it shut down, Wilbur took a sack of cash to Reno and bought his own club (the Bonanza) at 207 N. Center Street, just down from the Bank Club. It was a money-loser.

There was no way to compete with Bill Graham's casino two doors down, so when he returned to Vegas, he put his remaining cash (about $37,000) into the old Northern casino downtown, fronted for the Mob, and kept his mouth shut. His partners changed the name to the Turf Club. Then sent him to be the front-man job at the El Rancho.

Moe Sedway collected from every casino racebook in Las Vegas and never had to call Siegel or Cohen for help. Within a year, Siegel's end of the business was $25,000 a week. Hollywood was perfect for Bugsy: vile, obscenely greedy, and plagued by neophytes. Still, Vegas was a hole. He hated making the trip into town to get his share of the profits, but the heat was coming hard and fast in L.A.

So, Siegel put six months of race-wire profits into the Las Vegas Club and skimmed it hard. Then he pushed into the Boulder Club, the Frontier, and took over the racebook at Guy McAfee's Golden Nugget. He kept the skim strong, often $100,000 a week. It was a legal goldmine and getting better.

At the far end of Fremont Street, Marion Hicks and J.C. Grayson built the first "new" casino downtown. It wasn't just a rebuild or extension to an existing property. Built then for, and only for gambling, the El Cortez, the first major resort in town, ran a hefty $245,000. Locals scoffed that it was too far from the train station and unlikely to ever pay for itself. They were wrong.

Hicks and Grayson were builders, but J. Kell Houssels was a business owner and casino man. He'd received one of the first gaming licenses in Las Vegas back in 1931 for his Smoke Shop after converting it into a tiny slot joint with a roulette wheel and blackjack game. And, he'd purchased the El Cortez once it was finished. A fact that Bugsy Siegel was comfortable with.

The El Cortez was a casino Siegel couldn't muscle Houssels out of, so they agreed on a fair price of $600,000. A price so shocking to locals that even if they weren't gamblers, they were compelled to drive downtown to see it. Some were impressed with the size of the property. Most were confused about how it could be worth more than half a million dollars. None of them could fathom its earning power, much less its potential for serious skimming.

So, was Houssels happy to make bank on a massive sale after proving the club a monster earner? Certainly. Did he want to sell right then? Sometimes you get an offer you can't refuse – and how could you say no to Bugsy with his handsome good looks, smile, and shiny revolver? Sometimes you have to go along to get along. Now the New York Mob was stronger in Nevada than the Chicago Outfit.

In 1945, Davie Berman left his Minneapolis clubs and came west after clearing a deal with Frank Costello to take a piece of the El Cortez. Then, he gave Meyer Lansky his $160,000 front money and headed to the desert.

He brought his brother and business partner Chickie with him. While Davie was doing a stretch in Sing Sing Prison, Chickie was running their slots and pinball machines – and making a killing (when necessary) at racebooks with the silent help of Minneapolis Mayor Marvin Kline.

In the next election, Kline got clobbered by Hubert Humphrey, and away went their protection, so the Berman brothers decided to go straight to Las Vegas.

After arriving, Davie headed uptown while Chickie wandered downtown to shoot craps. He was an aggressive player. He was connected, got high limits, and seriously crapped out, losing the brother's combined cash of $160,000 in a game at the Golden Nugget before even meeting with Bugsy or Moe Sedway.

Davie hid Chickie away in a North Las Vegas dive and caught the next train home. Over three days, he convinced his Minneapolis partners to squash the hit they had ordered on his brother, finagled more cash from two outside partners, and returned to Vegas to try again.

May 10th, 1945, Berman turned over another satchel of cash himself, joining his New York partners Lansky, Sedway, and Siegel; his Chicago (by way of Phoenix) partner Gus Greenbaum; and introduced his Minnesota muscle and partner "Ice Pick" Willie Alterman. Alderman didn't get his nickname from chopping ice for drinks. No sir.

When Ice Pick didn't get the answers he wanted, he'd lean into a troublesome competitor and scramble their brains by shoving that long steel end of his ice pick through their ear and into the soft tissue of their brains. They'd never again breathe an air of resistance. Things seemed to go as well for him in Las Vegas as they had in Minnesota.

From 1941 until January 1949, the gaming license at El Cortez stayed the same. Nevada had no gaming control board until 1955. Who would lie on a gaming license, right?

During those years, a weekly satchel of cash went directly to Lansky, whether he was in Las Vegas, Miami, or New York. Lansky handled the skim for every group claiming a piece of the pie.

The El Cortez had limits as low as 10 cents at 21 and craps but also took on heavy hitters like Nick "The Greek" Dandalos, who played $500 on the line at craps. They also took huge bets from Billy Wilkerson, owner of The Hollywood Reporter. Both lost most of the time.

Over the next three years, Davie Berman worked at the El Cortez, the Las Vegas Club, and the El Dorado. As the pit manager, he took a 10 percent cut of the combined take. Siegel owned 25 percent with Sedway, and Greenbaum and Alderman each had 10 percent. The skim was constant, at 80 percent (with 25 percent rake off the top for Lansky to deliver to the bosses. The clubs only claimed 30 percent of the total take to their books.

Housing was short in the 1940s, with a war on and no supplies, but after the war ended, it was just a matter of paying the right administrators to get building materials.

The owners, even those with just a few percent, never had to pay for anything at the clubs. Free rooms, meals, booze, and broads. It was as American as apple pie.

The money Vegas was making took a decisive turn for the better after the Second World War ended. There was money and fun in the air every night.

Cocktail servers started wearing short dresses and taking drinks to the tables. Cigarette girls sold "cigars, cigarettes, and Tiparillo's," and showgirls were required to walk the casino for at least an hour after the dinner crowd left the showroom.

Many hung around the bar in skimpy costumes that accentuated their curves and could easily be talked into taking a look at a player's hotel room for, say, five dollars. Bellhops and valet attendants offered male and even female visitors a companion for the evening for only a slightly higher price. Ah, what Las Vegas could offer!

Dave Berman, then in his early 40s, was self-educated, personable, and had been a Canadian war hero. He took to being called Davie, even by new associates. He wanted to work in his casinos and spend time with his wife and little girl. His daughter, Susan, never suspected that her father was connected to the underworld.

She saw him as a loving father who worked long hours at his hotels. On the other hand, Mom had already seen too much of the Mob, spent most of her time confined to a sickbed at home or a Los Angeles psych ward, and passed away at a young age.

When singer Kay Starr played the casino for the first time, she thought she had to gamble and sing. She tried craps, messed up the game for the other players, and lost her first night's salary.

Berman strolled over and told her, "Stay away from the tables. How can you make people happy with your singing if you know you owe us your full salary because of your gambling?"

Lucky Luciano got released from prison in 1946. He wasn't allowed to stay in the US, so the government whisked him off to Ellis Island and then a freighter in Brooklyn harbor. On February 9th, he was allowed a spaghetti dinner with Albert Anastasia and five guests. In the morning, the freighter sailed to Naples. Luciano set up the Mob business in new offices, then flew to Cuba to take over The Commission again. Vegas and Cuba were both looking solid gold.

El Rancho Vegas circa 1940s - Frasher Foto postcard

Chapter Nine

Spin the Policy Wheel

While the Mob took a serious view of any violence in Las Vegas, preferring to keep the town looking squeaky clean, the streets of Chicago were as dangerous in the 1940s as they had been in Al Capone's 1920s!

As one gangster put it, "The coppers are just as crooked but even greedier, and if they don't get their weekly juice, you'll get hit as quick as if you were crossing Sam Giancana."

By the mid-'40s, Giancana was the Outfit's most powerful street boss. While doing time for bootlegging (yup, even after the end of Prohibition), Giancana met Eddie Jones in the Terre Haute pen, the biggest policymaker in town.

If you've heard of the numbers racket, the daily numbers lottery could make you some fast bucks, and as Giancana said, "Everyone's got a nickel, right? And a nickel gets you a fiver. A buck gets you a grand."

"Run correctly; the policy wheel chooses three numbers every day, like 6-6-6, and pays off 1000 to 1 to the winners. But you can't lose when you're doin' fifty-grand a day and paying back twenty-five!

Eddie and his brothers raked it in, taking baskets of coins and cash to banks across the city. They had it all, and Sam Giancana wanted his share — or all he could steal.

First, he convinced Eddie to let him in on the policy and help run things. Then, Giancana convinced Paul Ricca to let him move into the Colored wards, where Eddie and his partners ran the policy racket.

Ricca was game, but Tony Accardo's top men, Humphreys and Guzik, weren't convinced. Giancana moved forward anyway, and the money was as good as Eddie Jones had said.

When Jake Guzik balked, Giancana took him for a ride with Fat Leonard Caifano to a burned-out building in Cicero. "Listen, Jake," Giancana said, "you been good to me, I been good to you. This is the new deal, and you're too late to squawk."

"I got 200 grand, and you can hold that in your hands tonight, or you can hold your brains in them instead."

To his credit, Guzik held out until daybreak with a gun to his head. When the sun rose, so did his belief that there was only one decision: should he walk home or take a ride after accepting the cash?

Giancana and Fat Leonard dropped him at the corner of West Roosevelt Road, and nowhere and off he went. Giancana never had to meet with Humphreys. He called to say the policy was a great idea. Unfortunately, Guzik was tougher to convince about the wisdom of a partnership in policy than Eddie Jones's partners.

Giancana's ten years as a hitman, strategist, and go-to guy for the Chicago Outfit paid off big in 1946 when Tony Accardo made him his underboss. It was a day of surprise for those out of the loop. Everyone else knew his day was coming.

Sam and his wife Ange spent time in Florida, willing the snow in Chicago to subside and seeing friends. Giancana's reach expanded, and his circle of syndicate/Mob associates did the same.

The Chicago underboss was now free to travel anywhere business called him, from California to New York and even Cuba. There were deals to make with previous rivals that benefitted everyone, and only J. Edgar Hoover couldn't see the handwriting on the wall that the Mob was organized.

When the weather in Chicago got a little warmer, Giancana returned to find that Eddie Jones had been paroled and was finally back in the policy racket working with his brothers, George and Mack. The money in the African American areas was terrific. With the Jones brother's experience, the Outfit moved into new areas of town that included all income brackets and all races.

Three numbers were drawn from a spinning wheel each day with ten spots, 0 to 9. The three spins represented a 1 in 10 chance of guessing the number correctly, so with overall odds of 1000 to 1, the policymakers paid 600 to 1 to the winners.

A single nickel bet paid the winner $30; a quarter paid $150. Those were dream amounts for people working for just a few bucks a day! Agents or writers hit the street in the morning, collecting bets and taking the money to their bosses. For thirty years, you could bet your policy in barbershops, bookie joints, and cigar stores up and down Bronzeville, knowing the Jones brothers would pay your guess if you won.

There was little anger or condemnation of the policy racket in the city, and the profits scored by the Jones brothers got invested in black businesses, starting with their tailor shop. Later they boasted the only black-owned Ben Franklin store on 47th street.

The money also bankrolled law enforcement officers, politicians, writers, sports figures, and entertainers who filled the local bars and dance joints. The money was so huge that the policymakers had to hire CPAs and lawyers to keep the records and police right where they wanted them.

Keeping much of the money local, the proceeds also financed banks, restaurants, and Provident Hospital. It was all too much for the Fed and the Outfit. And Time magazine recognized that these businessmen were hugely successful, "The Policy King's engine is the center of black businesses in the United States."

Author Richard Wright said, "They would have been steel tycoons, wall street brokers, and auto moguls had they been white."

By the mid-'40s, the Jones Brothers were taking more than $18 million a year in bets and paying back just over half. And death threats, violence, and even jail time for Eddie had crushed some of the high points away.

Eddie took the fall for his brothers and did 18 months for tax evasion, meeting Sam Giancana behind bars. They talked, schemed, and when Eddie got out, he took Giancana and the Outfit as equal partners in his 3,000 policy locations.

Brother Mack was killed in a car accident, leaving just Eddie and George to defend their turf. "Tough Teddy Roe, a powerful policy broker, was the son of a black mother and Italian father, but he never trusted Giancana. He had good instincts and told him; you'll have to kill me to take me out of the game."

The Outfit enjoyed two years of increasing profits and power, and then Giancana got greedy. He turned on Eddie Jones and told his lieutenants to get ready for war; they were going to take over all the policy wheels in town.

On a clear night in May, Sam met with Fat Leonard and his three most brutal soldiers, and they drove in two cars to a policy wheel near Eddie Jones's home for a chat.

As soon as they were alone, Sam and Fat Leonard took him out the back door into an alley and drove him to Sam's unfinished home in Oak Park.

The kidnapping and payoff of Guzik had worked so well that Sam figured the same tactic would work with Jones, but with a twist. Instead of a payoff, Sam sent word to Eddie's brother George that he wanted $250,000 and the whole operation in exchange for a breathing brother. He settled for $100,000 cash and the brothers' exit in three days. Eddie, George, their wives, and children all took a train to Mexico.

Giancana knew the kidnapping was the easy part as he moved his men into the policy locations Jones had left him. His problem was Teddy Roe, who still owned at least a thousand of the policy racket locations in town and refused to partner with Giancana, knowing he'd get booted out of town too.

After several years of solidifying their power on the South Side, the Outfit called on the Jones brothers to return to Chicago and make the peace. It was an offer they couldn't refuse.

George Jones introduced Giancana to Teddy Roe, but Roe wasn't interested in selling. A few days later, a meeting was set for 5 pm the following evening, but Roe never showed.

Finally reached at home by Charles Craig, Roe said, "You fucking rats aren't going to shake me down. I handled the negotiations to get Eddie out of his headlock with Giancana, getting the price of his freedom down from $250,000 to $100,000 and personally putting the cash in George's car for the handoff. Go fuck yourself."

Things didn't get much better for Giancana after that. The colored newspapers backed Roe, incensed that the Italian gang was taking over their neighborhoods and making them unsafe for business people to work. And, the Outfit's connections didn't hold sway in all areas of the state.

Plus, Roe was a hero in his neighborhood. He'd come to the area from Galliano, Louisiana, via Detroit and taken a job with Mr. Edward Jones, a tailor. When Jones decided to enter the policy game, Roe got a job as his first runner, taking bets and delivering money and guesses for the lottery.

After the Italian gangs took most of the policy banks, Roe held out. He refused to move from his home in Chicago with his wife Carrie and wasn't loudmouthed. He was a businessman and a Robin Hood type who had put money into legitimate businesses like car dealerships, restaurants, and bars.

Roe had also paid hospital bills for down-and-out neighbors, funeral tabs for those who went before him, and stood up for gamblers who got cheated at competitor's joints. He'd take some muscle with him when he had to and get a player's money back. If you were hungry, Teddy would spot a buck for a meal, then slide you a twenty so your family wouldn't go hungry.

Roe kept his policy wheels for years until Tony Accardo told his underboss to cut his power. Giancana took one last swipe at buying him off, catching him at 49th and Lawrence Avenue in Washington Park, but the conversation went sideways.

Afterward, there were no more attempts at negotiating, and Giancana sent Fat Leonard and his group to kill him and anyone who stood with him. Leonard Caifano had recently moved into a $100,000 home in Oak Park after years of loyal service to Giancana and had worked with his brother, Marshall, a Mad Man, on extortion and mob hits. He was as tough and strong as anyone, but he misjudged Roe.

Caifano grabbed a couple of hitters and waited for Jones to cross

South Park Way on foot before bursting from their car to shoot him. Caifano's first shot missed; Roe's didn't; his bullet catching the fat man square in the forehead. He slumped immediately to the ground as Roe fired several more shots and ran unhurt from the scene. Caifano was transferred to a hospital, where he died.

The following day, Chicago Police detectives arrested Roe for murder. He confessed to the shooting but claimed self-defense in his first court appearance. Tough Teddy was taken from court to the Cook County Jail, where he got an extra guard, and his meals were prepared outside the prison to prevent poisoning.

Since the police figured he might beat the murder rap, they charged him with conspiracy to violate the Illinois State anti-gambling statute. He was denied bail six times.

In the meantime, Giancana took his frustrations out on the Black bookies and remaining policymakers. They were threatened, beaten, and several were shot.

When Roe was finally released after beating the rap (some of the prosecutors were proven to have Mob ties), Tough Teddy stayed home, telling his wife, "This will all be over soon."

On August 4, 1952, Teddy dressed in a sharp three-piece suit and put a hat on his head. He left his home at 5239 S. Michigan Avenue but only got a few steps before a call in the wind came, "Roe."

A second later, a fusillade of shotgun blasts echoed down the street as Tough Teddy's body was slammed against a tree. He died sitting up, proud as always.

Local friends provided a $5,000 casket, and Roe received the most prominent funeral in Chicago since Jack Johnson years earlier. The 81-car procession lasted half an hour.

Vegas and the Chicago Outfit

According to FBI Agent William F. Roemer, Jr., a wiretap caught Sam Giancana reminiscing years later. At the time, he said, "I'll say this. Nigger or no nigger, that bastard went out like a man. He had balls. It was a fuckin' shame to kill him.

Eloquent or not, Giancana had respect for few people, but he learned much from Eddie Jones and Teddy Roe. He learned that nickels make quarters, and quarters make dollars, and all those dollars make you rich and powerful.

In the coming years, as crackdown after crackdown hit the Outfit, Giancana insisted that most casinos in Nevada used slot machines from good old Chicago, Illinois. Did I mention that he got a piece of the action as they left the factory and a bigger piece of the action when they got used in Las Vegas? I should have.

Fat Leonard never got the funeral Tough Teddy Roe got, but he was buried along with his name at Mount Carmel Catholic Cemetery in Hillside, Illinois.

His brother, Marshall (Marcello Giuseppe Caifano 1911 – September 2003), wasn't the massive 400-pounds Fat Leonard was, but he was meaner. And he was more than happy to have been a part of taking out Teddy Roe with eight shotgun blasts. Marshall was happy to do the bidding of his bosses or work on his own, no matter what it took to get the job done.

In 1941, when things were falling apart in the Outfit because of the Hollywood union scandal, mobster Nick Circella was charged in the extortion case. His cute girlfriend Estell Carey knew about the jobs Circella handled, and she agreed to cooperate in the federal investigation. To keep everything quiet, they let her keep dating Circella, but he got wind of the scam and told Caifano.

In February, Marshall and Sam Battaglia went to see Estell at her apartment at 512 Addison Avenue. She let them in, they talked, they slapped her around a little, but she swore there was nothing fishy going on. So, they knocked her to the floor, tied her to a chair, hands and legs, and started a more serious interrogation.

They promised her that if she told them what they wanted to know, they would stop, but she was stubborn, so they beat her repeatedly about the head and shoulders until she was unconscious. When she finally came out of her stupor, bleary-eyed and mumbling, she told the truth. Then they used a hand-held blowtorch and burned her mouth and face before setting her clothes on fire and leaving her. The authorities found her after a neighbor called the fire department. Thankfully she had died earlier.

Marshall wasn't happy unless he was busy, so he looked forward to every chance to send a message or end a conversation. The Outfit frowned on anyone taking more than a tiny percentage of their business away or skimming their profits. They dealt in cash businesses, and those created problems. Problems that Caifano took care of.

When bookie Frank Quattrochi told his street lieutenant that he had taken a few bad bets, he got a beating from Caifano, but Giancana said Quattrochi was too smart to over-book several games and not lay off the bets. "He'd rather take a beating for losing than get dead stealing. Do what you gotta do with that fuck."

Caifano wasn't the smartest, but he watched Quattrochi's life with the aid of a few kids down the block for a week and then ambushed him as he walked to his car after a meal in a pricey restaurant.

It was windy (Chicago, right?), and the police found a hat under a car near the crime scene with MC stitched into the bill. Caifano got picked up and questioned. Then he got released. He was working a long game with plans for a warmer climate.

Tony Accardo circa 1960 – Associated Press / Public Domain

Chapter Ten

Bugsy Siegel Dreams of Flamingos

As well as Bugsy's new Mexican drug highway was working to enrich him and his friends in Chicago, he was struggling with the Hollywood union fiasco and the push by the authorities against Jack Dragna in Los Angeles to rid the city of crooks and gamblers. Those same gamblers, Guy McAfee, Tutor Scherer, and Farmer Page, had all decided the city police were too rough on them and resettled in Las Vegas. Bugsy wasn't convinced.

He was rich, but he wasn't impressed. At least not with Las Vegas. He had an inkling that perhaps his future wasn't in California but that damn desert – especially when he had to deal with his girlfriend Virginia Hill's total disregard for anything outside Beverly Hills.

Still, those few casinos he was skimming were doing great, and Moe Sedway was talking to Scherer about a race book in the new Pioneer Hotel downtown on Fremont Street. And knowing Moe, he'd twist a little juice out of the place they could skim. And then Bugsy got lucky. He walked into a half-finished casino project on the burgeoning Las Vegas Strip and took over. And once again, he didn't have to pull a gun.

Siegel knew Billy (William Richard Wilkerson September 29, 1890 – September 2, 1962) Wilkerson from his days as the owner of Southern California restaurants to the couture-like Ciro's and La Rue. Places you could blow a hundred bucks on a meal with wine even in the 1940s.

And Bugsy knew Billy from his frequent, frenzied days shooting craps at the El Cortez, where he often went off for twenty or thirty grand. All that at a time when you could buy a ranch house with land and a barn for less – with an orange grove no less, near LA.

Wilkerson was a hard-working, twenty-coke-a-day ball of fire who managed and owned the Hollywood Reporter, but he was heavily addicted to horse racing and casinos. After years of losing his ass at the track and playing craps, Wilkerson figured the best thing he could do to pull the reins in on his gambling was to own a casino, so he leased the El Rancho Vegas for six months at the cost of $50,000.

He didn't know how to run a casino, so some friends of Bugsy's helped him. And since he didn't have to be there to manage the place, he had time to shoot craps at the Last Frontier and the El Cortez, where he lost $120,000.

One day on the way back from the El Cortez and another disastrous outing, Wilkerson saw a "For Sale" sign on several acres of scrub and sand. Why not, he thought, and in January of 1945, Wilkerson got the lot, sand, and sage for just $84,000. Mrs. Margaret M. Folsom later admitted that she and her husband had paid $100 an acre for the 33-acre plot, but Billy was happy with a new project.

He drew plans, filled pages and pages with Hollywood-style extravaganza drawings, and hired architects to fulfill his dream for a two-hundred-room palace in the desert.

It was near the end of World War Two, and getting plans approved for building materials involved some finagling, so the single approved building needed archways, overhangs, and walkways attached to it branching off from the casino. Wilkerson envisioned an elegant showroom, fancy restaurants, and air conditioning. The architects and construction company he hired said his dream would come true for a zesty $1.2 million.

But there was a problem. With all the cash passing through Wilkerson's hands at his restaurants and advertising in the Hollywood Reporter, Billy came into the deal with only $30,000. He got a loan of $200,000 from Howard Hughes and a $600,000 hotel loan from Bank of America in Los Angeles, pulling up well short of the mark.

He took his $30,000 down to the El Rancho to run it up, but the tables swallowed the cash in one gulp. Out of options, he asked Gus Greenbaum and Moe Sedway if they wanted to run his new casino in exchange for a $450,000 cash advance. "No problem," was the answer. Yeah, right!

Instead of a check to the construction company, they gave the gambler cash, and before the end of the year, he'd blown $400,000 right back into the El Cortez craps tables. Construction that had started months earlier stopped. The project was dead in the water.

His plan was half-baked and half-finished, sitting idle in the desert sun. Sand blew against the walls of the main building, inside and out. Weekly, Wilkerson drove from LA to Vegas, wandered the empty acres, and cogitated. One afternoon, he had a visitor on the dusty lot when a beautiful new Buick slid beside him, pulled into the construction site, and sat idle.

Eventually, from the back seat, a Mr. G. Harry Rothberg from the East Coast emerged from the car. The man scanned the lot, looked pensively at Wilkerson, and introduced himself.

Billy was like a proud papa, happy to show off what had already been finished (it wasn't much), and this Mr. Rothberg was intrigued. He talked about the design, the total square footage, and whether the cost could be kept under $12 a square foot. They connected. They laughed. They got down to brass tacks.

Rothberg was serious. "What do you need to finish, top to bottom?"

Excited, Wilkerson shot for the moon and said, "A million dollars." Rothberg said.

"Fine. I'll cut you a check. You finish the job; I take two-thirds ownership but don't worry, it's your hotel. No problems."

Three days later, a contract was signed at the bank, and a check was deposited. Billy Wilkerson walked out into the Las Vegas sun, the happiest he had ever been. Construction crews returned to work immediately, happy to have a job again, and everything was hunky-dory for a week.

On Tuesday, Wilkerson saw that exact Buick arrive on the lot. There were three suits in the car. He knew all three men: Gus Greenbaum, Moe Sedway, and Mr. Rothberg, whom the two men admitted was from the east coast, but Wilkerson's new managing partner was Bugsy Siegel.

More importantly, the money he contributed had not all come from his pocket. Instead, Siegel took a $750,000 investment from Frank Costello in New York, and he and Berman, Sedway, Alderman, and

91

Greenbaum each put up a $50,000 bump.

Greenbaum and Wilkerson contracted with the Del E. Webb Construction Company of Phoenix, Arizona, to complete the project. Webb was a former semi-professional baseball player and part-owner of the New York Yankees when he and his firm were hired to construct the Flamingo.

The construction started and stopped as Siegel had architects make changes on the fly. He argued with Wilkerson, the construction crew's head man, his general contractor Del Webb, and his girlfriend, Virginia Hill, who had been in charge of decorating.

She was known to be temperamental, but Bugsy was just living up to his name. At some point, he finally told his wife Esta, whom he had left in Scarsdale, New York, with his kids, to go to Reno and take the cure (establish a six-week residency for a divorce). She obliged, and their lawyers agreed on $600 per month alimony and $350 a week for child support. You could do a lot with $2100 a month in the '40s when most workers were making $25 a week.

Supply trucks drove onto the property and parked, their loads carefully checked by a foreman. Late at night, they left the property still loaded and re-entered in the morning hours to be re-checked and re-billed to Siegel. He was so sure that only he could manage the project that the whole ball of wax started melting in the 110-degree Las Vegas heat.

By then, the $1 million he had kicked into the construction was nearly gone. So was his temper. Virginia Hill took a trip to LA to avoid the growing treats from Bugsy, but that didn't improve his demeanor.

Although he had rooms at the Last Frontier, his favorite place to avoid construction noise was a set of offices at the Las Vegas Club downtown. The one is still owned by J. K. Houssels but run by Bugsy. The one where FBI Special Agent memos confirmed years later that J. Edgar Hoover had wired and constant access to conversations with

Siegel, Sedway, and many other hoods. They called the offices the "Boiler Room" since that was where so many deals were discussed.

And although the conversations covered years of discussions, the Director of the FBI (remember him, the all-knowing and all-powerful Hoover) took the memos and did nothing. A very curious fact.

It is evident from the recordings that the hotel project was in severe financial trouble. Money seemed to be pouring into the sand with no end in sight. At that point, Siegel thought he needed $600,000 to finish. He was wildly optimistic.

Memos also show Siegel's movements. Trips to LA, then a series of flights to Chicago and New York as he begged for more cash from Tony Accardo, and then Frank Costello followed.

Meyer Lansky gave him the same advice as the last time he showed up wanting money, "Ben, stop fussing with the features and get the joint open," but the Flamingo had swallowed him up.

When he returned to Vegas, he had a new scam for Wilkerson: corporate stock in exchange for five percent more ownership. Wilkerson could read the writing in the sand and give in. Next, Bugsy gave Virginia Hill the go-ahead for her decorating ideas. Accordingly, she blew through the money like wind through a fishing net. She also took a trip to Paris and Switzerland, depositing some "emergency" cash in a numbered account.

The following month Siegel coerced Wilkerson to sell him half the land for another five percent total stock, but Siegel was relentless. The more he got, the more he wanted. Six weeks later, he got the remaining land for another five percent, making Wilkerson a 48 percent partner, but not in Mob parlance.

Bugsy needed more cash, so in June of 1946, he formed the Nevada Project Corporation of California, naming (drumroll..........)

himself president. Wilkerson was toast, and that's when Hoover finally decided to make a move.

The FBI had observed that the Chicago Outfit was making headway in Las Vegas, LA, and even at home in Illinois, so Hoover started Capga (Capone gang). A deep investigation to go with their other investigations that seemed to rely on other investigations that weren't working against the Mob. You know, organized crime in every big city from Newark to Philly, to Buffalo, to Kansas City. You get the point.

Hoover's big plan was to get approval for even more wiretaps, starting with Meyer Lansky and Bugsy Siegel in LA, Las Vegas, and New York. Homes, businesses, oh, and a United States Attorney General's approval for hotel rooms and even mail drops meant Special Agents could steal US mail, read it, and then return it to mailboxes. Just in case anyone divulged a murder or something else in a letter.

After another six weeks of snooping, did J. Edgar stop the project? Did he stop the skimming at the Las Vegas Club, the Frontier, or the El Cortez? Nope. He called Wilkerson personally and told him he was mixed up with an extremely dangerous character and might want to "extricate himself from the project." Wilkerson was candid with J. Edgar, saying, "It's too late."

Hoover's next salvo was to leak a story to Walter Winchell, who went live via his radio show on July 14, 1946, to tell his audience that a prominent West Coast newspaper publisher was getting pushed out of his interest in a hotel project. It didn't take a genius to figure out who the story was about.

When friends told Winchell it was Siegel and Billy Wilkerson, both of whom he knew, he was sweating bullets. He made phone calls; he wrote letters and met with Wilkerson personally and babbled in his ear until he agreed to write a letter to Siegel. Eventually, his groveling was enough to keep Bugsy from killing him. Since they were friends, he caught a break once he admitted that Hoover was his source. Well, that and the fact that nobody in Vegas cared.

Siegel was still pissed, and FBI recordings from his motel room (401) at the Last Frontier caught him talking to Virginia Hill and saying, "I'll get him (Winchell) to make the Director meet with me, and I'll make that cock sucker tell me how he got the info, and I'll kill the people who gave it. If this makes it so I can't get a license here, what am I going to do with the hotel, stick it up my ass? I'll knock his fucking eyes out."

On August 5, 1946, the first gaming license for the Flamingo was denied by the Clark County Commissioner's office.

Siegel put another $62,500 into the construction himself, asking Meyer to do the same. Lansky agreed, forwarding a check, but told him, "Ben," the well's dry. Get the damn club open. It was never designed to be a $2 million front." If only that were all Bugsy had spent.

According to FBI memos, even after getting Meyer to kick in the extra cash, he still had one more favor to ask. "Meyer, I need a carload of beer," he said.

It was more than a few six-packs. What he wanted and got was a railroad carload, direct from Arthur H. Samish, who represented the California State Brewers Institute. Samish directed Alfred Hart Distilleries of Los Angeles, California, to ship the beer via rail into Las Vegas and drop it off. Then Siegel offered it directly to the commissioner's office. His liquor license got rubber-stamped a week later.

There wasn't a peep from the FBI, but the Salt Lake City office running Capca assigned a fourth agent to the investigation and sent him to become the new Las Vegas Resident agent. His first assignment was verifying bribery-related allegations involving several politicians, including Senator McCarran of Nevada.

US Senator Pat McCarran rearranged priority lists to allow the

Flamingo to get materials unavailable to other builders. Whatever was needed, McCarran could get. The price was still no object for Bugsy. He needed the supplies, and he needed to get open.

And then, in the middle of all the chaos, the Las Vegas newspaper carried a story about the construction of the Flamingo when veterans desperately needed materials for the construction of homes. Prompted by the newspaper story, the Civil Production Administration (CPA) put a "Stop Order" on the entire project and instructed Siegel and his architect to meet with the directors at the CPA West Coast office in San Francisco in October.

Not to worry. Although Siegel had changed his construction plans several times without authorization, a $20,000 bribe was plenty for the CPA in San Francisco. He couldn't find the original plans, so Del Webb swore that the March 1946 plans were the original January plans. Everything went fine after Senator McCarran explained, "I have the greatest respect for the CPA's job, and with all the construction going on, it is understandable that an error or two might be made."

Bugsy borrowed $950,000 from a Utah company, while Del Webb waited for $435,000 in payments before resuming construction.

To get them working again, Siegel drained his other Vegas joints, telling Greenbaum, "Listen, Gus, get $10,000 from Dave Berman and get $10,000 from the Golden Nugget. Then, take the remaining $45,000 from the Las Vegas Club racebook, make a check for $60,000 and another one for $40,000 to the Nevada Projects Corporation, and date them November 1. Then, call Del Webb and tell him there's $100,000 ready to be cashed in November." Siegel was walking on thin ice in the desert, and he could hear it cracking.

Phoenix contractor, Del E Webb, was waiting for a check one Friday afternoon in Siegel's room when Virginia came in and started throwing everything that wasn't nailed down at Bugsy. She had good delivery, but her aim was lousy, so she yelled and rushed at Bugsy, who grabbed her arm and forced it behind her back while she screamed and kicked him with her favorite $100 heels. Eventually, the room quieted, and she slunk out of the suite.

When she did, Siegel called someone downstairs and threatened to kill them if they let her back in the suite that afternoon. Then he remembered Del Webb was waiting in the wings. "Don't worry, we only kill our own, Del," Bugsy assured his contractor.

Del Webb and his construction company were now close to bankruptcy too. His lawyers and the Nevada Project's lawyers agreed: Webb would forget about the $770,000 profit he was expecting and would keep construction going if he was paid for all materials and current costs. To finish the construction, Gus Greenbaum got a $500,000 loan through Tony Accardo in Chicago at 4%. Now the Outfit would get 20% of the skim.

The only problem with that plan was that once the casino opened on December 26th, with no hotel rooms finished, it immediately lost money. All of Bugsy's big plans, planes flying in from Los Angeles and Hollywood stars as attractions, couldn't stop a terrible winter storm from killing the opening. Even with movie star George Raft losing $65,000 across the green felt tables, the joint took a loss.

The hemorrhaging continued for the next two weeks and totaled over $300,000. Dealers were stealing; slot attendants were stealing, and everything that could go wrong did.

Amazingly, Siegel was able to borrow another $500,000, even though he had sold 250% of the property and had no intention of paying any of his shareholders anything. And that's when Meyer Lansky called.

"Ben, you've got to fly to Cuba to see Lucky."

Well, Siegel was busy. He oversaw Vegas. He was Bugsy Siegel! And he was in deep shit because Lucky Luciano was still the boss.

In Havana, he was told, "Ben, the casino's not the only problem. There's an issue with the wire service, too. We expect to see our investment very soon from the casino, and you need to let Chicago have the wire."

Bugsy flipped, he yelled, he even threatened, but he was trapped, knowing his last source of income was withering away. "So, what's my end here? I lose the wire, all my income, and have nothing to show for the work I've put in?"

"Of course not, Ben, you've got your share of the bookies but not the wire fees, and you'll get something from Chicago, we're not there yet, but it's happening," Lansky told him.

He also said, "Ben, you've got your clubs in Las Vegas, and you've got cash coming to clean up the Flamingo, but that's the end."

Siegel left fuming but still relieved he would get another chunk of cash, even if it wasn't enough to finish building. He did not know he wasn't the only person in town to meet the boss. He was just one of 17 others, including Meyer Lansky, Tony Accardo, Sam Giancana, Frank Costello, and Albert Anastasia.

On March 1, 1947, the Flamingo reopened. There were hotel rooms. There were $7.95 steak dinners in fancy restaurants, but there still weren't any crowds. The casino broke even and then finally started to make a little profit, but it wasn't enough for Luciano or Lansky.

Meanwhile, things weren't any calmer between Virginia and Bugsy. They yelled, shoved, and had no compunction about airing their dirty laundry in public. One afternoon Hill caught him chatting up a busty young cigarette girl. The fight turned serious when Virginia clunked the girl across the mouth and pulled her hair. Bugsy yanked the women apart, but then Hill started kicking them both.

"Sure, save her young face, you gangster," Hill screamed as the now enraged casino owner pushed her towards a side door to the hotel grounds. "You're a murderer and a gangster," she cried, "you all are!"

When she pushed back at Siegel, he gave her a backhand across the face, bloodying her nose. "I'm through with you; I'm going to kill myself," she cried loudly. Siegel forced her to his penthouse, and the casino returned to business like it was an everyday occurrence. Maybe it was.

The third-floor penthouse featured bullet-proof windows overlooking the pool, steel-lined walls, and a floor safe for cash and jewelry. And there was an escape tunnel in the walk-in closet, just in case. They didn't need it that night.

In the morning, Bugsy took Virginia to Clark County General Hospital and admitted her for a drug overdose. She was released the following afternoon. When she returned to the Flamingo, she went to their room, packed her bags and a trunk, and headed to the airport.

From Las Vegas, she flew to Los Angeles and saw her brother, Charles Hill, who was staying at her home with his girlfriend, Jeri Mason. The following day she flew from coast to coast, and Joey Adonis picked her up at the airport in New York. They spent the night together; then, in the morning, she met with Frank Costello, who bought her first-class plane tickets to Paris, where she stayed until told she could return.

The next day, June 13, 1947, Tony Accardo announced that the Trans-America wire service was shutting down because he now owned the Continental Service.

Siegel was livid that the Continental was now a part of the Chicago Outfit's holdings, and the West Coast profits would go directly to Mickey Cohen. He had been pushed out of his own deal. He was defunct.

Ben spent the afternoon of June 20th with Allen Smiley and his lawyer in Los Angeles. That evening Smiley, Jeri Mason, Charles Hill, and Siegel drove out to Jack's Café at Ocean Park. The new restaurant offered complimentary newspapers for their guests. Ben took one with him. They drove to the Linden Drive home, where everyone stayed for the evening.

Jeri and Charles were upstairs; Ben sat reading the paper while Allen Smiley sat four feet away. It was Virginia Hill's home, but she was still in Paris. Outside, with his rifle propped up on the lattice work surrounded by tall bushes, a shooter waited patiently.

Ben snubbed out a cigarette and leaned back. Smiley sat quietly. Then, the glass windowpane shattered, and nine rifle shots echoed about the room, the bullets finding soft flesh and hard wood. One pierced a painting; one shattered a marble statue of Bacchus. Another crushed the bridge of Siegel's nose, while another of the five that found their mark passed through Bugsy's right cheek and sent his eyeball skittering fifteen feet away. Allen Smiley was not hit. When the shooting started, he fell to the ground and hugged the floor. He didn't stand for two minutes and didn't call the police for another ten minutes.

The shooter crouched and ran back to the car where Frankie Carbo sat waiting. Carbo ground the car into gear, and they moved smoothly up to touring speed and headed towards California Coast Highway 1. As they drove, the .30-caliber Army carbine rifle was cut down with a hacksaw, and its pieces were tossed from the moving car. They stopped to refuel in Carmel, grabbed a bite at a greasy spoon, and continued to San Francisco. Once in the City by the Bay, they holed up in a seedy apartment in South San Francisco.

The following morning, they boarded a plane for New York. In the city, they spent three days at 136-05 Sanford Avenue in Flushing. After a tip, they hit the streets running and split company. One headed to Florida, the other to North Shore Lake Tahoe on the California/Nevada border. The FBI raided the empty New York apartment hideout on June 25, 1947, and continued following imaginary footprints for years.

When the shooting was over and the hit confirmed, a phone rang in the El Cortez and was patched over to Davie Berman. He summoned Morris Rosen, and they met with Gus Greenbaum at the Flamingo casino less than 20 minutes later. Business continued as though nothing had happened.

In Los Angeles, bookies all over the coast rejoiced, knowing they didn't have to pay for two different wire services anymore, and now this, Bugsy was dead too? Mickey Cohen reminded them quickly that he was still taking a cut of their income. As for Benjamin Siegel, his body sat unclaimed for five days at the Los Angeles County Morgue.

When the Coroner's Inquest was over, Dr. Maurice Siegel, Ben's brother, who was a rabbi, claimed the body, and services were held at the Groman Mortuary in Los Angeles. The service lasted five minutes and was attended by six mourners: Siegel's divorced wife Esther, his two children, Barbara and Millicent, his brother Maurice, and his sister, Bessy. At the time, the police still had not returned two strange, 14-carat gold keys with "BS" monogrammed at the top, which they found in Siegel's pocket. What they went to has never been disclosed.

Months later, Beverly Hills Police Chief Clinton H. Anderson said, "The gun used to kill Mr. Siegel, a 30-30 carbine, is an unusual type of firearm, though it is kept in all police arsenals." The FBI ran ballistics tests on several similar weapons but found no perfect matches. However, months after the shooting, Chief Anderson took a trip to New York and stated, "I know who did it; now I have to wrap up enough evidence to justify an indictment."

Nothing came from Anderson's statements, and the FBI never added anything concrete to the investigation. We knew as much then as we know now about Bugsy going away.

As for the Flamingo, Sanford Adler and Charlie Resnick, owners at the El Rancho Vegas, were chosen to run the property. Rosen, Berman, Sedway, and Greenbaum tossed out the old deals and started a new one. He said the property was worth $5 million, and partners needed to put up 10% of their piece, so a deposit of $5,000 per slice was required. Adler ponied up $225,000 for a 45% cut. The others split the rest. Meyer Lansky took the cash.

Afterward, Adler had some pull, but Greenbaum and Berman ran the casino and the count room.

Adler wanted access to the finances but was locked out as the real owners skimmed 80 percent of the profits and sent satchels of cash across the states to Lansky, who distributed most of it to Chicago and New York.

When Adler threw a fit in the gaming pit one night about a high-roller's comps, Gus Greenbaum listened for thirty seconds and then gave him a quick punch to the face. Adler went down in a heap, and Greenbaum said, "Throw this bum out," and that's just what two-armed security guards did. He was still shouting as he was tossed out the door. Gus shouted in response, "You better get the hell out of Las Vegas, buddy, and never come back."

Adler steamed, he schemed, and he fled to Los Angeles. Then he drove to Carson City, Nevada, to protest his dismissal to the new Tax Board in charge of gaming licenses, and finally the State Supreme Court, but it was all for naught. He'd lost his investment.

Not to be deterred, he sold his home in Las Vegas and his businesses there and bought the Club Fortune at the corner of Second Avenue and North Virginia Street in Reno.

With Adler gone, Greenbaum got a better deal from his bosses. He took out a personal loan of $1 million with Chicago that NY agreed to, including Lucky Luciano, Frank Costello, and Meyer Lansky, who had the final say-so on the Bugsy going-away party.

The loan helped the Del Webb Corporation pay off and build a few more hotel rooms. Miraculously the club showed a profit of $4 million, even after Lansky's group skimmed $16 million. Las Vegas would boom over the next ten years as more properties joined the Flamingo on the "Strip."

If you are wondering how a casino could generate so much money in the 1940s, keep in mind that the Chicago Outfit wasn't the only business booming after WWII, and owners were making gobs of money. As for Nevada, casinos all over the state were also booming.

Flamingo Casino circa 1950 – Public Domain

Chapter Eleven

The Rise of Sam Giancana

With Bugsy Siegel disposed of, the Flamingo proved his vision and immediately earned gobs of money for the crime families that had staked the cash (mostly New York and Chicago). Las Vegas was the real thing.

In Lake Tahoe, two casinos had ties to Chicago, one to Kansas City, and then came "Russian Louie" Strauss in 1947 to front the Tahoe Village. As chronicled in *Mob City: Reno*, Nick Abelman had sold his casinos at the lake (Tahoe Village and Stateline Country Club) to concentrate on a vast new project in Reno. So Tony Accardo in Chicago expected a significant cut of the profits from the Tahoe Village. He just needed the proper frontman, and Strauss was his first choice.

Unfortunately, Strauss's license was denied, making him the worst front in history. Still, he'd spent years working for Bugsy Siegel and Tony Cornero, so he stayed connected and followed the word from Chicago - bring in Harry Sherwood to get licensed.

Sherwood was a character, having once robbed the SS REX – one of Cornero's floating casinos off Long Beach, California, in 1936, and living to tell the tale. But now, he owed $80,000 to the Flamingo in Vegas, and Greenbaum and Lansky were tired of waiting.

They helped get Sherwood into the Tahoe Village, expecting payment after the summer season, but Russian Louie said the books didn't look right. Only Sherwood and the Russian had access to the cash and the books. Someone was a rat eating all the cheese.

Near the end of the summer gambling rush, Louie and Sherwood had a knock-down-shoot-'em-out fight. Sherwood did the knocking down. Louie did the shooting. One slug from Strauss's gun passed through Sherwood's right elbow and lodged next to his heart.

When questioned by the police, Strauss claimed he had confronted Sherwood about the $100,000 in investor's money that his partner had gambled away. He also claimed that the 250-pound Sherwood had knocked him down, and only then had he drawn his gun and fired two shots in self-defense.

Doctors removed the bullet from Sherwood's chest, but the operation left him paralyzed from the waist down. During surgery, Russian Louie left town. He was caught in his truck at the California border, towing a trailer, and in the company of his 18-year-old girlfriend, a chorus girl Strauss claimed was his bookkeeper.

Sherwood never recovered, and Strauss went on trial for murder. A Nevada judge ruled, "No evidence was produced to show who fired the fatal shot." Louie walked out of court a free man.

Afterward, Strauss returned to Las Vegas, where he was often in the company of Marshall Caifano, who kept a close eye on him. They came up with a new frontman for the Tahoe Village, but neither Caifano nor Meyer Lansky was happy. They lost the $80,000 Sherwood owed the Flamingo partners, and a quiet investigation pointed to Russian Louie as the actual thief. Oh, and Sherwood was dead, but these things happen.

Sam Giancana

Back in Chicago, everything was going Sam Giancana's way. He'd done a fine job as an underboss, and with Tony Accardo happy, Sam pushed the Outfit's influence into rackets farther from home.

In 1947, he gave his brother Chuck a plumb job working the pinball machine and juke rackets in the Marquette District. Local Police captain Andy Akins was well paid each week and didn't see any problems with the new vending machines popping up everywhere.

Chuck got more than 200 of the illegal pinballs into bowling alleys, roadhouses, and bars and collected more than $10,000 a month in profits that he dutifully delivered directly to his brother. When he did, Mooney would slice $1,000 for Chuck and $2,000 for himself before the remaining $7k went to his boss, Tony Accardo.

Later in the year, Giancana sent Chuck to Cuba to see Meyer Lansky. He carried a half-million dollars of Sam's money to buy a piece of the Hotel Nacionale, one of Havana's best-earning casinos.

Chuck said later that he only met Lansky for a minute, handed him the cash, and with a wave, the small Jewish man said, "Thank you, tell Mooney hello."

Home again in Chicago, his brother told him there would be more trips, more casinos, all over the world. According to Chuck in his book **Double Cross**, Sam said, "Listen, we're moving fast now. I got two points, two percent of the skim for myself at the Flamingo in Vegas. They cost me $35 Gs apiece. Those points were a helluva buy. And after we're done locking up Cuba, we're going to look at the Arabs, the Dominican Republic. When we're done with the dictator in the Dominican Republic, he'll give us the whole fuckin' island."

In 1948, New York and Chicago moved in on the latest casino on the Strip, The Thunderbird. The brainchild of Guy McAfee, Tutor Scherer, Marion Hicks, and Clifford "Big Juice" Jones, the twinkling lights of the club sat just a mile north of the now financially successful Flamingo. Across the street was the El Rancho.

Unlike the Flamingo, the club wasn't named for a girlfriend's long, luscious legs but for a Navajo legend, "The Sacred Bearer of Happiness Unlimited."

The Flamingo casino had a three-story cascading waterfall of lights. The new bird had a three-color neon sign winking and blinking at the cars as they passed. It also had a Navajo-style Pow Wow showroom and dining area with native stone, unlike the more refined Flamingo restaurant and showroom. There were 76 motel rooms for weary travelers, plus Lil' Joe's Oyster Bar, named after partner Joe Wells and his Wells Cargo Freight Line.

Well's daughter was ten years old, born and raised in Reno, and later was crowned Miss Nevada in 1959. Miss Wells went on to even greater fame as Dawn Wells when she landed the role of Mary Ann in the 1964 TV show Gilligan's Island.

At the helm of the Thunderbird, the partners had Marion Hicks and former Lieutenant Governor and lawyer Clifford Jones, the king of connections and juice, to persuade any deal or business to find a way to thrive and survive. It was a good thing he was a partner because the first night in action, the casino got into trouble.

In early Vegas, it was a custom for existing businessmen to try restaurants, shows, and their luck in the casinos. The opening of the Thunderbird was no different as several prominent businessmen enjoyed a good meal and hoped for good luck at the gaming tables. None were successful until about 9:30 pm when two competing casino owners, Jake Katleman of the El Rancho and Farmer Paige of the Pioneer, hit the craps table.

Vegas and the Chicago Outfit

With a rush of luck rarely seen, the two men hammered front-line winner after winner and watched as security guards brought three "fills" of new chips to the game as Katleman and Paige raked winnings into the rail surrounding them. Eventually, they called it quits and hit the cashier's cage.

It took two cashiers ten minutes to verify their total of $160,000, but only two minutes for the Thunderbird's owners to realize they had no way to pay their cross-street rivals. Oh, the embarrassment!

Fortunately, the ownership included "Big Juice," who patched a call to Meyer Lansky, happily sitting in his penthouse suite in the Hotel Nacional in Havana, Cuba.

The conversation was easy but costly: "Sure, I'll be your partner," Lansky said, "and make sure you get my brother Jake a good job."

Ten minutes later, $150,000 in cash arrived from the Flamingo's vault, and ten days after that, Jake Lansky was listed as the "casino manager." Concerning the Thunderbird's illustrious owners, the skim at the Thunderbird was tapered down to just 30%. Jake Lansky handled the satchels going east.

His job was to watch over the casino games and slot machines, personally watch the money sorted in the "count room," and make sure that 30% got squirreled away every morning so he could hand it over to two couriers every week. One went straight to Chicago. One went to Florida.

Jake liked to say he never lost a bag, and long-trusted, non-made experts were standard. So were stars. Johnny Roselli used his charm and excellent eye to choose rising young Hollywood stars and fading actors as cash runners. Sam Giancana agreed, "They made great bagmen; everyone's too busy being dazzled and asking for autographs to ask what's in a briefcase."

But truth be told, bags occasionally went missing. Jake did lose one from the Thunderbird when a courier missed a delivery to Chicago in 1950. He got off the train two stops early and had a nice dinner and a nice woman. He'd done it before, but he'd never do it again.

That trip was his last after he awoke barefoot on a park bench, severely hung-over and without his bag. Rather than calling his contact and pleading out (and finding a way to pay back the $42,000), he went into hiding. He was found three weeks later by two hustlers in a neighboring state. Then he was beaten, questioned, and beaten again. A decision on his fate was sealed when he pleaded out that he was too poor to repay the debt.

The two street soldiers took him to a nearby sawmill, where he was pulped out, and his remnant remains became part of the company's next delivery for paper products. Hollywood never missed him.

A less-known event involving craps occurred later in the year when Rex Allen and the Sons of the Pioneers performed at the resort. Allen brought his horse Coco onto the stage during the dinner show. And you guessed it; the horse took a crap while the spectators watched in surprise.

Also crappy was the treatment of minorities in Las Vegas. Nat King Cole was a much sought-after entertainer in the 1940s, but he wasn't allowed to use the front entrance or visit the casino in 1949 when he was a headliner at the Thunderbird.

Instead, he had to stay across the tracks in some decrepit wooden shacks he dubbed Dust Ville. If he and his manager wanted to gamble, they could only go to a local Chinese – owed club with dice games. Sadly, Vegas wasn't much different from other parts of the country.

While the Strip was growing, the downtown area of Fremont Street was still a great earner. Moe Sedway was the listed owner at the El Dorado Club, and he took what he felt was a fair share of the profits before sending satchels of skimmed cash off to Chicago and New York.

Chicago's platform downtown hadn't diminished after Bugsy went away, and they concentrated more on the Strip. The El Cortez and the Las Vegas Club were great earners too.

Benny Binion was the biggest gaming earner in the Dallas area, but he lost his political strength, and Las Vegas, Nevada, was the next obvious choice. He also hoped to shed his killer background since he'd always asserted that when people around him (AKA competitors) got dead, it was always an act of self-defense that had caused their demise.

In 1936, Binion and his partner Buddy Malone gunned down Ben Frieden, a gamer moving into his territory, but no charges were filed. Likewise, in 1940 when Sam Murray dared to try and open some floating craps games in Dallas. This time, Binion and his bodyguard Ivy Miller caught Murray as he tried to enter a bank, leaving him filled with bullets and bleeding on the steps.

Murray died on the spot, but the outcome would have been different if his bodyguard, Herbert Noble, hadn't been paid off to take a sick day. Charges were filed against Ivy and Benny, but enough money crossed palms to get the case dropped – on the last day the District Attorney held office.

Binion and Noble's agreement allowed Murray's policy wheels to fall to him and his partner, Ray Laudermilk, but Benny still wanted a cut. The wheels were highly profitable, so Benny demanded more money. Noble refused. A month later, Benny's gang lit a fuse, and Laudermilk's car blew into a million pieces.

In retaliation, Binion's top bodyguard was ambushed and killed by a shotgun blast. The gang fighting intensified.

A week later, the gang caught Noble in his car and plastered him with bullets, but he lived, so they bombed his first lieutenant's car, who wasn't so lucky. Neither was Noble's wife, who borrowed her husband's car one hot sunny afternoon, and she too went away after a bomb attached to the car's ignition demolished everything within 10 feet of the driveway.

Amazingly, as those around him died, Noble lived on, even after being caught in a crossfire and shot six times. While recuperating at a local hospital, a sniper took a few stray shots at him too, but the man refused to die.

District Attorney Henry Wade of Dallas stated he had information that there was a $10,000 contract out for the death of Noble. Noble said he had heard $50,000.

About that time, the Chicago Outfit backed Binion's rival in the local Sheriff's race so they could control the local gaming, and Benny was forced out of town. He arrived angry in Las Vegas in '47, dragging his wife, five children, and a trunk full of cash.

He may or may not have known that the Outfit had been instrumental in bouncing him from Dallas, but in Vegas, he was welcomed as an old friend. Why not? His money was as good as anyone's, and boom, he was a partner at the Las Vegas Club. Very handy!

But his time at the casino was short since he wanted to run things differently than his new buddies. And, he didn't take kindly to his profits going to the Mob. So, Binion opened the Westerner Gambling House and Saloon with Louis "Russian Louie" Strauss, where he was quickly licensed. Still, his luck faded after Cliff Helms, one of his bodyguards, killed Johnny Beasley - a two-bit hustler trying to blackmail Binion - in the casino's restroom.

The club was tainted, so Moe Sedway and the gang sold Benny a piece of the El Dorado club with the enclosed Apache Hotel, which he reopened as Binion's Horseshoe Club. Governor Charles Russell said, "The license is predicated on Binion's affidavit and proof that he is not engaged in gambling in any other state where gambling is illegal."

Apparently, Nevada was strict. Shootings, car bombings, and other nefarious activities notwithstanding, they wanted to make sure Benny wasn't involved in any illegal gambling.

For the record, one fine morning in August of 1951, Herbert Noble drove from his farmhouse and stopped at his mailbox to get his mail. With the engine idling, a man waiting on a bluff 60 yards away pushed a switch connected to 60-yards of wire. The result was an electrical impulse that triggered a Delco battery hidden 18 feet from a box at the base of Noble's mailbox.

Attached to the box was enough explosive to demolish Noble's 1951 sedan and leave a hole four feet deep in the roadway. Herbert's body, bones, and flesh were scattered 200 feet in every direction. It was the 12th attempt on his life.

Police traced the killer's use of the battery and the wiring to the spot on the bluff where tire tracks were evident. Ironically, the hood from Noble's car flew and landed just a few feet from the spot.

Just a few weeks before Noble's big blast, Binion and Russian Louie Strauss were driving in Las Vegas when a gunman took six shots at their car. Probably just a cranky gambler, right?

Regardless, Binion hired a new bodyguard, Glen Bodell, and kept the lights at his ranch house lit 24 hours daily. The gated enclave was patrolled by two vicious Great Danes dogs so mean that they had even attacked Mrs. Binion, scarring her for life.

At the new casino, Binion set his limits higher than his competition as soon as his gaming license was rubber-stamped back into action. To get players in the door, he hosted a month's-long poker game featuring the Southern Circuit's best player Johnny Moss and the deep pocket gambler "Nick The Greek" Dandalos.

The crowds came, they gambled, they lost what they were expected to, and Binion's Horseshoe Club became a local favorite. The

Outfit was happy with their sale price, but it's hard to say today how long they got a monthly cut of the win.

Binion was old school and likely shared, as an event that happened right after Bugsy Siegel went to his eternal gangster-land home might infer.

From a spot in his room at the Last Frontier, "Fat Irish" Green, a sometime bodyguard and race book operator for Bugsy, took out the suitcase he was holding for Siegel. He boarded a plane for New York and met with Meyer Lansky in Frank Costello's office, where the suitcase was opened.

Inside sat $300,000 in cool green cash. Lansky was so happy to see the money that he called the El Cortez and told them to set Mr. Green up with Penthouse 1 for life. Oh, and free food for life too.

Lansky's word was good, and even after Jackie Gaughan purchased the property in 1963, Fat Irish Green (who was getting fatter and fatter) stayed in the hotel, gratis.

Benny Binion offered to take the Fat Man in for meals, and Mr. Green ate at the Horseshoe for free for the rest of his life. Of course, this wasn't uncommon. Even Moe Sedway admitted to the Kefauver Committee, "I get my room; I get my board." You're an owner; you don't pay for nothing!

Desert Inn Casino Pool circa 1950s - Ferris H. Scott / Public Domain

Chapter Twelve

Wilbur and Moe's Desert Inn

With Bugsy Siegel gone, Las Vegas casinos fell to a triumvirate of Gus Greenbaum, Morris Rosen, and Johnny Roselli. Greenbaum and Rosen handled the casinos with backing from Davie Berman and Israel Willie Alderman. Moe Sedway kept a watch on the racebooks in town, and Johnny Roselli watched everything.

Roselli was released from prison in 1947 after his sentence for participating in the Hollywood Union scandal. While the Los Angeles FBI office continued to produce memos saying he was employed as a movie producer at Monogram Studios, he traveled continually to Las Vegas, where he was the Chicago Outfit and Los Angeles mob's enforcer.

With a standard skim of 75%, the Outfit's casinos were much more valuable than Nevada regulators or the IRS ever knew. And, that skim money had to get to the most trusted bagmen – and a couple of bag women – so it could find its way to Meyer Lansky for final distribution.

At the El Rancho, the owners continued to lease out the casino, and Wilbur Clark did very well with his piece of the pie, parlaying a $200,000 investment into $1.5 million in less than three years. He sold out in 1946 with dreams of grandeur.

Like Bugsy Siegel, Clark learned to grind out everything possible from his casinos, and while his partners skimmed, he got rich too. After starts and stops at four casinos, Clark salivated over the idea of owning a new casino. And like Billy Wilkerson, he had plans for a new joint with real panache and style. Sound familiar? It was.

Located across from the Last Frontier, Clark bought the Players Club – a hot-spot bar and band joint – for $75,000. He got the land surrounding the upscale roadhouse and told the local press he was building Wilbur Clark's Desert Inn.

His due diligence priced the project at a little over $1.5 million, and he hired ex-El Rancho design and remodeling partner Wayne McAllister to head his project. Records show Clark listed a 7.5% expense for the architecture of the proposed $1.5 million building cost for the hotel (62 units), casino, and restaurants.

He also included $2,500 monthly for his president, $1,000 for his manager, $225 for a night auditor and secretary, and $700 for four gardeners.

Frank Sinatra saw the casino being built and offered to buy out Clark and change the name to New Horizon, but Moe Dalitz told him to "back the fuck-off". Shortly after, Clark realized he couldn't finish the project without a loan, and no banks in town would touch the project.

Then, like knights in shining armor, Moe's Mayfield Road Gang (Morris Kleinman, Ruby Kolod, Sam Tucker, et al.) came to the rescue with $3.6 million to finish the project. Cash is king, and while Clark may have crowed about his property from then on, he held less than 10% after what Moe and his gang took.

And where did Moe get the cash for the final $6.4 million-dollar opening on April 24, 1950? Well, from the Teamsters Union! The DI was the first to harness the power of the Teamsters and the first to bask in the glow of pre- and post-opening publicity on a national scale, including a spread in Life magazine.

Unlike Bugsy's disastrous opening of the Flamingo, the Desert Inn was an unqualified success from the start. Aside from hundreds of newspaper and magazine reporters invited by publicist Hank Greenspun (founder of The Las Vegas Sun newspaper), the marketing department had hundreds of players on their lists for future events.

Wilbur Clark personally invited 150 high rollers he knew from his other casinos and offered every one of them a $10,000 starting credit line. Most lost, and the DI was paid for in less than a year, but those sweet Teamster loans were paid back a drip and a drop at a time.

In 1949 when the Detroit Teamsters local demanded a five-day workweek for their workers, a strike seemed imminent. Moe contacted Jimmy Hoffa, and for $25,000, the problem went away.

The FBI kept detailed records on Dalitz, whom they characterized as the "head of the Mayfield Road Gang," dating back to 1938. Dalitz denied to agents that he was ever a part of the Purple Gang of Detroit, although he grew up with several gang members. He also told the FBI that he left Detroit for Akron, Ohio, where he engaged for approximately four years in the bootleg alcohol business before moving to Cleveland, where he continued to sell bootleg whiskey.

The FBI agreed with his statements and noted that Dalitz "Muscled his way into gambling, pinball, slot machine, and other rackets. His major competitor in the slot-machine racket in Cleveland, Nathan Weisenberg, was ambushed and killed. Dalitz was never charged."

Clark was the perfect host and the perfect ego for Las Vegas. He was a legend in his own mind and minted 3,500 $1 slot tokens with his likeness on them. He liked them so much that he made key chains and lucky bucks with his picture, then chips. The property was spacious, with plenty of parking right in front of the casino. It became a favorite of locals for meetings, and plenty of deals originated at the bar.

There were also plenty of Hollywood types in attendance on any given weekend in Las Vegas. With stars like Ronald Reagan playing at the Sahara, Sinatra playing at the Sands, Jimmy Durante, Rosemarie, Joe E. Brown, Bing Crosby, Bob Hope, and Zsa Zsa Gabor often seen hobnobbing around, Vegas was the place to be in the 1950s.

Moe Dalitz was a big golf fan, playing the resort's course every morning and taking lessons from the club's resident pro, Howard Capps, who is credited with the idea of pitting the winners of the previous year's PGA Tour events in a Tournament of Champions. Dalitz and Allard Roen came up with the prize – the most on tour – of $10,000. When the first year's winner, Al Besselink, captured the tournament in 1953, he was presented with a wheelbarrow filled with 10,000 silver dollars. Dalitz suggested he make a sizable donation to charity, so he promptly donated half the money to the local Damon Runyan Memorial Fund for Cancer Research. "Honestly, I wanted to," he said.

Down in Cuba, Meyer Lansky convinced Fulgencio Batista to let him run the National casino. Pan Am's Intercontinental Hotels Corporation took over the management of the hotel in 1955. Lansky took a wing of the grand entrance hall to refurbish, including a round bar, a restaurant, a showroom, and of course, the luxurious casino with chandeliers, deep carpet, and a new job for his brother Jake.

New chips were made for his frontman, Wilbur Clark, and again they featured the smiling man from Las Vegas, who managed to visit the club more than once while it was in operation. Wilbur Clark's Casino International opened with Eartha Kitt in the dinner theater, and flights from Florida were packed with tourists. The casino was a huge success. Dalitz and Lansky scored most of the income, while Batista's wife helped collect her husband's ten-percent fee nightly.

Around the island, casinos were going up faster than in Las Vegas, and why not? The government was matching, dollar for dollar, all construction costs. George Raft, Bugsy's old pal, fronted for the Capri casino. Everyone was getting rich but the locals.

After the Desert Inn property opened in Las Vegas, Beldon Katleman expanded his Last Frontier casino and opened the Silver Slipper at 3100 Las Vegas Boulevard South.

The casino was the perfect glamour and glitz of Las Vegas, with a huge 20-foot spinning slipper made of silver and mirrors that dazzled passersby with a continuously changing display of spotlight-reflected light beams.

And then, right in the middle of some seriously upbeat win and skim numbers, a little-known senator from Tennessee tried his best to spotlight what was happening with gambling all over the United States.

His results in state after state were massive, not so much in Nevada or Las Vegas.

Frank Costello at Kefauver Hearings circa 1951 - Al Aumuller, World Telegram / Public Domain

Chapter Thirteen

The Kefauver Commission

This section contains direct information culled from the Kefauver Commission. According to records of the United States Senate, in 1949, more than 10,000 cities nationwide petitioned the federal government to combat organized crime, something the FBI refused to do since, according to Director J. Edgar Hoover, it did not exist.

To the Senate's credit, Senator Estes Kefauver of Tennessee drafted a resolution to create a special committee to investigate. To the Senate's condemnation, there was a great debate about whether this was necessary, and the Commerce and Judiciary Committees debated long and hard for their sides.

Eventually, Vice President Alben Barkley's tie-breaking vote established a special committee that Kefauver would head with a budget of $150,000 to study interstate crime. The five-member committee spent fifteen months investigating, and while some authors have whitewashed the effects, they were pretty profound.

The committee met in 14 major cities and interviewed hundreds of witnesses, prominent crime figures were served subpoenas, and many testified under oath. Some weren't as candid as the senators had hoped, but they all made for good TV material.

Frank Costello, by that time, considered the head of the Mob, took the Fifth Amendment at all costs, refusing to testify as his answers might incriminate him. He was eventually jailed for contempt of court and later for tax evasion.

Bugsy Siegel's ex-girlfriend testified, but some of her remarks were bleeped from TV screens, including an exasperating time for the senators when she tried to explain why the men she knew gave her mink coats, jewels, and money:

Senator Tobey: "But why would Joe Epstein give you all that money, Miss Hill?"

Virginia Hill: "You really want to know?"

Senator Tobey: "Yes, I really want to know."

Virginia Hill: "Then I'll tell you why. Because I'm the best cocksucker in town!"

Senator Kefauver: "Order! I demand order!"

After her testimony, Hill swept her hair back behind her wide-brimmed hat, pulled her $5,000 mink coat closed and pushed her way through a sea of reporters, one of whom asked an innocent question. Hill's response? A slap in the face to the female scribe.

"I hope the atom bomb falls on every one of you," Hill shouted as she left the building. But when she got to a taxi, she stopped long enough for the photographers to get a few good shots.

Hill was a valuable party favor for the Mob's get together's and also a formidable bag person who was trusted with carrying millions of dollars in cash from fenced jewelry robberies, Las Vegas casino skim, and likely a bit of mad money stashed away for her and Bugsy in a Swiss bank account.

The committee also established through tax records, CPA trails, and sworn testimony that the Mob and its branches in New York, Miami, Detroit, New Jersey, Kansas City, and especially Chicago were running a profit game that most viewers could hardly fathom – the money was that huge!

Many of the findings involved the illegal drug trade, much of which was initially facilitated by Waxey Gordon's group on the east coast until his run-in with Bugsy Siegel. Ironically, Bugsy worked with Virginia Hill in the early '40s to establish a new supply route through Mexico. She mingled well with the power groups, and he had the money and workforce to establish Tony Accardo's Outfit with a perfect trade route.

However, the Kefauver committee spent an inordinate amount of time with gaming since that seemed to be where the money was. To that end, they suggested:

The transmission of bets or wagers, or the transmission of money in payment of bets or wagers, across State lines by telegraph, telephone, or any other interstate communication, or the United States mails, should be prohibited.

The prohibition against the transportation of slot machines in interstate commerce should be extended to include other gambling devices susceptible to gangster or racketeer control, such as punchboards, roulette wheels, etc.

Vegas and the Chicago Outfit

Early in the investigation, states started cleaning up their acts before "That crazy Kefauver's group" showed up. A grand jury report in Los Angeles named 60 persons as defendants in connection with a $7,000,000 bookmaking operation. Imagine that!

Crime legislation received particular attention in nearly every State legislature which held 1951 sessions. Eleven States tightened their narcotics laws; eight imposed new controls on horse racing; five introduced new book-making laws, and ten States revised their gaming laws.

In New York City, 505 members of the police department retired when they realized their weekly graft was going away.

In New Jersey, Joseph Doto, alias Joe Adonis, labeled by the committee as a co-leader with Frank Costello of the east coast underworld, was sent to prison.

In Maine, a 5-month secret probe produced 146 indictments in Cumberland County, and the legislature adopted a new gambling law-making bookmaking, lottery, numbers, and similar felonies.

Around Chicago, 1,200 slot machines were seized and destroyed by the State police, and two large bookmaking establishments --one grossing more than $6,000,000 a year - were raided and closed.

In Louisiana, slot machines previously found in practically every business were outlawed – and the laws enforced after the committee's hearings in New Orleans. The case against "Dandy Phil" Kastel, an associate of Frank Costello, was dismissed.

John J. Fogerty, co-owner and operator of the local wire service, entered a plea of nolo contendere and was given a fine, while Carlos Marcello, recognized kingpin of Louisiana racketeering, was convicted and received a sentence of 6 months in prison and a fine of $500.

Again, according to the committee, "The Accardos, the Guziks, and the Costellos who direct the big-city syndicates have their counterparts in the smaller cities. Territories may be more restricted, but the modus operandi of the small-town racketeers is virtually a carbon copy of that followed by the big-city mobs.

"Gambling is controlled by former bootleggers, and the emphasis is on illegal bookmaking which is dependent upon the wire service emanating from Continental Press Service, controlled by the old Capone syndicate."

"A bookmaker cannot do business without prompt racing information. And this he cannot obtain except through the interstate monopoly of the mob-controlled Continental Press Service, which obtains the news from the track illegally and broadcasts it through an elaborate system of wigwag, telephone, and telegraph. The $2 bet placed with a local "bookie" is a contribution to a $5,000,000,000 mobster operation."

More specific information was detailed for individual locations, including Atlantic City, where it was concluded that the city was "riddled with rackets, including nearly every known type of gambling operation. Its famous Boardwalk is lined with stands operating devices purporting to be games of skill but looked upon by their customers as games of chance. It contains two powerful numbers syndicates, and nearly every cigar store is a front for a book-maker."

A former operator of a Boardwalk game testified that to obtain a license, he paid the license fee of $1,000 plus an additional $1,000 in cash "under the table" to Joseph McBeth, the treasurer of the Republican County Committee, and a $250 cash payment directly to Senator Farley made in Farley's kitchen.

In Kentucky, where at least a dozen fancy gaming houses graced the countryside, the committee noted the Beverly Hills Country Club, the Latin Quarter, the Yorkshire Club, and the Alexandria Club operating openly.

"At the Beverly Hills Country Club, about 150 persons were observed in the casino where there were four dice tables, two roulette wheels, a black-jack table, and a chuck-a-luck table. About 100 persons were observed in the Latin Quarter, which featured three or four dice tables and two roulette wheels."

Other counties' smaller clubs included the Lookout House, the Kentucky Club, the 514 Club, the Kenton Club, the Press Club, the Gold Horseshoe, and the Turf Club.

According to testimony, the counties in question had Grand juries in session "for a total of about 27 days each year and the rest of the time gambling continues unhindered." Nice!

In Kent County, it was estimated that there were 1,500 slot machines in operation. When the committee subpoenaed business records from 1948 and 1949, the partners' shares at the large casinos included some substantial payoffs: Marion Brink, wife of James H. Brink, $33,860; B. W. Brink, $16,930; Charles V. Carr, $16,935; Mitchell Meyer, $20,858; John Croft, $10,429; Samuel Schroeder, $39,583; Louis Rothkopf, $41,765; Morris Kleinman, $41,765; Moe Dalitz, $41,765; Louise Tucker, wife of Samuel Tucker, $41,765; and Charles Polizzi, $33,352. Most of those were from the Cleveland group, or Mayfield Road Gang, who relocated after that to Las Vegas.

In Newport, the city manager (Mr. Rhoads) stated that the casino owners had offered him $1,000 weekly to look the other way. They could easily afford that amount since the books at the Beverly Hill Country Club showed similar payouts distributed to their owners: Samuel Tucker, Moe Dalitz, Rothkopf, and Kleinman, $44,019 each; Charles Polizzi, $32,014; T. J. McGinty, $34,301; John Croft, $26,583; Harry Potter, $20,008; Mitchell Meyer, $17,150; Samuel Schroeder, $54,024; and Marion Brink, $40,017.

In addition, Tucker was paid a salary of $10,000 annually from 1945 to 1948, Meyer and Potter were paid $3,900 each for 1948 and $4,110 each for 1949. The money wheels took in $70,000, chuck-a-luck, $17,000; blackjack, $51,000; craps, etc., $244,000, and slots, $69,000.

To be thorough (and redundant, sorry), the committee found that the operations at the Yorkshire Club produced $1,526,000, with a gross profit of $614,000 and a net of $427,597. Those dollars went to some of the same owners, plus point holders in Kentucky, Cincinnati, Tucson, and Detroit.

Downhome in Scranton, PA, Police Captain McElroy said there were independent gaming operators and a syndicate headed by Mr. Cohen that grossed more than $30,000,000 a year.

One small operator, Ralph S. Kreitz, or Reading, had 100 slots at what he deemed chartered clubs and bars. They did an average of about $180,000 a year, which he split 50-50 with the owners. Then he stopped himself and added, "of course, I really only made about $60,000 due to the goodwill expenditures for beer and lunches. Sandwiches were 75 cents, and beers were 50 cents. That means Mr. Kreitz ate about 20,000 sandwiches and drank 60,000 beers that year!

In New Jersey, that $60,000 annual salary of Mr. Kreitz pales compared to Abner Longie Zwillman's income, according to the States Treasury, which conducted an intensive investigation of Zwillman. Testimony showed:

Senator: Now, Mr. Baldwin, as a result of your investigation, can you give us an approximation of how much this syndicate collected from 1926 to 1933?

Mr. Baldwin: We uncovered bank deposits of around $25,000,000, then we found out that was only part of the syndicate's operations. We found that the cash they took in they never deposited. Mr. Joseph "Doc" Stacher, at one time told me that they collected at least as much cash as they collected (checks).

Senator: So that means roughly that the Reinfeld Syndicate collected approximately $60,000,000 from their illegal liquor distributorships?

Mr. Baldwin: Based on my investigation, I would say yes."

Much of the money received was sent in $100,000 and $500,000 lots, frequently in gold, to Cuba "so that in case this country got too hot for them, they would have something if they had to flee."

Later, the bootlegging operation was owned by several people in a legitimate operation – including Zwillman, Frank Costello, and Stacher. The new corporation was named Browne-Vintners.

In 1940 Browne-Vintners was sold to Seagrams for $7,500,000, but some of the owners failed to report the correct percentage of their ownership on the tax forms. Most were prosecuted in 1950.

Zwillman was a partner in Public Service Tobacco, a distributor of cigarettes through vending machines, with "Big Mike" Lascari, a close friend of "Lucky" Luciano. Gross sales 1949: $1,421,881.38. Plus Federal Automatic, E & S Trading Company, and a General Motors distributorship. Oh, and 42,000 shares of Barium Steel Corporation valued at $600,000.

What wasn't explained was why Zwillman offered Democratic candidate Elmer Wene $300,000 in exchange for the right to approve the man-appointed attorney general of New Jersey.

In Chicago, the mood was also sour as the committee subpoenaed many of the Outfit's highest members and some of their associates in other states.

Murray Humphreys read into the record a statement claiming his privilege against self-incrimination, as did Rocco Fischetti. However, he did admit he had used the alias of J. Harris in the past but refused to say why. Others testified they didn't know Outfit members like Jake Guzik,

Al Capone, Frank Nitti, and especially James Ragen, whose death got a lot of coverage.

When Committee counsel asked Humphreys, "Do you know who killed James Ragen?" He replied, "I am going to have to claim my privilege on that also, sir."

Well then, "Do you know who killed William Drury?"

"I am going to have to claim my privilege on that also, sir."

It's good that he did because the same man who arranged for Ragen to die also arranged the death of Drury. William Drury was a good cop in Chicago, at least for a while. In 1944, Drury was fired for looking the other way while Tony Accardo flooded the city with gaming joints and slot machines.

Taking his firing to court, Drury got reinstated but was fired again after refusing to appear before the grand jury. Then, he and his partner avoided criminal prosecution for their refusal after a witness to the grand jury probe was found murdered.

Called before the Kefauver Commission, Drury was set to testify. His body was found slumped behind the wheel of his new Cadillac, covered in his own blood. Four large holes had penetrated the windshield. There were more holes in his chest and neck.

Marshall Caifano read the reports of the killing and got a sour look on his face when he read, "Drury had six $100 bills in his pocket when he was shot."

Said Caifano, "What a fuckin waste. I'd a taken a minute longer if I'd a known that."

Marvin Bas, an Outfit attorney ready to testify the same day about Chicago gaming operations, was also murdered. Sam Battaglia knew about the hit but never admitted he was involved. Other big names in

Chicago got press that year.

Cases presented to United States attorneys included players from a dozen states. In Chicago, those names were:

Anthony J. Accardo, Chicago, Ill.

Murray L. Humphreys, Chicago, Ill.

George S. May, Chicago, Ill.

Rocco Fischetti, Chicago, Ill.

Jacob Guzik, Chicago, Ill.

Joseph Aiuppa, Cicero, Ill.

The Kefauver hearings let the cat out of the bag and the wind out of the sales for most small gaming operators. For the big boys, Union infiltration and manipulation became more critical. As for the gambling, everything pointed to Las Vegas.

The hearings held in Las Vegas were more of the same. Still, interesting dialog explained how Siegel and the Outfit had denied service to some racebooks to demand they share a weekly rate and a piece of the overall action.

When racebooks refused, they got nothing. If they controlled a series of bookie's joints, they paid heavily, as outlined by the Last Frontier's manager, William Moore.

Senator Tobey: How much does your establishment pay for the service?

Mr. Moore: For the race-wire service?

Senator Tobey: Yes.

Mr. Moore: Approximately $200 per month. It's just a new

establishment.

Senator Tobey: It might interest you to know, Mr. Moore, that we examined the Continental Press directors and officials in Washing- ton and asked how many receivables they had, and they had 20 or 24 receivables. The first name on his list, we asked them what they paid for the service, and it may surprise you that they said $6,000.

And I said, "$6,000 a year?"

"Oh, no, $6,000 a week."

So there is one that pays $312,000 a year to Continental Service.

Does that surprise you?

Mr. Moore: No.

Senator Tobey: $312,000 a year?

Mr. Moore: That doesn't surprise me.

Mr. Halley, Do you have any other concessions?

Mr. Moore: In the gambling?

Mr. Halley: Yes.

Mr. Moore: Yes, there is a fellow by the name of Waterman that has 50 percent interest in the penny roulette; a fellow by the name of Phillips that has a 50 percent interest in the commission room.

Mr. Halley: Why do you have these concessions?

Mr. Halley: Would you explain why you have the other concessions?

Mr. Moore: Well, the penny roulette is an illustration, and the reason we have that concession is that we know nothing on earth about penny roulette, and it is a unique game all within itself, and I have seen many people try to operate it and never make a quarter. Others operate it and do all right.

And Phillips on the commission room, frankly, that is a dangerous game. You can win or lose $200,000 or $300,000 or more in one day.

Mr. Halley: Would you explain what the commission room is?

Mr. Moore: The commission room is a lay-off room for the racehorse book. In other words, they lay off bets that are received in the racebook.

Senator Tobey: Reinsurance?

Mr. Moore: Reinsurance, yes.

Mr. Halley: Do you lay off all your bets or only a part?

Mr. Moore: We lay off the ones we want to lay off.

Mr. William J. Moore was the builder, with J. Kell Houssels, of the Last Frontier casino. It's funny to hear him saying the penny roulette game had an operator of its own because "we know nothing on earth about penny roulette."

This is a qualified, experienced resort owner in Las Vegas – but an investor and builder – not a casino operator. That's why when the same men built the Showboat hotel and casino in 1954, they leased the casino to Moe Dalitz and his partners.

As for the commission room and the racetrack, the sportsbook pays the actual winning totals at the track. Racetracks run a parimutuel system where they keep over 20% for themselves, and the payout to the winners is based (at that time) only on what is bet at the track? Total betting at the track might only be $20,000 on a single race, while the total bet at racebooks might be millions.

A steamer or unknown horse with great ability often shows up and wins races. The owners usually make their bets at racebooks to keep the odds at the track and their returns very high. The commission room might take $250,000 in action on a single horse running at 15-1 odds. Then the commission room has to share their bets with other bookies and reduce the chances of getting wiped out by a steamer.

And, the commission room would often call a connected bettor, or beard, at the actual track the horse was running at to make a wager of $5,000 or more to knock the odds down from that scary 15 to 1 to a manageable 3 to 1 or so.

It was a dangerous game, especially if past-posted bets were taking you off. Jimmy, "The Weasel" Fratianno, explained how that worked in Ovid Demaris's The Last Mafioso.

In 1947, Jimmy and Chico Marx partnered with a fellow who had a house facing the finish line at the New Orleans Fairgrounds. It took the three of them to scam the El Rancho casino, but it wasn't too hard.

The fellow at the racetrack called Jimmy as the horses neared the end of each race, and if a horse had a five or six-length lead, Jimmy would call the El Rancho racebook and ask for Chico. Sometimes the announcer for the race wire in Chicago would be a minute or so behind giving the results from another track, and Chico could bet the horse to win and place, getting down bets that nearly always won.

Fratianno said that during the Marx Brother's three-week engagement at the El Rancho Opera House, he and Chico split nearly $40,000 in winnings.

He and Chico were able to scam the Vegas racebooks, but stealing was another thing. When Tony Trombino and Tony Brancato hit Hy Goldbaum's commission book at the Flamingo, Gus Greenbaum and Tom and Jack Dragna got angry. Then they got Jimmy to do something about it.

Jimmy told Nick Licata he needed Charley Bats to help when the two Tonys picked them up in their car. Charley sat behind Tony number one, and Jimmy took a seat behind Tony number two. As soon as he closed the door, Jimmy shoved his revolver against Brancato's head and popped him twice, the bullets entering his skull with so much force that his body jerked up in the seat.

Charley Bats froze, so Jimmy turned slightly and let Trombino have three quick shots in the head before he could even react to his partner's death. All the car's occupants caught a film of bloody brain tissue.

That's the kind of person Mooney and Momo needed in Las Vegas to watch over things.

The Rat Pack - Frank Sinatra, Dean Martin, Sammy Davis Jr., Peter Lawford, Joey Bishop at Sands Casino circa 1960 - the Creative Commons Attribution-Share Alike 2.0 Generic – Don Graham https://www.flickr.com/people/23155134@N06

Chapter Fourteen

New Casinos Skimmed to the Bone

The building boom in Las Vegas as the 1950s dawned was a great sign of success for Nevada and the Mob. It didn't matter that local banks were reluctant to risk their precious dollars on casino loans, not when the Teamsters and their bosses were happy to pay the freight.

Over a dozen casinos used Teamster funds Jimmy Hoffa, and Allen Dorfman provided to build their resorts. Dorfman was born in Chicago, where his father, Paul "Red" Dorfman, was the Chicago Waste Handler's Union head.

Vegas and the Chicago Outfit

Father Paul asked Jimmy Hoffa, the then head of the Teamsters in Michigan, to fund a new insurance business his son was setting up with his mother. It all sounded so wholesome; how could Hoffa refuse the offer – and a chance to meet with Red's most important contact, Tony Accardo?

Hoffa, Red, and Allen were all millionaires when the synergy came together. Accardo and the Chicago Outfit were unstoppable. Later, Hoffa was elected head of the International Brotherhood of Teamsters.

With Frank Fitzsimmons in Michigan, Hoffa designated the Michigan Conference of Teamsters Welfare Fund to the new Chicago branch of Union Casualty Insurance. Next came the Central States Health and Welfare Fund and more than $3 million in commissions and fees for the Dorfman's.

Then came the loan fees for Hoffa, Dorfman, and anyone connected (Accardo, Giancana, and others) with an active loan from the Teamster's fund. When a Las Vegas casino needed cash, an emissary would arrange a meeting with Dorfman, who would greenlight the loan. The emissary got a finder's fee, often about 10 percent, but smaller if Hoffa got a substantial kickback.

The Sahara

Soon-to-be casino owner Milton Prell arrived in Butte, Montana, and made friends with Frank Shivo, whose mother ran a café and bar. After a getting-acquainted period, the friends opened an illegal casino in the back of the bar, keeping them busy and well-financed for several years.

They arrived in Las Vegas in 1945 and opened Club Bingo on the Las Vegas Strip, which became the Sahara hotel-casino, a $5.5 million project financed by (drum roll ....) the Teamsters in 1952.

Loans came with obligations and fees. To lessen the impact of any obligation, money was skimmed to avoid taxes. It was the way of Vegas for forty years.

The owners called their new Sahara "The Jewel in the Desert," which was certainly a jewel in the saber rattled by the Chicago Outfit. There were restaurants, a pool, 240 rooms, and a casino that did quite well; thank you!

Prell may have trusted Frank Schivo as his key employee and Frank's sister, Eda, as his private executive secretary, but Jake Lansky had run of the property.

In 1955, the Las Vegas Sun published articles about the Thunderbird casino. It stated that Jake Lansky was involved with counting the daily win at the casino, so the Nevada Tax Commission investigated.

Marion Hicks and Clifford Jones did their best to spin a story that might be plausible and acceptable by the Tax Commission after the club had run short of cash on their grand opening (remember that crazy craps game?). Hicks stated that they received a $160,000 construction loan from Jake Lansky's friend, George Sadlo, that night in 1947, and he had been collecting on the loan through Jake. But there was another problem.

In 1948, since Sadlo was the go-between to Meyer Lansky and wanted a piece of the action for himself, he paid Hicks $37,500 for a five-percent slice. Hicks accepted, and the "loan" was on the club's books for the use of the gaming operation.

Unfortunately, Nevada again stood by their decree that current investors and licensees could have no "illegal gaming operations" in other locations. George Sadlo was a known gamer with friends like Jake and Meyer Lansky. The Tax Board considered him a silent partner and stated:

"The individual interests of George Sadlo and Jack Lansky in Citees' gambling operation was a material fact which was required by law to be reported by the Citees to the commission."

Under questioning at the Kefauver hearings, Jones had earlier admitted that he once owned 50% of the Thunderbird, but his ownership had been reduced to just 11%. He also admitted that he held 1% of the Golden Nugget and received $12,000 a year and 5% of the Pioneer casino, for which he received $14,000 a year. His take from the Thunderbird was zero for the previous two years. The skim Lansky was taking away on monthly trips to Meyer in Miami was strangling the property.

What's crazy is that the Nevada Tax Board stated, "the criminal and corruptive elements engaged in unlawful gambling, tend to organize and thus obtain widespread power and control over corruptive criminal enterprises throughout this country; that the existence of organized crime has long been recognized and has become a serious concern of the federal government as well as the governments of the several states."

They openly admitted that organized crime existed, as did the Kefauver hearings, but the FBI stood by their director and refused to admit any such thing!

In a heated frenzy, the state closed the Thunderbird, created the Nevada Gaming Control Board, restricted owners from entering the count room, and revoked Marion Hicks and Clifford Jones's gaming licenses.

The Thunderbird wasn't closed long; the owners just found some new front men, so a Los Angeles investment group called Harris and Schulz took over the property. No fuss, no muss.

As for the Sahara, Prell sold out his Sahara to Del Webb in 1961. And Webb eventually became the owner of other casinos, including the Sahara Reno (which had been the Primadonna) and the Sahara Tahoe, which Webb built in 1963 and ran until the 1980s.

Chicago's Tony Accardo kept a low profile during the late '40s and early '50s, allowing Sam Giancana the limelight if he wanted it. Along with Paul Ricca, the three men took more and more of the Outfit profits without worrying the well would run dry, especially with more clubs opening in Las Vegas.

The Sands

Other large casinos opened in the mid-'50s, including the Sands, the Riviera, the Hacienda, and the Dunes. Their openings involved more cooperation between Mob families across the country.

When Max Kufferman bought La Rue's restaurant on the Strip and started building the Sands, there was an outcry that his known associates included people mentioned in the Kefauver hearings (those damn hearings were a pain in the collective butts of every crime family). Kufferman found The Big Texan, Jake Freedman, to buy into the project and help shield the associate owners like Meyer Lansky, New Jersey's Joseph "Doc" Stacher, New York's Joey Adonis and Frank Costello, Kentucky's Eddie Levinson, and Minnesota's Isadore "Kid Cann" Blumenfeld.

Freedman partnered with Jack Entratter of New York's Copacabana to turn a pile of sand into the soon-to-be world-renowned casino, The Sands. Carl Cohen, a local New York dice man, ran the casino for the boys back home.

And although a known mobster, Doc Stacher strolled the grounds and had a permanent room in the hotel. Sam Giancana was also seen on the property from time to time. According to Chuck Giancana, the Outfit continued to lean on known entertainers for charity shows and Las Vegas openings.

After the opening of The Sands, the local newspaper said, "It's amazing to see opening act Danny Thomas and his rise from $50 per week shows at the 5100 Club in Chicago to its present pinnacle in the

Copa room."

However, Thomas was a bit over-sung by the second evening and begged off the stage. Instead, Entratter asked a few friends in the audience to entertain in his absence. Those taking the mike included Ray Anthony, Frankie Laine, Jane Powell, Denise Darcel, Jimmy Durante, Eddie Jackson, and the Ritz Brothers.

Strangely enough, Las Vegas had pulled it off. The shows were sleek and sophisticated, even if the town wasn't, and soon the whole world wanted to come to town and catch a show with Hollywood stars like Ronald Regan, Joey Bishop, or Marlena Dietrich.

Frank Sinatra headlined at The Sands in 1957, and soon his friends Dean Martin, Sammy Davis Jr., Peter Lawford, and Joey Bishop were part of the act, too, often referred to as the "Rat Pack."

Not surprisingly, they rarely traveled alone. Beautiful starlets like Marilyn Monroe, Angie Dickinson, Juliet Prowse, and Shirley MacLaine were sometimes called the "Rat Pack Mascots" when seen with their Hollywood male friends.

Sinatra was paid $15,000 weekly at The Sands, but the club could afford it. Even with a substantial skim of the profits, the $5.5 million resort was paid for in less than six months.

Sinatra was a star, and when he asked for more cash, he was offered more credit in the casino. It wasn't what he wanted, but it was better than nothing. Often, he just told a friendly Pit Boss to "lose" his credit marker. They obliged for a while.

On a stormy night, Sinatra blew through $100,000 and wanted more. "Look," he said, "if I can't get another $50,000, I may have to consider doing my show elsewhere."

He was playing 21 and pounded the table, so hard chips flew out of the tray and onto the floor. Sinatra wasn't a quiet person or one who expected to be stiff-armed when he wanted anything (from money to cars to a woman for the evening).

He screamed at the dealer, pushed a cocktail server away, and told the pit boss, "Listen, you're never working in this town again," and grabbed the railing of the 21 table and nearly turned it over. Chips rained to the floor, but the pit boss never moved. Sinatra stormed across the casino, his face twitching, searching for Carl Cohen, the Casino Manager.

When he found him in the coffee shop, Sinatra grabbed his table but couldn't pick it up because it was bolted to the floor. He did manage to spill Cohen's coffee cup. The 55-year-old Cohen looked at Sinatra for a moment and then rose from his chair. When he got to his feet, he delivered a short, quick punch to Sinatra's mouth, knocking out two front teeth and leaving him with a bloody nose.

He was done for the evening, but the Rat Pack continued to draw enormous crowds to Las Vegas, and casinos continued to pop up in the desert. None of the large properties were paid for with personal wealth. Every club had a Teamsters loan and a special skimming fund going to a series of crime families.

The money trail was always hard to follow, as were the efforts to get licensed or, more importantly, get paid. A little story about "Doc" Stacher should cast more light on the situation in Nevada.

Up in Reno, the Bank Club was the largest earning casino and the state's largest employer in the early 1930s. By 1950 it was a more sedentary earner but still plugging along with a twenty-year lease good through 1966. When partner Jack Sullivan decided to retire and sell his one-third interest in the club, Bill Graham and James McKay chose Joseph "Doc" Stacher to join the fun.

According to court documents, after the United States canceled his Certificate of Naturalization, Stacher had already purchased his interest in the club before filling out all those pesky license papers:

(a) Defendant, up to June 17, 1950, had resided in New Jersey. At that time, he went to Reno, Nevada

(b) In July 1950, the defendant purchased "an interest" costing roughly $91,000 in two corporations; the Bank Club of Reno, Inc. (50,000 shares) and Golden Securities Co. (250 shares).

(c) According to the appellant's 1952 Income Tax Return, he sold these shares on April 30, 1952. According to his tax attorney, Mr. Burton, he sold his interest in the Golden Hotel (Golden Securities, Inc.) and the Bank Club of Reno in May 1952. According to the appellant's 1953 tax return, he sold the shares of the two corporations on April 30, 1953. The 1952 date is undoubtedly correct. Appellant received $86,000 cash, a one-third interest in the Earl Carroll Theatre Building in Hollywood, valued at $97,000, and "Installment Notes" of $1,166,000. At any rate, "early in 1952" and on May 29, 1952, he moved to Las Vegas, although he frequently returned to Reno to collect on and watch his second and third purchase price mortgages on the hotel.

(d) In Reno, he looked at houses to buy, but they "were too much money, and my wife wouldn't live there." Appellant lived at a Mr. Emmons' house, at the Golden Hotel, and at a Mr. High's house. He lived with High for over a year, off and on.

(e) He had stayed at The Desert Inn in Las Vegas in May or June 1951 and various times before October 1952.

The Nevada tax commission investigated the good doctor's background and found he had Mob connections dating back to the old Bugsy and Lansky gang of Murder, Inc., so he was denied a license.

A confidential report from the Chicago Crime Commission also states that Joe Stacher had recently met with a large group of known gangsters at the Kenilworth Hotel in Hollywood, Florida. Abner "Longie" Zwillman was at the meeting and had recently purchased some property at Lake Tahoe. Stacher and Lansky were in close conversations, often joined by Moe Sedway.

Then, when Stacher got charged in the Saratoga Spa fiasco, extradition papers were transferred from New York to Nevada. Stacher surrendered himself under the warrant in Las Vegas, paid $5,000 cash bail, and had a hearing set for a week later.

Next, Stacher drove up to tiny Ely, Nevada, before White Pine County Judge Harry Watson asked for the extradition order to be quashed. Watson had extra deputies on guard to ensure outside authorities didn't take Stacher to New York. He later ruled Stacher was "not a fugitive subject to extradition" and released him. The friendly Judge had done a similar service for Lincoln Fitzgerald and Dan Sullivan of Reno's Nevada Club when they were similarly charged in Michigan.

When Stacher was finally extradited weeks later, the wheels had been sufficiently greased. He was charged with twenty counts, pled guilty, paid a $10,000 fine, and was placed on two years' probation. He returned to Las Vegas to open the Sands and help run other properties such as the Fremont Hotel for Lansky's partners.

According to the court documents, Stacher sold the casino interest in the Bank Club he was never licensed to own for cash, one-third of a theater, and "Installment Notes" of $1,166,000. That was a hell of a fortunate purchase, right? Or just the Mob moving money around from one Mob owner to the next?

When Stacher was denied a license, he brought in David High to watch the East Coast's share of the club. High had worked at a casino in New Jersey owned by Joe Adonis and Meyer Lansky but swore he was just the restaurant manager. At the Golden, he was listed as the hotel's managing director.

In February 1952, the Golden Hotel was purchased for $6 million. The price included $3.5 million for McKay and Graham's interest in the casino. McKay retired permanently from the gaming industry and lived in Reno for the rest of his life.

Graham was awarded a new twenty-year lease for the entire downstairs, which had previously held both the Bank Club and the Golden Gulch Casino. Graham and High applied for a gaming license in the new Golden Bank Casino. Graham was approved for licensing but not High.

When asked by the State Tax Commission where he had gotten the money to purchase twenty-five percent of the casino, High stated that Bill Graham had given him $500,000 after the sale of the Golden Hotel for his excellent work. His application was denied.

The FBI, as usual, was watching everything, taking notes, and telling no one. Even former boxing champ Jack Dempsey was a subject of surveillance. In 1953, according to official memorandums from the SAC Salt Lake City, to Hoover, Dempsey "stayed at the Golden Hotel, and is an old friend of William Graham, who is the owner of the gaming concessions of the establishment, and who made a chorus girl available for Dempsey's pleasure." Thank goodness they had that information.

Graham held the license for 272 slot machines and 34 table games, as well as keno, pan, and a cabaret bar. With 40,000 square feet on one level, it was now the largest casino in the world and took 400 employees to run.

The property was large, Bill Graham was getting old, and at the request of Tony Accardo in Chicago, Graham offered the manager's spot to John Drew. The manager had keys to the count room. Need I say more?

Previously Drew had been in Las Vegas, working as a go-between in several casinos for Accardo. In Reno, Drew applied for a gaming license as a twenty-five percent owner of the Golden Bank Club Casino, for which he told the state he was paying $100,000.

Aside from the purchase price suddenly being just one-fifth what High said his twenty-five percent interest was worth, the state had other concerns and was reluctant to issue a license.

Drew had been arrested several times, including incidents where crooked dice were used to fleece victims in rigged craps games. Losses in those games were as much as $250,000. He was also questioned regarding his association with Lester "Killer" Kruse.

Although Drew first denied knowing Kruse, he later admitted that he had hired him as a floor man in a casino. Drew stated he would have no interaction with Kruse, nor would Kruse have any interest in the club under his licensing.

As for the Golden Bank Club casino, he denied any current connection to the club but said he had visited it a few times. Commission Secretary Robbins Cahill and another member visited the club and asked a pit boss who was in charge. The boss took them to John Drew.

When questioned about this strange occurrence, Drew suggested the pit boss must have been confused about the question put to him. The commission denied his license. However, six months later, he reapplied and was miraculously licensed for the same twenty-five percent he had been seeking earlier. Who got paid and how much? Who knows, but Drew immediately hired old friend Lester Kruse as a pit boss.

In reality, Kruse was the money man for the Chicago Outfit. He secured financing, stashed cash, paid associates, and suddenly the Outfit had for free, what Graham had been charging a 15% fee for 20 years: a money-laundering service. What better way to move bad bills than across the cashier's cage for chips bought at the tables with clean money?

In December of 1955, John Drew and Bill Graham sold their interest in the casino and the remaining seventeen years on the lease for

$425,000. Considering the previous owner had paid Graham, McKay, and High $4 million, this was the bargain of the century. An expanded, nicer casino was now apparently worth only ten percent of what it was just two years earlier. Of course, the money from that purchase was nice and clean, and much of it was already out of the state.

Reno managed to maintain an air of independence from the Mob, but the truth was out there. The Riverside casino was run for years by the Wertheimer brothers, and when the Mapes was built, the straight Charlie Mapes leased his first casino out.

It was extremely popular, with even Mickey Cohen and Sam Giancana spending time at the hotel and casino checking the action. **Time** magazine was on hand to open the public's eyes. Their 1950 article titled, *The Sky Room's the Limit*, let the cat out of the bag.

Central to the story was that the U.S. Government's Reconstruction Finance Corporation had loaned the Mapes Hotel in Reno $975,000, "which drew 30% to 40% of its income from a thriving twelfth-floor gambling casino called 'The Sky Room.' The casino operators, said Committee Chairman William Fulbright last week, was 'lawbreakers and thugs' and the casino's boss is Lou Wertheimer of Detroit Wertheimer's gambling."

Also seen at the hotel was Virginia Hill, Bugsy's old girlfriend. She arrived regularly with a dozen pieces of luggage and her friend Joe Epstein, the Outfit tax expert and top Chicago bookie. Epstein, who liked to be called Joey Epp, had taken care of Hill since she turned tricks for a buck a pop in the early '30s. He was a friendly, middle-class accountant with thick glasses who ran the Outfit's racetracks, so he put her to work as a bagger, carrying cash from one scam to the next. She dipped her fingers into the pie regularly, but Epp loved her anyway and never said a word.

As for Stacher, he left Reno and, although unlicensed, ran the gaming at the Sands and the Fremont until 1964, when he was arrested for tax evasion. He lost his citizenship and was deported in 1965 to Israel, where he was "gifted" with citizenship under the "Law of Return." He passed away in 1977.

The Dunes

Raymond Patriarca, head of the Patriarca Crime Family in Providence, Rhode Island, wanted a share of the desert bloom in Vegas. He dispatched Joe Sullivan to find a suitable front for their casino.

Meyer Lansky pointed Sullivan to Al Gottesman, a retired movie theater chain owner living in Miami. In a series of meetings like many other casino starts, Sullivan convinced his fish to front a little less than $100,000 to buy the proposed property and hire an architect. In exchange, Gottesman was to get his cash back when the land was resold and 9% of the resort's profits.

As usual, the casino got built on International Brotherhood of Teamsters' loans, and the place was jammed, but somehow it just couldn't make a buck for Mr. Gottesman. What a bummer!

The new "Miracle in the Desert" offered an Arabian Nights theme with a 35-foot sultan guarding the entrance. Inside were 200 hotel rooms, a 150-foot lagoon, and a 90-foot V-shaped swimming pool.

The opening show featured Vera Ellen and future stars gracing the stage inside the Arabian Room, including Liberace, George and Gracie Burns, Judy Garland, Phyllis Diller, and Frank Sinatra.

In less than a year, Gottesman wanted out since, instead of taking down a bundle of cash, his partners kept asking for more money to keep the marketing strong. He sold his share to Major A. Riddle and Jake Gottlieb. Strangely enough, both men were from Chicago.

Riddle had been an illegal casino boss in the Windy City, tied to Tony Accardo. Later he had done even better with oil leases in Texas. At one point, his interest strayed to Virginia Hill before she moved on to Bugsy Siegel. After Riddle took control of the Dunes, Virginia agreed to handle some skim drops for Sam Giancana.

Riddle made several changes at the Dunes, including adding Minsky's Follies, the state's first topless show. The State Legislature considered it rude and vulgar (because everything else in Nevada was as pure as the newly fallen Tibetan snow). Still, as they say, "the show must go on," and it did — to a record single-week attendance of 16,000.

Still, the casino seemed to struggle to make a profit. So Riddle and Gottlieb got another $4 million from the Teamsters and hired Jayne Mansfield to work the showroom for $35,000 weekly.

An 18-hole golf course opened soon after, as well as a 24-story tower. The casino still reported trouble making a profit — for the next 30 years. Strange.

Also opening in the '50s was the Riviera, which went through the usual reshuffling of owners for several years before finding just the right ones to satisfy the gaming board.

The Detroit Partnership's Lefty Clark, who applied as William Bischoff to capture a piece of the project for Joe Zerilli, was forced to withdraw, as were several others until the mix finally had Gummo Marx and his brother Harpo as two of a dozen owners with Clarence "Bucky" Harris (owner of the North Shore Club at Lake Tahoe) as the casino manager. The latter would receive a salary and 5% of the net win.

The club was licensed for four dice games, four roulette tables, four blackjack games, and 200 slots. But it took some time to finish the $7.5 million resort with several union strikes and some confusion when the Teamsters pushed their way into what was originally an AFL Union job. Chicago helped smooth the waters they had turned into waves and took a piece of the casino in return.

Liberace and his brother opened in the Clover room, and Joan

Crawford was paid $10,000 for a week of glad-handing the resort's first guests. Liberace got $50K. The showroom was huge, and the show included a 50-piece orchestra, most of whom had to be brought in from Los Angeles.

The Maxwell Company of Miami did the interior, and it took 105 railroad cars to deliver all the chairs, tables, mattresses, beds, linen, and you name it, to get open. Las Vegas didn't have any bedding or furniture industries; they dealt in dreams only.

After a smooth opening in April, the resort started having financial difficulties. Surprise surprise, with newbies at the helm of the casino. Debt was piling up, and Chicago had its chance to grab a bigger handful of the resort with Meyer Lansky's blessing.

Tony Accardo personally met with Gus Greenbaum in Scottsdale, Arizona, where he had recently retired from his job running the Flamingo, but Gus turned him down flat – not interested.

"Sorry, Tony, my wife Bess don't want me back in Vegas, and she don't want to go there neither. I'm retired."

The next day, Accardo sent his bodyguard to talk to Gus's brother, Charlie, and his wife, Leone at their home at 317 West Wilshire Drive. He asked the couple to talk to Gus, but they weren't too worried until the man grabbed Leone by the throat and said it wasn't a request; it was a matter of life and death.

Two days later, Charlie headed to the racetrack while his daughter Betty visited with her mother in the other room. The last things Leone said was, "Don't leave me here alone," then she said, "give me a kiss, the next time you see me I'll be dead. She was right.

Dr. Daniel J. Condon, the Maricopa County medical examiner, said she had been smothered by a human hand. Before he made that announcement, Gus Greenbaum was back in Vegas, bringing Davie

Berman with him from the Flamingo to save the Riviera.

Did I mention that Gus and his two brothers moved from Chicago to Phoenix in 1928 to run the Outfit's race wire? Yup, that toddling town of Chicago sure had some winners.

Greenbaum and his group agreed to lease the property for $1,250,000 per year and invest $500,000 cash immediately, with another $1 million coming soon. Their license application was approved.

Before the end of the year, the property was miraculously back on its feet but not as profitable as the state had hoped. Too much skim.

Meyer Lansky was so happy with the success of the Riviera casino in Las Vegas that he used the same name for his new 440-room hotel in Havana. Wilbur Clark was his frontman, while Meyer was listed as the Kitchen Director and nowhere else in the financial papers. Neither were his partners, Accardo or Dalitz.

When the $8 million-dollar project opened in late 1957, the 21-story hotel was the finest Mob-owned casino in the world. There were beautiful chandeliers and crystals across the ceilings, gold-leaf walls, beautiful Caribbean tile throughout, and the property had its own bakery. Stars like William Holden and Ava Gardner flew in to see the new beauty, and Steve Allen even taped an episode of his Sunday night TV show. What's not to like?

Ginger Rogers headed the Copa Room Cabaret floorshow, and while the casino was busy and lucky, Lansky remarked later, "That Rogers girl can sure wiggle her ass, but she can't sing a goddam note."

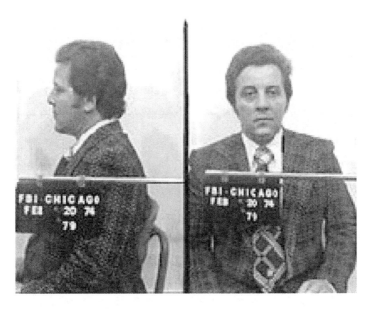

Tony Spilotro circa 1974 – FBI – Government Mugshot / Public Domain

Chapter Fifteen

Chicago Outfit Enforcers in Las Vegas

With the plethora of casinos in the desert and the pesky Tax Commission making it tougher to get at the day's win to skim, Mob bosses appointed enforcers to oversee their interest in Las Vegas.

The Outfit was no different and had Johnny Roselli - the top guy since Bugsy went away – doing their bidding and coordinating the cash transactions back to Chicago. But a change was coming. Business was business, and perhaps Johnny wasn't tough enough, thought Tony Accardo. He needed someone with the right outlook and the right demeanor. Nobody was meaner than the man he had in mind.

Roselli was smooth as silk and had eyes that turned to ice when he needed a movie star to do a fundraiser, a down-on-his-luck baseball player to drop a fly ball, or a boxer to take a dive.

Marshall Caifano, on the other hand, was about as smooth as broken glass. He had a heart of ice if he had one, and only two ideas in his tiny, one-track mind: money and power.

So, Sam and Tony send Caifano on a little mission to Las Vegas as a final test. While he hung around with "Russian Louie" Strauss, Marshall met with Jimmy Fratianno on the sly.

According to Fratianno, Strauss had been trying to blackmail Benny Binion about the killing of Johnny Beasley at the Westerner years earlier. It seems Beasley knew something and told Strauss, so Binion had him whacked. Nobody knew what Strauss or Beasley knew, but Binion told Nick Licata he had a problem, and Licata relayed the information to Jack Dragna in LA. Dragna asked what was in it for him — to dispose of the smelly Russian.

When Licata passed the question to Binion, he walked to the front of his downtown casino and pointed across the street to a vacant lot off Freemont. "I'm expanding soon. Tell Dragna he's good for a share."

Licata sat on the response for a long time, trying to figure out how he would best profit off this new turn of events. In the meantime, Strauss was named by the Gaming Control Board as one of four people who slipped 68's into a craps game at the tiny Savoy casino downtown (the dice were mismarked and rolled only sixes and eights) and caused the casino to lose their license after they couldn't pay the winners.

Also involved were Allen Smiley (who lived to tell of Bugsy getting whacked), Harry Barber (who kept getting turned down for gaming licenses — we see why), and Jack Durant, a Pit Boss at the Flamingo.

Eventually, Licata passed the hit to Fratianno and waited.

Then Dragna got permission from Tony Accardo (who was still angry that Strauss had killed his Tahoe Village casino partner before collecting the $80,000 he owed to the Flamingo), who sent Caifano and Philly Alderisio to get the job done.

At the last minute, Accardo decided he wanted Caifano safe from any possible charges (he had another plan) and had him stay back. At the same time, Philly and Jimmy took the Russian into California, leaving his wife Naomi behind and telling her they were going to Palm Springs. Jimmy took a nap in the back seat until they passed the San Bernardino Mountains and were close to their rendezvous.

When they stopped the car, Fratianno said, "Philly, go see if the guy's home." Then after a few minutes, Fratianno got out of the car, saying, "Let me see what's takin' this guy so long."

A minute later, he held open the door to the secluded house and waved to Russian Louie. The second the Russian crossed the threshold, Frank Bompensiero and Joe Dippolito grabbed his arms while Jimmy tugged with all his might on one end of the garrote Bomp had wrapped around his head. The big man fought back, but in vain, and the look of surprise held on his face, even after his eyes bulged and he bit his tongue nearly in half.

In the living room of the murder house were several capos, plus Louie Dragna, LA Boss Jack Dragna's nephew, to make sure the job got done right.

When Accardo got word that the Russian was taking a dirt nap, he figured he'd be safe to take Caifano's wife, Darlene, away from him, but Caifano already knew his sultry Kentucky girl was shaking up with Accardo. Why? Because in a strange twist, the FBI had let the cat out of the bag.

Special Agent Bill Roemer was detailed to follow the Chicago bosses around town and had planted several microphones and some tape recorders in their offices. One night he followed Giancana to the Thunderbird hotel in suburban Rosemont, where he saw Caifano's big raw-boned wife with the boss.

Roemer hoped that if he spilled the beans, Caifano might flip out and kill Accardo or flip and become an informant. Roemer misjudged Marshall; he thought he was human.

Instead of being angry, Caifano just smiled when Roemer told him. Caifano wanted Las Vegas as his territory, and Giancana wanted him out of Chicago, so the two men got what they wanted without ever admitting anything to each other.

Caifano changed his name to John Marshall and bought expensive suits to saunter around the casinos in, but his taste was so atrocious that he looked like a clown. He could be seen from a block away with his bright green and yellow pants and heavy gold jewelry.

He pushed his weight around the Outfit's casinos and chased the front men around their clubs when he didn't get his way. He grabbed showgirls right out of chorus lines and dragged them to his room, where he assaulted them. He kicked dealers when they lost too much and insulted Gaming Control Board members.

The heat in Las Vegas was boiling, and Tony Accardo was getting similar heat in Chicago from the IRS and decided it was time to take an extended vacation in 1957. It lasted ten years.

During that time, Sam Giancana took the reins with Paul Ricca, leaving Accardo as an immensely powerful consigliere.

While Ricca and Accardo had tried to keep a low profile, Giancana enjoyed his power and wealth, often painting the town with movie stars and famous singers.

And while other capos had squandered their earnings on gambling, Giancana spent his buying a personal piece of several hot casinos in Las Vegas, Reno, Havana, and even Iran and Central America. He was wealthy, and he didn't care who knew it.

After the Russian Louie hit, Jack Dragna failed to get a piece of a downtown casino because Benny Binion was on trial with the government over tax issues from his time in Texas. He lost his trial and was eventually convicted, so Benny sold most of the casino to New Orleans oil millionaire Joe W. Brown.

Benny lost his license and was never allowed to hold one again, but the family regained partial control in the '50s and complete control of the property and casino in 1964. By then, Benny was the Director of Public Relations and grew to be thought of as the kind-hearted grandfather of Las Vegas. That of the man who said he followed the golden rule: "He who owns the gold rules."

When the Binion family got the controlling interest of the Horseshoe back, Stanley Burke was finally turning a little profit at his Hacienda casino. Frank Sinatra knew Stanley Burke and wanted a piece of the club, but Chicago told him to stay out; they would share some of the Dunes with him. He waited.

Meanwhile, Beldon Katleman at the Last Frontier contracted the beautiful Gabor sisters (Zsa Zsa and Eva) to compete against the talent at the Sands and the Sahara. They featured Red Skelton and Anna Maria Alberghetti.

Stan Irwin at the Sahara had a miniature replica of the club's "Garden of Allah" swimming pool built for a billboard marque, where young ladies were seen swimming and frolicking about in the mid-day sunshine of Los Angeles with a giant arrow pointing to Las Vegas.

Down the Strip, the Tropicana opened in April of the same year, but not on Mob money. Instead, in tried-and-true fashion, Miami Beach Fontainebleau hotel owner Ben Jaffe bought some land on the Las Vegas Strip and started building a casino. See a pattern yet? Sure you do!

Then, due to excessive construction overruns and union issues

153

(caused by the Mob), the project stalled, and Jaffe was forced to sell his share of the Fontainebleau in Miami Beach and give up control of the new casino before the resort opened on April 4th of '57. Margaret Kastel handled the décor. Indeed her husband, Frank Costello's pal "Dandy Phil" Kastel, couldn't be involved in the project. Wouldn't the Nevada Gaming Control Board have issues with that?

Eventually, they did, but once Kastel bowed out, the Trop got licensed. Owners of record were Theodore Shimberg of Chicago, Charles Baron of Chicago, and Las Vegas casino owner Lou Lederer.

On May 2, Frank Costello was walking through the lobby of his Manhattan apartment building when he heard, "This is for you, Frank." When he turned, a gun blast knocked him off his feet, and he sprawled across the tile floor, bleeding profusely from a scalp wound. Vincent "The Chin" Gigante walked triumphantly from the building only to learn later that he had given Costello just enough warning to turn slightly and keep from having his brains blown out.

Police picked up Gigante, but Costello refused to identify him as the shooter, and he was released from custody. Vito Genovese, who had controlled the hit, knew Albert Anastasia was furious over the assassination attempt and would seek revenge. He fortified his squad of goons and laid low. In Mob parlance, they went to the mattresses.

By then, the police were puzzling over a folded paper they found in Costello's pocket while he lay unconscious. The note said, "Gross casino wins as of 4/27/57 - $651,284," with individual wins for each gaming department. To be even more specific, the final line said, "Mike $150 a week, totaling $600; Jake $100 a week, totaling $400; L. - $30,000; H. - $9,000. The initial "L" stood for Meyer Lansky, the Mob's main financial wizard, and "H" stood for Murray Humphreys, Chicago's chief financial manager.

After Costello had got caught with the casino's gross gaming numbers in his pocket, Louis Lederer, whose handwriting was detected on the slip in Costello's pocket, was forced to sell his interest in the Tropicana. This, of course, would make everything fine, and no hoodlums would be involved in running the club, right? The Gaming Control Board was delusional again, but it looked good in the press.

So did the Tropicana's winnings when it was announced it was the highest earning casino in Las Vegas, and that was after the standard skim. According to the records of the Gaming Control Board, Harold's Club in Reno and Harrah's Club at South Shore Lake Tahoe were the biggest-earning casinos in the state at the time. When Bill Harrah purchased George's Gateway Club at Lake Tahoe in 1955, he remarked, "We were doing great in Reno, and here was this tiny club in Tahoe doing twice what we were."

However, believing that a beautiful new hotel-casino in Las Vegas could be out-earned by a seasonal property in the Sierra Nevada Mountains with no hotel was ridiculous. The skim in Las Vegas was enormous, and casinos like the Fremont, Stardust, Desert Inn, Riviera, Sands, Dunes, and Flamingo provided most of it. The Tropicana, right there with the best, continued to grow and provide a steady income for their owners, and even a little for their frontmen.

Back in New York, Costello feigned ignorance. He was taken before a judge but refused to explain the amounts on the note. The judge slapped a 30-day sentence on the Mob boss for contempt of court.

In Nevada, the Gaming Control Board said about the memo Costello had, "We are aware of it, and will take any action indicated by it," whatever the hell that means.

In October of 1957, Albert Anastasia went for a shave at New York's Park Sheraton barbershop, and what a shave he got! Two shooters entered the barbershop when his face was draped with a hot towel, and Anastasia exited the world. His photo on the front page of hundreds of newspapers reminded readers of a picture from a decade earlier of Bugsy Siegel: a top-notch Mob Guy lying in a pool of blood.

Not too much had changed in those ten years. After Frank Costello recovered from the assassination attempt, he and Vito Genovese made the peace. But things still got dicey.

The following month, the country became familiar with the town of Apalachin, New York, when dozens of men in expensive suits ran off through the woods trying to escape a raid on their meeting of The Committee. On a lucky break, state troopers stumbled on a gathering of some very powerful men. Carlo Gambino, Vito Genovese, and Joseph Profaci were among the best known. Santo Trafficante, Jr. was also present, and so were at least 100 others. The local police and state troopers rounded up 58, while dozens of others escaped through the woods with nothing more than torn suits.

The massive meeting of crime family members forced the FBI to finally admit there really was an overall power behind the Mob or Mafia and that the heads of the families did meet, make decisions, and work as a group. Twenty of the apprehended bosses were fined $10,000 each, and several received prison sentences for "Conspiracy to obstruct justice by lying about the nature of the underworld meeting." Yeah, that sounds strange. The sentences were all overturned on appeal.

In Las Vegas, the Riviera was still making bank, but Davie Berman died unexpectedly during a routine ulcer operation, and Gus Greenbaum was spinning out of control. A good man at home in Scottsdale, Arizona, Gus was too close to the action when living in Sin City, and drugs and women were taking too much of his time. As the casino owner of record, it was expected that he would sweeten his pay, but it is never right to take too much of the big boss's skim.

Even after a warning, Gus couldn't shake his drug or gambling habit, and things went sideways. First, his friend in Phoenix, William Nelson, who had come to visit Gus at the Riviera, turned out to be Willie Bioff, the man who had turned state's evidence (squealed like a rat) and sent his bosses, including Frank Nitti, Paul Ricca, and Johnny Roselli to the slammer.

When Sam Giancana found out, he sent Marshall Caifano to Phoenix with a demolition expert. Then, Bioff exited his home at 1259 East Bethany Home Road one crisp, clear morning, got in his truck, and turned the key.

The explosion forced his body through the evaporating roof and windshield, breaking his neck and tearing his arms from his shoulders. He was found nearly fifteen feet away, a mass of exposed flesh and bones. Bioff's feet and legs had broken, and his chest was smashed by the steering wheel where a half-circle was embedded into his torso. Bits and pieces of the truck were found in yards a block away.

Afterward, Gus spent most of his time at the bar in the Riviera, and this time it was Johnny Roselli who came to visit. "Gus," he said, "there's a gentleman's way out. Sell your 27 percent and move on; everything will be forgiven, even the skimming."

"I can't, this; this town is in my blood now, Johnny."

Invariably well-dressed and smooth as silk, Roselli used to hand out his business cards when asked about his profession. They had one word on them: Strategist.

Marshall Caifano, Roselli, and Tony Accardo had a sit-down. They discussed the issue with Lanksy, who said: "Go." Marshall Caifano went. A few days later, a plane from Miami arrived in Phoenix. Two men got out and climbed into a car waiting for them in the private plane's hangar.

On December 3, 1958, Pearl Ray, the Greenbaum's housekeeper, arrived for work to a blaring TV. There were no other sounds in the house until she screamed when she found Gus in the master bedroom, clad in his usual silk pajamas. He was stretched across two joined twin beds, pillows on either side of his head, holding it still. His neck was sliced through the muscle and tendons and down to his spinal cord. Blood caked the pillows and cascaded across the bed, over the sides, and down to the floor.

Bravely, Mrs. Ray continued down the hall, where she found Bess Greenbaum face down on a floral couch. Her hands were tied severely behind her back with one of Gus's silk ties. Her throat, too, was slashed open, her skull bludgeoned by a heavy bottle that lay on the floor beside her.

The murder weapon, a knife from the kitchen, lay on a plastic bag the killer used to avoid fingerprints. Surrounding Bess's head were two pillows and a bathroom towel used to keep the flow of blood from a beautiful oriental rug. It was worth more than her life.

Things continued to go wrong for the Mob at the end of the 1950s. In Havana, before Meyer Lansky's $8 million Riviera casino property had earned back even half of its cost, Fulgencio Batista lost his grip on the Republic of Cuba. Fidel Castro took over, renounced the casinos, then retracted his statement and said they could stay.

By then, the slot machines, gaming tables, and even the parking meters in the city had been destroyed by happy vandals. Soon after, Castro reversed himself again, refusing to let the casinos reopen.

When Castro was assured of his new dictatorship, the rebels faded slightly, allowing hundreds of dealers and pit bosses to leave the battered casinos and search for a way home.

According to Associated Press, as reported from a long-distance phone call from a detainee, Joe Warren, there were still 26 Las Vegas dealers penned in the National and the Havana Hilton, waiting for the rioting and looting to end so they too could leave. When the rioting finally stopped, boats from "paradise" to "freedom" took the dealers away with nothing but the clothes on their backs.

In 1959, New York's Genovese was convicted of selling heroin and sentenced to 15 years in the Atlanta Federal Penitentiary.

In late 1960, the Republic of Cuba confiscated Meyer Lansky's (and everybody else's) holdings in Cuba. The loss of capital spent in Cuba by the NY Mob and Chicago's Outfit was devastating.

Massive spending had been going on in Havana, half the Mob's money, half-matched by the government of Cuba. The loss of cash expected revenue and the high-income jobs of higher-ups came crashing down on organized crime just as states in the US pushed harder to close down policy rackets and illegal casinos. It was a one-two combination of nearly lethal force.

As for Meyer Lansky, his fortunes were significantly impacted, and It would be up to his investments in Nevada to support him for the next twenty years.

Stardust Casino circa 1959 - Unknown photographer / Public
Domain

Chapter Sixteen

The Stardust Opens in Las Vegas for Record Skim

Number 13 isn't always lucky, but it was for Chicago when the
Stardust became the 13th casino to open on the Las Vegas Strip. As it
was often called, the Dust provided skim into the 1980s, the last
significant property to go down fighting. It was profitable, and it was
famous, but it was never easy.

The idea was Tony Cornero's, who ran out of town in 1931 when
his casino, The Meadows, had a suspicious fire after he refused to share
his profits with Meyer Lansky. But Tony never quit. He just headed back
to California and, with three partners, Bill Blazer, Cal Custer, and Jim
Lloyd opened the SS Tango, anchored just over three miles from Santa
Monica pier.

Players were ferried to the casino-in-a-ship via water taxis from
Long Beach and San Pedro. They lost, and the partners got rich but not
happy. The owners spend endless nights discussing who should sell their

share, and the four cranky partners eventually got in a winner-take-all poker game. Tony was the first out.

Instead of taking the loss and moving on, he bought a new ship, the Kenilworth, and spent a half-million dollars upgrading it and buying a fleet of skip boats to bring players to his new SS Rex. It was so successful he figured he might have to bribe California Attorney General Earl Warren, but it didn't work. The man was impossibly straight and called the gambling boats off the California coast "The greatest nuisance operating in the country."

Warren must not have gotten around much because there were hundreds of illegal casinos in Cleveland, Toledo, Detroit, Covington, Louisville, Miami, and Hot Springs, Arkansas. And, including Galveston and New Orleans properties, many were much bigger than the floating casinos could offer. That didn't matter; the US Coast Guard seized the SS Rex in 1939.

Cornero wasn't a quitter, so when Warren left office as Attorney General, Tony took another shot at the floating money off California's coast with the launching of the SS Lux in 1946. It took exactly two days before he got arrested – Earl Warren might not have been Attorney General, but he was the Governor of California. Jeez, Tony!

After Cornero was jammed into a private jail cell and all his little speed boats seized, the 800 players stranded in the casino just kept right on gambling. What else could they do? Six hours later, the Coast Guard allowed limited water taxi service to get the people on board back to shore. Generally, they weren't worried and considered the whole affair an adventure. Tony sent in a team of lawyers, but he never even got his ship back. What to do? Why open a casino in Los Angeles, of course!

He bought a building, spent $25K renovating, and then met with Mickey Cohen, who wasn't impressed. Instead of making a deal, Cohen pulled a snub-nosed .38 revolver and lodged it in Tony's left ear. They agreed that Tony would never open a club in Los Angeles.

With no other options, Cornero called the owner of the Apache Hotel in downtown Las Vegas, Orlando Silvagni. They agreed on a lease, and the now land-based SS Rex gaming hall moved towards licensing. The casino was voted down, but it was close, so Cornero bought the final vote he needed and opened his new club. Other club owners (the Outfit and the NY Mob) weren't too happy about Cornero in their midst and arranged a new vote. Strangely enough, the license was denied, and Tony was told to get out of town, which he did. Benny Binion took the lease, refurbished, and opened Binion's Horseshoe Casino.

Back in Beverly Hills, Tony "The Hat" found backers for a casino in Baja, but the local Mexican businessmen were no happier to see him than the Mob in Vegas was. On February 9, 1948, Cornero opened his door in Beverly Hills and was handed a package. Once his hands were full, the two men pulled their weapons and fired four bullets into his stomach. Somehow the feisty and unpopular man lived. He laid low for several years until the lure of Las Vegas was too much for him.

In 1954, Cornero and partner James Bradley began selling stock in "Stardust, Inc." and started constructing a new hotel and casino. Tony applied for a gaming license, which was immediately opposed by the governor and the Nevada Tax Commission. But that wasn't all.

The Federal Securities and Exchange Commission had serious issues about the stock the partners had sold since it was unregulated and therefore worth nothing. Kind of like the stock Bugsy had sold in the Flamingo – the Nevada Project – and Moe Dalitz and Meyer Lansky watched and waited for Cornero to get desperate. It didn't take long.

Dalitz knew Cornero was stuck, so he loaned him $1.25 million to finish construction and took a nice slice of the pie. It was just enough to get the place ready but not open, especially after Governor Charles Russell said, "As long as I'm Governor, Cornero will never get a license."

Most of that was based on new information that went public when Hank Greenspun's Las Vegas Sun ran an expose' – a series of articles involving casino owners and prospective owners who got caught on tape. So, Nevada was "being more careful."

One of the tapes had Lieutenant Governor Cliff Jones telling a prospective buyer of his Thunderbird Casino some exciting things. Jones asked the buyer if he had a record, and the man said, "A little narcotics, bootlegging, murder, manslaughter." Jones replied, "You're all right, but not until after the first of the year when Pittman takes office. Believe me; I've been called a lot of names...one thing nobody ever called me, and that's stupid."

Lou Weiner, Jones's lawyer (and previously Bugsy Siegel's), admitted even more on tape:

WEINER: "It's important to us to have Cliff in there because there are a lot of things that Cliff can get."

BUYER: "I know that on the back, Jake Lansky, Meyer Lansky, everybody's in it, on the Algiers, everything runs smooth. The Rancho over here, I got a good friend from New Orleans over there."

WEINER: "But nobody bothers them; they don't care. What everybody else does is their business."

WEINER: "Cliff can take care of it (Carson City gaming licensing), but not...." (Until the first of the year).

WEINER: "They know Doc Stacher is in the Sands. What do you think; they don't know Doc's in there. You think they don't know Meyer and Jake are in the Thunderbird, huh?"

After the six-week sting operation, Reid started a series of twelve articles revealing the many conversations with "business owners" in Las Vegas. Pittman, destined to win the Governorship, lost to upstart

163

Russell. Lieutenant Governor Clifford A. Jones resigned as Democratic National Committeeman, and lawyer Louis Weiner shook off the expose' and continued practicing law.

As for Carson City, the politicians set up the Nevada Gaming Control Board to oversee all gaming applications and appointed a former FBI agent as the first director. It helped a little.

Cornero heard the Governor's response to his application for a gaming license and replied, "I'll get a license or be carried out feet first." His partners chuckled, probably thinking, "Your proposal is acceptable."

While construction continued, Tony spent his time shooting craps at the Desert Inn, sometimes happy, sometimes sad, and always loud and demanding. If you ever saw the movie Goodfellows, Tony would be Murray, who had the idea for the Lufthansa heist and was always bugging everyone for his share of the $5.75 million. Dalitz would be Jimmy, who held the cash after the job was done.

One night Tony was shooting craps and arguing with Dalitz, who didn't appear to be bothered by the blustery Corner. When Dalitz crapped out at the dice game, he turned back to Dalitz and started arguing again. Cornero bent his knees towards the table, grabbed his drink off the low railing, slammed a gulp of a new seven-and-seven, and then stopped mid-sentence. He grabbed for the craps table rail, twitched his head back and forth, and collapsed to the dirty rug, littered with cigarette butts.

There were no attempts to revive the dying man. Cornero's doctor was called, and he asked that the body not be sent to the coroner's office. He was confident it would be Tony's last wish to be taken to his family in Beverly Hills quickly. He was. "Quickly" was the operative word.

The story continues that the cocktail server who witnessed the death and brought the poor man his last drink was shaken up. To help her get over her grief, the casino sent her on a week-long stay in Cuba, where she had full reign of the facilities at Wilbur Clark's Casino National. Dalitz and Lansky got controlling interest in the Stardust Hotel and Casino, and poor Tony got an immediate burial. There was no autopsy performed to see what was in that last drink.

It was three years before the 1,000-room hotel emerged from Federal Bankruptcy Court and opened to the public on July 2, 1958. The actual owners drew out the process, who couldn't drop more cash into the project with Cornero gone and the court system involved. So, arrangements were made to bring in John "Jake the Barber" Factor and his beautiful wife Rella of the Max Factor family, and they paid off the outstanding construction costs. The smaller investors and stockholders, rumored to be in the neighborhood of three thousand, were quietly ignored.

Jake the Barber had a rap sheet longer than Tony Cornero's, including the time he orchestrated his own kidnapping to take down Roger Touhy, a competing gang head, and the time he was sentenced to 10 years in prison for selling $1 million in non-existent whiskey. He was also denied a gaming license for the Stardust, and while it wasn't a big surprise, it was still inconvenient, but nothing couldn't be worked out. When the Stardust did open, Dalitz held 22 percent of the Stardust Casino operation, which was operated on a lease basis from John and Rella Factor, who ran the hotel.

In reality, Chicago and Tony Accardo owned a piece since he had fronted $3 million, and nearly half the skim traipsed back to Chicago weekly. Then the Stardust group changed names. The United Hotel Corporation, the Dalitz group that owned the Riviera and Desert Inn (in the eyes of the Gaming Control Board), got licensed to run the property, and the D.I. Operating Company was licensed to run the casino. If you aren't confused by that, you should be.

The D.I. Operating Company listed 13 applicants who put up the casino "cage cash" of $300,000. The names were familiar: Wilbur Clark (just 5.5 percent), Thomas McGinty, Morris Kleinman, Moe Dalitz, Sam Tucker, Allard Roen, Bernard Rothkopf, Robert Kay, Ruby Kolod, Clifford Jones, Joseph Bock, John Drew, and Milton Jaffe. Most were long-time members of the Purple Gang. Most had a piece of the Desert Inn.

One of Dalitz's most trusted partners in Cleveland was not on the list, Samuel "Game Boy" Miller. He helped keep the clubs in Ohio going when Dalitz moved permanently to Las Vegas. Game Boy also purchased a house in Miami, where he kept regular company with Meyer Lansky. In 1955, Game Boy tried to get licensed at the Riviera but was turned down. He turned his interest to the Royal Nevada, where he took a silent role. The club struggled but still provided an untaxed profit.

Nevada regulators turned a blind eye to the final deals at the Stardust. They had an image to uphold as a safe and prosperous gaming capital and a 1,000+ room hotel and casino to get open. The following month the Desert Inn purchased the Royal Nevada Hotel adjacent to the Stardust and diagonally across the street from the Desert Inn.

Royal Nevada was used as a convention center and had motel rooms slightly different than those at the Stardust. In modern terms, they were nothing more than inexpensive motor lodge rooms. Inside the Stardust, the casino was a good size, with room for 60 gaming tables, a keno lounge, a poker room, a racebook, and a restaurant.

Also in-house were a lovely showroom with two additional restaurants, one a steak house and one a 24-hour café. Also, when the casino first opened, there was room for a bingo parlor, which drew a great deal of business over the first ten years the resort was open.

The property also had a large pool, obviously a big hit during the summer months when Vegas temperatures are usually in the 100s. When the show got out at 10 pm, parents often had to retrieve their children from the pool area (where the kids could order enough 25-cent hot dogs and hamburgers to make themselves sick) because the temperature was still 90 degrees at night.

All in all, the Stardust provided a friendly, inexpensive place to stay for a few days. There were a series of gift shops and a gas station 100 feet from the parking lot. Everyone involved with the Stardust was making money, but with owners, co-owners, hidden interests, and the Mob all over Las Vegas, it was hard to tell who owned what. Licenses often named ten or more owners, but many of those were Los Angeles law firms just fronting for silent owners.

Fulgencio Batista with Meyer Lansky and his wife in Havana circa 1948
Havana - http://carlosbua.com/los-italianos-en-cuba/ Public Domain

Chapter Seventeen

1960s Mob Madness

As the 1960s dawned, more and more Nevada casinos fell into the
hands of organized crime. "Fell" might be incorrect. "Pushed" is
probably closer to the truth. There were no corporate owners of
casinos, and no publicly traded companies owned or offered shares. It
was still the wild west.

Unfortunately, many properties fell into disarray because the
Outfits casinos were so heavily skimmed. Inventory control was shotty,
and routine maintenance was ignored. Planned upgrades and
refurbishing didn't happen. Money that should have gone into
expansion went into little satchels to bosses from New Orleans to
Miami, Newark, Philadelphia, and a dozen more stops.

And, because the money was huge – a million dollars a week could
go north-east from the Flamingo casino to Sam Giancana for his small

percentage – managers who wanted to upgrade their departments couldn't. And the enforcers were the most powerful men in Vegas.

Johnny Roselli was cool, but Marshall Caifano had some severe issues. He had fights with casino managers, connected and otherwise, and a running feud with Beldon Katleman, owner of the El Rancho Vegas, is said to have come to a head over a denied free room and a showgirl on June 17, 1960. That night, while Harry James and Betty Grable were performing on stage, a suspicious fire broke out in a dressing room and the kitchen. It raged all night and destroyed the El Ranch Vegas.

When Chicago didn't do anything to slow him down, Nevada finally did. The Gaming Control Board had legislation passed that allowed them to bar certain "unsavory" characters from the state's casinos, and guess who the first character was? Bingo! Marshall Caifano is number one in the Black Book. Any association by licensees with people listed in the Black Book would result in fines and possibly revocation of gaming licenses. Nevada had finally acted. It was 1961.

Caifano refused to take the hint and continued to strut around the Mob's casinos. When he was asked to leave the Stardust one evening, he returned ten minutes later. The next time he was told to go, he went to dinner but returned. This time, agents from the Gaming Control Board were on the property, and he was arrested, but the thick-headed mobster still couldn't get it through his skull that his days in Vegas were over.

To make matters worse, he did what his Chicago bosses never wanted any made guy to do; he hired a lawyer and sued the state for his arrest and inclusion in the Black Book.

The added spotlight on the Mob was too much for Tony Accardo, who reassumed control over the Outfit and brought Caifano back to Chicago. Of course, the next enforcer in the city, Tony "The Ant"

Spilotro, wasn't any quieter, and neither was Chicago in the early '60s.

From the first of the year 1960 until November of 1963, there were at least 40 known (and nearly all unsolved) gangland killings in the Windy City.

Most of the murders were retaliation killings, you know, like "hey, you didn't pay your loan shark, you didn't pay your bookie, you didn't pay your juice to the boss for your latest jewelry heist," and of course the old favorite – skimming a little too much from the Outfit's earnings.

And then there were the M&M Murders, where some stupid kids (Jimmy Miraglia and Billy McCarthy) shot up a bar and killed the owners and a waitress. The joint was Outfit owned (weren't they all?), and Mad Sam DeStefano and upstart killer Spilotro took out their frustration using tried and true methods, including a shop vice.

DeStefano asked Miraglia nicely, "Who da fuck you workin' wit" as he stood over his bloody body, but the 24-year-old hesitated. So, Spilotro picked him up, shoved his head into the vise sideways, and asked again while turning the crank and tightening the vice.

His jaw cracked on the third turn. On the fourth, his eye popped out of its socket. He gave up McCarthy and was rewarded with a slit throat.

The killers found McCarthy the next day and tortured him into the night before slitting his throat too. Chicago was tough, and DeStefano saw Spilotro as a star. He sent him to find real estate broker Leo Foreman, whom DeStefano said screwed him on a commission deal.

Tony and Chuck Grimaldi brought Leo to a house in town, and there they met with Mad Sam, who took Foreman by surprise when he whacked him with a hammer. Once he had his attention, he got a little information and then went back to business, knocking McCarthy down and smashing him below the waist over and over. Spilotro and Grimaldi got their fists and feet into the mix before Mad Sam brought out an ice pick. Twenty or more punctures later, the poor man passed out from blood loss and unimaginable pain.

Spilotro got tired and shot him twice in the head. Then he and Grimaldi wrapped him in plastic, carried him to a stolen car, tossed him in the trunk, and dropped the car at the bus station.

Spilotro was well known by the police in Chicago. He'd been a punk kid in the '50s, boosting a car or two, stealing purses, and heisting goods from open trucks. But he'd grown up (well, he only sprouted to 5-foot two inches) since then.

Like so many criminals, Spilotro was egocentric. He didn't mind being noticed and was confident his way was the best way. Still, he listened to his bosses for years before branching out into a mini crime spree of his own while still killing whenever he was asked.

Life was a bit more civilized out In Reno, and the boys from Detroit were doing quite well at the Riverside, thank you. George Wingfield leased his hotel and casino to Mert Wertheimer, and his brother Lou was carving up the Mapes. Mert expanded the casino and did whatever was necessary to keep his backers happy. Lou and Mert had similar success in Detroit and Miami, and Meyer Lansky and Bill Tocco (as well as Tony Zerilli and Mike Polizzi) were happy with their cut but wanted more.

Tocco and Joseph Zerilli, alternately running the Detroit Partnership in their home state of Michigan, were quiet compared to other Mob Family bosses. With the obvious exceptions of the Jimmy Hoffa disappearance and Zerilli's son being indicted for hidden ownership at the Frontier Hotel Casino in Las Vegas, the Partnership was kept out of the news. Their involvement in several casinos was never reported in the national press, and skim heading to Detroit was done expertly, quietly.

In 1958, Lou Wertheimer died; two months later, his brother Mert

171

died under mysterious circumstances, and "Jimmy the Weasel" Fratianno said that Bill Graham had ordered a hit on Mert, carried out by Reno hitman and jewel thief Frankie Frost.

The upshot was that the Wertheimer's had a 10-year lease on the Riverside casino in Reno - which Graham had a piece of - with nine and a half years to go, and Tony Zerilli and Mike Polizzi wanted the whole property instead of the slice that the Wertheimer's were sharing. So Graham has Frost pop some amphetamines into Mert to speed up his heart, which couldn't keep up since he was weak with leukemia, and the autopsy winds up reading that he died of acute monocytic leukemia. It's like today when you die after having leukemia for five years but test positive for Covid, so the death certificate says "Covid."

It's all plausible since the Detroit Partnership was running the New Frontier (since 1955, when the casino changed its name from the Hotel Last Frontier), enjoying some major skim, and always ready for more. And that's what happened, as the Riverside casino changed hands after the Wertheimer's went away.

There were several owners of record, and in September of 1960, Bill Miller paid close to $5 million for the property. He was an investor in the New Frontier (shocking!) in Las Vegas and was approved for 95% ownership. Hmmm.

The remaining 5% went to Gerald Layne, also from Las Vegas, brought in to be the casino manager. His application was denied when the Gaming Commission disclosed that Layne had been arrested two years earlier in Tulsa, Oklahoma, with a carload of crooked dice and cards. Oops!

Although he had no license, the 35-year-old Layne still had access to whatever he wanted as the General Manager of the Riverside. On January 10th, he filled a satchel with cash from the casino to play in a high-stakes poker game in Placerville, California, organized by Glenn F. Lucas, another Las Vegas resident.

Layne's car was later found abandoned at Harrah's Lake Tahoe casino. Layne and the cash were never seen again. Lucas was a suspect in the disappearance but swore the game was canceled. Also canceled were several checks Lucas had passed at Harrah's casino the week before. They all bounced.

In April, Lucas went on trial for the bad checks while Layne's ex-wife was filing papers to represent Layne's business interests. Her lawyer of record was Mead Dixon, who famously brokered the Harrah's estate and its sale to Holiday Inn during the late 1970s.

Things didn't improve much at the Riverside in Reno, which was sued in 1962 by gambler Jack Berman who alleged altered dice. However, the case was thrown out since Nevada Supreme Court rulings stated that money lost in gambling is not recoverable. Jeez, you can't make this stuff up!

Shortly after that, another sucker, I mean buyer, was found for the casino when Raymond Spector, a New York cosmetics executive, bought the club when some new friends at the casino got him a $2.75 million Teamsters Union Loan to finance the purchase.

Eventually, Spector realized he had no control of the casino or the cash boxes and ducked out of the picture. The property was closed in December and reopened in July 1963 with new owners who knew the score.

Frank Sinatra had purchased the Cal-Neva Lodge at Lake Tahoe by that time. Frank was a long-time friend of many otherwise wholesome gentlemen who just happened to be in the Chicago Outfit. He was also a 9% shareholder in the Sands casino in Vegas and was paid $100,000 a week to perform in the showroom, so he should have been a happy guy. Especially after getting into the Cal-Neva for what amounted to a few autographs and a few measly pennies.

So, FBI Special Agent Bill Roemer was interested when one of his microphone bugs in Sam Giancana's Chicago hangout caught the boss saying, "What's up with Frankie? He don't seem happy."

Ironically for Chicago and Giancana, the Cal-Neva was the club that Sanford Adler and Charles Resnick bought in 1948 after they were thrown out of their jobs (and $195,000 ownership) at the Flamingo after Bugsy was removed from the picture and the state licensing board had calmed down.

Giancana was happy because he had arranged a Teamsters Union loan for $1.75 million for Sinatra to buy the casino and upgrade the facilities. And he was happy because he got half the club for nothing. Then, as a special added thank you to Sinatra, Sam took his half directly out of the count room, so the club always looked like it was cash poor (it was, I suppose) and paid little in taxes.

The club was a great money maker, dating back to the 1920s when the Hollywood elite would gamble away $10,000 and think nothing of it. But that was when Bill Graham and James McKay owned the property. By the time Sinatra came along, it had been through many owners, but in 1961 Frank had Lewis McWillie watching over the club as a Pit Boss who never worked.

Johnny Roselli had sent him to keep an eye on Giancana's investment. And it was the same McWillie working at the Thunderbird casino in Las Vegas during the 1960s.

As for the 1950s at the Cal-Neva Lodge, "Wingy" Grober did big business at the lake, enjoyed himself, and often had Joe Kennedy (his liquor supplier) at the casino. There wasn't a hotel, but several cabins, so Hollywood socialites visited. So did Giancana. And then suddenly Wingy said, "I want to sell," for the bargain price of just $250,000. Dean Martin would be partners with Sinatra, but he got cold feet when he heard who his partners would be.

Besides visitors like Robert Kennedy and his wife, Ethel, Teddy Kennedy, Peter Lawford and his wife, Patricia Kennedy, Dean Martin, and the list goes on.

Sinatra also counted as friends like Carlo Gambino, Tony Accardo, Sam Giancana, and Willie Moretti, who some swore got him out of his contract with band leader Tommy Dorsey by forcing a gun down his throat (I'll make him an offer he can't refuse"). It might be true.

Whether that was true or not, William F. Roemer, Jr., FBI Special Agent who had access in Chicago to microphones all over town, repeatedly heard about Sinatra and the Cal-Neva Lodge directly from Sam Giancana. One microphone, "Little Al," picked up detailed conversations and helped the FBI piece things together.

Sinatra convinced many Hollywood friends to come to the Cal-Neva, filling the showroom with stars such as Trini Lopez, Buddy Rich, Tony Bennett, and the McGuire Sisters. Phyllis McGuire was dating Sam Giancana at the time. Sinatra was trying to have an affair with Marilyn Monroe. John F. Kennedy and his brother, Robert, had also been involved with Marilyn. It was a healthy situation.

Sinatra had several tunnels expanded under the lodge. One ran from the closet of his cabin to the main tunnel, which had access to the back of the lodge, and to two other cabins. Only special guests like Sam Giancana, JFK., Marilyn Monroe, and a new lady who was also sleeping with both John F. Kennedy and Giancana, named Judy Campbell, were issued the cabins with tunnel access. Giancana preferred lodge 50 when he stayed at the resort, his resort. The FBI followed Campbell, and documents show that she was with the President and Giancana at one point in Chicago on subsequent days.

Also, in the tunnels beneath the casino, Sinatra built a room for himself, completely encased in steel. He wanted to feel safe while he was cooking the books.

Marilyn was going through a breakup with her husband, Arthur Miller, at the time. She was less spunky than the cinema queen who had once so glibly explained her nude Playboy magazine photos and toyed with the press so effortlessly once was. Monroe did some interviews then, and when a journalist asked what she had on during the photo shoot, she replied, "the radio." When asked what she wore to bed, she said, "Channel Number 5," and cultivated a world full of fans and admirers.

By the summer of 1960, her life was daily torture. She couldn't sleep without pills, and she couldn't work before noon. She and Clark Gable were filming the movie The Misfits in Reno when Frank invited the entire crew up to the Cal-Neva to see his show. The film would be the last for both Gable and Monroe.

Inside the casino, Paul D'Amato took care of the money, and everyone was happy, even after D'Amato started a prostitution ring from the bell desk. Hookers from the San Francisco Bay Area were brought to the lake weekly to entertain guests. The casino made plenty of money, and Sinatra was happy with his pie cut. However, Giancana was hoping for payback from Joe Kennedy for helping get JFK elected. Instead of a governmental relaxation on organized crime and Giancana, the opposite was happening.

When Giancana realized that Sinatra couldn't deliver on his promises, he started pushing harder for Frank to do something. Giancana perhaps realized that Frankie wasn't as close and influential with the new President as he had bragged.

The President's brother, Robert F. Kennedy, had already been a thorn in organized crime's side for ten years. He started working for the United States Department of Justice in 1951. In 1952, he became an assistant counsel for the Senate Permanent Subcommittee on Investigations and later was chief counsel for the Senate Labor Rackets Committee.

Now, Robert F. Kennedy was even more vigilant against organized crime than before his brother was elected, and Giancana felt betrayed by both Joe Kennedy and Sinatra. During the new Attorney General's term, convictions against notorious organized crime figures rose 800%. His policies and strategies often clash with J. Edgar Hoover's.

Hoover's "bugs" routinely picked up reams of data, but little seemed ever to come of the information. As early as 1944, Hoover's men were watching Bugsy Siegel and listening to conversations at his home, in hotel rooms at the Flamingo, at the St. Francis Hotel in San Francisco, and in his Las Vegas Club casino offices (which they called the boiler room) as well as following his every step around the country. However, they seemed woefully unaware of what was transpiring at the Flamingo construction site, the casino after it was built, or that he was the target of a coming Mob hit. If they were aware, they never shared.

In Reno, former heavyweight boxing champion Jack Dempsey was a subject of surveillance. In 1953, according to official memorandums from the SAC Salt Lake City, to Hoover, Dempsey "Stayed at the Golden Hotel, and is an old friend of William Graham, who is the owner of the gaming concessions of the establishment, and who made a chorus girl available for Dempsey's pleasure."

The strange thing about this report is that the FBI knows Bill Graham but is not watching him; they are watching Dempsey. At the same time, John Drew was also on the property, sent by Tony Accardo from Chicago. Even the state of Nevada had a problem with him until he was caving for whatever reason and allowed his purchase of a 25% stake in the casino, but hey, let's watch the ex-boxing champ and the chorus girl.

Frank Sinatra, trying very hard to hold on to his relationship with the Kennedys, and Giancana, was also pursuing Monroe, for whom he purchased a puppy. With her usual sense of humor and fun, she called the dog Maf, short for Mafia. She also confided to a friend, "Sure, the men like the sex part, but I don't understand what all the fuss is about."

Sinatra got a taste of the Dunes casino profits, too, gratis. He routinely snubbed the state's gaming agents and assumed he was invincible, although he and Dean Martin were forced to sell their holdings in the Berkshire Downs racetrack in Massachusetts. They were directors of the track, and other owners included New England Mafia boss Gaetano Lucchese, the head of one of New York's five families.

Near the end of June 1962, D'Amato's prostitution ring began to unravel. The FBI was there to investigate, and an agent ran into one of Giancana's men, Chuckie English, who was drunk, and told him, "If Bobby (Robert) Kennedy wants to know anything about Momo (Giancana), all he has to do is ask Sinatra."

The following day, Sinatra was told by Deputy Sheriff Richard Anderson to stay away from his wife, who worked at the Lodge as a waitress. She had dated Sinatra before marrying Anderson, and the friction was like two blocks of sandpaper rubbing together.

The two men ran into each other again in the restaurant's kitchen later in the week. Sinatra stormed up to Anderson and demanded to know what he was doing there.

"This is for employees only; what the fuck are you doing here?"

"Just waiting for my wife, Frankie," said Anderson. "Mr. Sinatra, it's Mr. Sinatra, you fucking ass," Frank said as he tried to remove the heavier Anderson.

Anderson popped Sinatra hard enough to keep him off the stage for a week in the ensuing scuffle. On July 17, Anderson and his wife drove down the mountain on Highway 28 near the Cal-Neva when Richard noticed a convertible bearing down on them at an excessive speed.

"What the hell is this joker doing?" Anderson asked. Before his wife could reply, the maroon sports car closed in on them and sideswiped their vehicle. The impact forced Anderson and his wife off the road, where the car fishtailed before striking a tree. Both were severely injured in the crash. Richard died before reaching the hospital. Likely just another Outfit coincidence.

At the urging of San Giancana, Sinatra talked Marilyn Monroe into coming up to the lake again. She was reluctant, but he promised Robert Kennedy would be there, and she changed her mind, just as Giancana thought she would. Frank arranged to have her flown up for the week, and the second night she had dinner with Peter and Pat Lawford, Sam Giancana, and her host, Sinatra. During the dinner show, Marilyn had just two drinks but became heavily intoxicated and violently ill. She was escorted back to her room, where she passed out on the bed. Giancana had the room wired for sound and film the week before with a plan to get Robert Kennedy into the room with her for a little blackmail insurance package, but he was a no-show, so Giancana went another way.

Conversations picked up by the microphone "Little Al" in Chicago later revealed that not only did her escort, Giancana, have sex with her. At the same time, she was passed out, but so did several other male and female "friends" allowed into the room. Sinatra was in the room at the time when the photographs were taken. The film made its way to Hollywood photographer Billy Woodfield, who developed the pictures. Then the pictures made their way to Robert Kennedy, who told Peter Lawford to tell Monroe that he never wanted to have any contact with her again. When she protested, Lawford showed her two of the photos. She continued trying to see Robert, but whether she ever did was unknown.

The emotionally distraught starlet died a week later at her home in Brentwood, California. There is a four-hour gap between the time her body was discovered (according to the housekeeper) and the time the first phone call to the Los Angeles Police Department was made. The first officer on the scene claimed it looked as though her body had been "posed." When he arrived, the live-in maid was doing the laundry.

Friend Peter Lawford, Kennedy's brother-in-law, said he talked to her earlier on the phone, and she "Sounded groggy like she was taking sleeping pills." However, there were no signs of a drug overdose, and the autopsy showed no trace of the barbiturates Monroe often used to get to sleep in her mouth, stomach, or intestines. There were no bottles of pills or drugs in her room or house. Lividity was present, a settling of the blood in various body parts, which strongly suggests that the body had been moved after death.

Indeed, questions remain about her tragic death. Peter Lawford's home was nearby and offered a convenient rendezvous spot for friends and lovers, but he offered the alibi that she was at home and talking to him on the phone when she died. FBI documents show Robert Kennedy was staying in Gilroy, California, about a four-hour drive away at the time. The FBI knew her situation at Lake Tahoe, and government officials were undoubtedly uncomfortable that she had a relationship with the Kennedy brothers and knew Giancana.

Some also believe Giancana could have been involved in her death to " push" the Kennedy administration into backing off their pursuit of the Mob. Again, the Mob felt betrayed by the Kennedys. JFK had written a personal note to Sinatra before the election, saying, "Frank – How much can I count on from the boys in Vegas? JFK." Norman Biltz worked hard for Kennedy, collecting nearly $15 million in the state, virtually all of it from the Las Vegas casino owners, for the Kennedy war chest. But what had they gotten in return? Nada. Life and crime went on.

The Cal-Neva continued making money, and Sinatra provided star power for Giancana's Villa Venice Supper Club in Wheeling, Illinois. Picked up on phone taps, it is evident that Frankie was helping Giancana for some reason, as the stars who appeared on November 9, 1962, all worked for free. The bill that evening included Eddie Fisher, who opened the festivities; Sammy Davis Jr., who sang and danced for the well-heeled crowd; Dean Martin, who joked and sang; and finally, the headliner, Frank Sinatra.

Guests attending the show were then shuttled a few blocks to an ugly warehouse facility surrounded by rusting car parts. Inside the building was a plush casino. Sources say revenue for the evening was over 1.2 million dollars.

The FBI, as usual, provided little information to other authorities, and Sam Giancana was a welcome guest of Sinatra's at the Lodge for another year. Eventually, the FBI did provide information to the State Gaming Control Board after Giancana was involved in a fight at the Cal-Neva.

Ed Olsen, the Gaming Control Board's Chairman, sent two investigators to the Lodge and got an interesting response. They were told, "Don't worry about it; nothing's happening," and one of the agents had a $100 bill tucked into his pocket.

Olsen talked to his agents and then called the General Manager, Paul D'Amato. He was unavailable, so a message was left. The following day, Sinatra was the one who returned the call. He was told that between the dates of July 17 and July 28, 1963, Sam Giancana was using the facilities at the Cal-Neva Lodge with the knowledge and consent of the licensee.

Sinatra never denied the charge, but he did ask Olsen to come up to the lake from his offices in Carson City so they could talk. Olsen declined the offer, and Sinatra flew into a rage.

"You're acting like a fucking cop; I just want to talk to you off the record," Sinatra said.

Now Olsen took offense. Frank was told in no uncertain terms that it would be better for all parties involved if he concentrated on his enterprises elsewhere.

"Don't fuck with me; I don't take this shit from anyone else, and I'm not going to take it from you, a pencil-pushing cock sucker," sputtered

Sinatra.

Then, thinking better of his outburst, he asked Olsen again to come up to the lake. Olsen said, "No, I'm setting a formal hearing date for October 7 in Carson City. You can come down from the lake!"

Grant Sawyer, the governor of Nevada, received multiple phone calls from people who talked about their ability to supply significant contributions for his coming election campaign. They also expressed hope that Mr. Sinatra's problems could be resolved amicably. Sawyer refused the campaign funds.

Both Sawyer and Olsen were very interested in finding out how much money was leaving the casinos as skim but were severely stymied by a part of the Nevada Gaming Control Act, which guaranteed casino owners that their financial data would not be disclosed. What a fantastic law the state allowed the casinos to use to steal. Sawyer was defeated for reelection.

After the Gaming Control Board met with Sinatra, he read a statement to the press. It outlined how he had decided to devote more of his time to the entertainment industry and would divest himself entirely from any involvement in the Nevada gaming industry. The board gave him ninety days to sell his casino holdings.

Giancana continued getting a slice of the cash at the Cal-Neva for two more years until it was shut down for renovations. Later, the club was graced with a hotel tower, but the new "owners" couldn't seem to get licensed. It was a tough time at the lake, especially for Giancana, who got left out in the cold. Of course, he hadn't invested a dime, so the cold air was probably tolerable.

Santo Trafficante circa 1955 San Souci's bar, Havana, Cuba -
https://oncubanews.com/en/cuba/society-cuba/cuban-history/the-
sans-souci-and-the-artists/ Public Domain

Chapter Eighteen

The Chicago Outfit Goes International

The 1960s were radical for millions of Americans who saw war, assassinations, hippies, rock and roll music, and a new thing being touted by J. Edgar Hoover's FBI: La Cosa Nostra.

Hoover looked the other way for decades when the Mafia moved stolen goods, prostitutes, loan sharking, and union corruption across state lines. And they listened intently to crime figures on tapped phones and implanted wires discuss business and skimming at legal casinos in Las Vegas and Cuba and illegal ones in Ohio, Kentucky, Arkansas, Florida, Texas, Louisiana, New York, and, well, you get the idea.

But after the vast Apalachin Mob meeting bust and the Kefauver hearings, Hoover looked terrible. He looked weak. So, he came up with a name that nobody in the Mafia ever used to describe themselves – La Cosa Nostra – feeling that it made him sound like he had inside information. Often, he did. Rarely did he use it. Still, the heat was on organized crime like never before.

In Chicago, all the usual illegal activities were happening with increasing labor union issues and even increased newspaper coverage about crime. That was a surprise. Chicago Outfit Boss Tony Accardo had stayed out of the limelight as much as he could during his reign from 1947 to 1957. He lived with his wife and family in a six-bedroom, six-bath home in River Forest, Illinois. The family estate included an indoor pool and two bowling lanes, enough to pique the interest of the IRS, so he bought a less flashy home on the 1400 block of North Ashland Avenue. Still, the IRS dug for unreported income.

In '31, Accardo inherited a street gang after Al Capone was convicted of tax evasion. Although he was implicated in the Saint Valentine's Day Massacre and questioned, cited, or arrested 172 times, he spent just one day in jail - and only because it was a holiday, and the courts were closed - so nobody could do him a favor after he was stopped in downtown Chicago by two rookie cops regarding an ongoing gambling case. The mistake kept the rookies beat cops their entire careers.

Governmental heat increased on all crime families in the late '50s and early '60s as they drew blanks due to witness intimidation, beatings, and disappearances. So, as they had in the 1920s when Elliot Ness prevailed in getting Al Capone convicted of income tax evasion, the government turned to the IRS.

According to Paul Ricca, crime boss of Chicago before Tony Accardo, "Accardo had more brains for breakfast than Capone had in a lifetime." And Accardo saw the writing on the wall and turned the reins over to Sam Giancana in 1957 when the IRS came calling, taking a diminished external role (with Ricca) but retaining an internal role as consigliere and ultimate counsel on all significant business.

Accardo gave Giancana a long leash and a long speech with stern words to tone down his flamboyant lifestyle, but he didn't listen. Sam loved his high profile. He partied with known criminals, mingled, and commanded Hollywood actors, padded the payroll of police, sheriffs, and politicians, and even bragged to his brother Chuck that he gave "steamer horses" to FBI Director J. Edgar Hoover so he could make guaranteed bets on fixed races. The man was a killer and a celebrity who liked to see his name and photo in the newspaper. Strange.

Although Accardo was the primary force behind getting slot machines into mainstream Chicago businesses and locations throughout Illinois and the Midwest, Giancana took credit (and millions in undeclared cash) from the operations. Accardo was also at the helm when Nevada turned to Mob control in the 1940s.

The Chicago Outfit not only owned and operated casinos like the Flamingo, Stardust, and Riviera, but Accardo's slot machines were in dozens of other clubs where the Outfit got a healthy slice of the pie. Their brothels in several states were converted to girls on call. The call girl switch reduced the Outfit's exposure to prosecution and increased profits. So did the group's reduction in union issues like labor racketeering and extortion.

Tony Accardo stayed in the background while Giancana expanded the Outfit's reach by opening casinos in foreign countries with the help of the CIA (as countries like Iran were helped by creating free elections – take that as you will).

Background or not, an income tax evasion trial eventually found Accardo in a precarious spot. After a year of legal wrangling, Federal District Judge Julius J. Hoffman sentenced the Outfit's former boss to six years in prison with a $15,000 fine and an order to pay the cost of the

Federal prosecution. It didn't stick.

Instead, the US Court of Appeals cited judicial errors, reversed the conviction, and sent the case back to the Federal Court. Accardo was acquitted in a second trial. No prison, no fine.

****

On the face of things, the sixties were becoming a crime family bonanza, with New York and Chicago scoring major victories. Santo Trafficante Jr. (November 15, 1914 – March 17, 1987) took over the Trafficante crime family from his father, Santo Trafficante Sr., and controlled organized crime operations in parts of Florida and Cuba. Florida had been an open state, with Ft. Lauderdale, Miami, Miami Beach, and Palm Beach controlled by New York crime families and financially managed by Meyer Lansky.

Trafficante, Jr. funneled Chicago money from drug deals in Asia, Central America, and the Caribbean. Giancana was cagy about working with Carlos Gambino in New York after Albert Anastasia was clipped at his barber shop in midtown Manhattan, and his picture splashed about the papers. Still, Giancana included the New York Gambino crime family with a split of his European casinos, with Meyer Lansky (living in Florida) arranging cash transfers.

A portion of Florida was also under the control of Carlos Marcello (February 6, 1910 – March 3, 1993), the crime boss of New Orleans who also wielded power in Texas. There was also a piece of Florida carved out for Angelo Bruno (May 21, 1910 – March 21, 1980), the crime family boss of Philadelphia.

While still Tony Accardo's Chicago Outfit consigliere, Sam Giancana set terms with Marcello for a working relationship with Chicago that included no more underground casinos in the Lone Star State except his, now that Benny Binion was safely out of Texas and getting richer in Las Vegas at his Horseshoe Casino.

In the mid-1950s, Giancana took a piece of the Thunderbird and Sands in Las Vegas with an overall personal cut of over $3 million. In exchange for safe passage between Tampa, New Orleans, New York, and Chicago for his couriers, Giancana shared 5% each with Marcello and Trafficante as long as his jewelry fencing business could move through the same spots safely. Later, gaming in Georgia and Alabama came under Marcello and Giancana's control. The money was huge.

And then there was the CIA again asking for Giancana's help with impossible to work with dictators who needed to be deposed and gun running to friendly rebels. Drug smuggling paid the bills, with a small chunk going back into black ops at the CIA and hidden away in Swiss, Italian, and Caribbean accounts.

According to Chuck Giancana, his brother's plans included using money skimmed by Jimmy Hoffa and the Teamsters Union to buy any necessary drugs or guns and coordinate with Chicago FBI agent Guy Banister and former FBI agent turned CIA operative Robert Maheu, Howard Hughes's soon-to-be front man, and Outfit go-between. But things began to spin out of control.

Some of that spin coincided with the Apalachin meeting fiasco and dozens of crime figures rounding up in the tiny New York town. Other issues were also holdovers from the '50s, chief counsel of the Senate Labor Rackets Committee, Robert F. Kennedy's public challenge of Mob-beloved Teamsters President Jimmy Hoffa. Still, others included the takeover of Cuba by rebel boss Fidel Castro – and the loss of millions invested in Mob casinos in Havana. And still, there was the Bay of Pigs fiasco.

Sam Giancana took it personally that he had lost millions in Cuba, and Bobby Kennedy was appointed United States Attorney General and was now challenging organized crime. It was a personal affront, considering Giancana swore he personally carried Illinois and Nevada for JFK's election as president. Where was the support now? Where was the gratitude?

Verifying some of Sam Giancana's stories about CIA cooperation in his overseas casinos and drug operations, Robert Maheu approached Johnny Roselli in September 1960 about connecting Santo Trafficante Jr. and Sam Giancana to a plot to kill Castro.

Roselli represented the Outfit in Las Vegas. That meant he watched over the skim of several casinos, making him highly skilled and highly trusted. He met with Trafficante and Giancana. They were all for the idea of dropping Castro since their Havana casinos had been seized and millions lost.

"Handsome" Johnny was offered $150,000 for Castro's removal after other plans, such as spraying his radio studio with LSD to make him incoherent on the air, were rejected. Declassified CIA files show Giancana suggested poison pills to lace Castro's food. The pills were manufactured by the CIA's Technical Services Division and handed to Juan Orta, Giancana's contact in the Cuban government with access to Castro.

Orta tried three times to spike Castro's food, but each attempt became more complicated and evident that he was acting strange. He begged off the job, and Trafficante chose Anthony Varona, leader of the Cuban Exile Juna. He was supplied with botulinum toxin pills, but Castro missed his next visit to the restaurant chosen for the poisoning. And then came the Bay of Pigs.

The Bay of Pigs was a crazy plot begun by the CIA – with President Eisenhower's blessing and $13 million in defense funds) to fund, train, and supply rebels with guns to overthrow Castro. CIA Director Allen Dulles was confident the plan would work since the CIA-led 1954 Guatemalan coup d'état had gone smoothly.

However, by the time the CIA was "ready, "President Kennedy was in charge. He had campaigned heavily against communism, and overthrowing Cuba seemed like an easy job, so it was greenlighted.

Unfortunately, the entire effort was riddled with mistakes, judgment errors, and the commitment of JFK the CIA was hoping for. When things went badly on April 15 (yeah, that's Tax Day) and the CIA and US cover was blown, Kennedy canceled the second round of bombing scheduled for the next day – stranding hundreds of dedicated soldiers in battle with no backup and quashing any chance of taking over Cuba. More than 100 US-funded and trained fighters died.

Director Dulles said, "CIA planners believed that once the troops were on the ground, Kennedy would authorize any action required to prevent failure – as Eisenhower had done in Guatemala in 1954 after that invasion looked as if it would collapse." Sorry, not happening. Dulles blamed Kennedy. Kennedy blamed the CIA.

Kennedy was later quoted as saying, "What I'd like to do is splinter the CIA in a thousand pieces and scatter it to the winds. The first advice I'm going to give my successor is to watch the generals and to avoid feeling that because they were military men, their opinions on military matters were worth a damn."

Now it was more than just the Mob and Giancana and Trafficante who hated Kennedy. Now it was the CIA, military personnel, officers – generals, and of course, Jimmy Hoffa. And then came November of 1963.

President Kennedy made several public appearances in the latter months of 1963 as he geared up for a reelection bid. The missile crisis of October '62 was a year past, and economic growth was expanding. When congresspersons said reducing taxes without spending cuts was unacceptable, Kennedy disagreed, saying, "a rising tide lifts all boats" and that strong economic growth would not continue without lower taxes. Ah, what a time to be alive.

The following story, corroborated over the years by multiple reliable sources, didn't make it to the public until 1975 when Edwin

Black, a reporter first for **Atlantic Monthly** and then the **Chicago Independent,** where his article appeared November 1975: *The Plot to Kill JFK in Chicago.*

These first notes may sound familiar if you know anything about the JFK assassination. The first suspect interrogated was a former marine. He had served at Marine bases in Japan that hosted the U-2 spy plane, code-named Dragon Lady. The US Airforce and US Navy flew the spy plane, but the CIA had majority control over the project. Who knew?

Strangely enough, then President Eisenhower wanted non-American to fly the planes that the CIA referred to as "articles" but eventually settled on USAF, who had to resign their military commissions to join the CIA as civilians – a process the agency called "sheep dipping." Pilots were then referred to as "drivers."

The interrogated suspect was involved in anti-Castro Cubans, an organization stirring the pot against Cuba and Castro. And, the suspect had a new job overlooking the planned presidential parade where he could fire down on the motorcade during a slow 90-degree turn.

But wait, the suspect's name wasn't Lee Harvey Oswald. It wasn't Dallas, not yet. It was Chicago, where the President was scheduled to appear on November 2nd and attend the Army Airforce game at Soldier Field. This man's name was Thomas Arthur Vallee. But how was he found?

Edwin Black's article stated, and eventually, the FBI admitted, that they received a tip that four right-wing extremists would assassinate the president as his motorcade traveled the Northwest Expressway to downtown Chicago.

The first lead came from a woman who rented rooms to four men only to find four rifles with telescopic sights in a room the next day. She called Chicago police on Thursday, October 31. The Secret Service dispatched all their agents to follow leads and monitor the rented room.

Agent Jay Lawrence Stocks sat outside the rental location and spotted two men fitting the landlady's description.

When the men got in a car and drove off, Stocks followed. In a parking garage, the suspects turned around and passed Stocks, who had a two-way radio in his car. As the suspects passed his open window, he received a call that they heard. Cover blown. The two suspects were apprehended and interviewed soon afterward. No guns were found.

The following day when Thomas Arthur Vallee was out of his room at an uptown dive, two agents picked the lock on his door and found evidence, including a handgun, a carbine, an M-1, and 2500 rounds of ammunition. The findings were reported, and two top Chicago police officers (Daniel Groth and Peter Schurla) tailing Vallee in his Ford Falcone vehicle were alerted.

When Vallee made a turn without using his blinker, he was pulled over. The officers saw a hunting knife on the front seat, and Vallee was told he could be charged with unlawful use of a weapon and failing to use his turn signal. Searching the vehicle, they found 750 rounds of ammo in the trunk. He was arrested at 9 am Saturday, just hours before President Kennedy was to arrive at O'Hare airport.

Although the two men held for questioning were still in custody, their two accomplices were in the wind with their weapons. Kennedy canceled his trip. Then the two men in custody were released. They have never been identified.

A week later, the FBI teletyped a new assassination threat to their New Orleans field office, similar to the Chicago threat. Kennedy was scheduled for a drive-thru motorcade parade on November 17. There are no notes or corroborating evidence of arrests before his visit.

Perhaps the conspirators were found – the second team of killers – or the FBI and Secret Service were comfortable knowing no danger existed. Kennedy arrived on time, and there were no specific hazards noted. A copy of the telex was shown during a CBS news broadcast in 1975, including an interview with the gentleman on duty. No other information about the threat exists.

On November 22, 1963, President Kennedy's motorcade traveled through Dallas and slowed for broad curves around Dealey Square. Upstairs on the 6th floor of the Texas Book Depository on Elm Street, a shooter aimed his gun at the President's vehicle.

Lee Harvey Oswald was a new employee at the Texas Book Depository - on his lunch break then. He was a former Marine stationed at Atsugi, in Japan, where the U-2 was located and where he worked in radio communications. Where he taught himself rudimentary Russian, where he was court-martialed twice, busted in rank, but somehow allowed a hardship discharge, and placed in the United States Marine Corps Reserve.

A month later, he was on his way to Russia as a tourist but told his guide once inside the country that he wanted to defect because he was a communist. It has been rumored that the CIA sent him with a set of active, secret radar codes to ensure his believability as a defector. He was admitted to Russia, given a factory job, and met his wife Marina Prusakova before writing the US Embassy and asking for a return of his passport. Amazingly his request was granted, and he and his wife came to the US.

Years later, the Warren Commission investigating the Kennedy assassination stated that the loss of radar codes Oswald may or may not have been given by the CIA caused a new system of codes to be developed and implemented.

Most recently, Oswald had been in New Orleans distributing Pro-Castro flyers and trying to infiltrate the Fair Play for Cuba Committee for a local politician, lawyer, and former FBI agent Guy Banister. Back in Dallas on November 22, Oswald was a work.

He had carried an extended, slender package to his job and placed it upstairs. Weeks previous, he had purchased a Mannlicher-Carcano rifle by mail. His wife took photos of him with the rifle. The rifle found on the 6th-floor shooting nest had Oswald's fingerprints and palm print on the trigger and barrel, respectively. Ballistics tied the rifle to the bullets that killed President Kennedy. That's all we know.

Was Oswald the only shooter? Make your own decisions. Was he a patsy, set up in Dallas in case Chicago and New Orleans attempts failed? Who knows. Did he act alone? Based on the Chicago and New Orleans incidents, it doesn't look like it.

As a side note, there are verified accounts of the evidence in Chicago and New Orleans being destroyed and buried. Nothing would look worse than the Secret Service not doing a better job of protecting the president. The FBI also failed to find evidence of early reports that Oswald was a security risk. Why?

Author Edwin Black also found while researching his story in 1975 that the original arrest report for Thomas Arthur Vallee was short on information. There were no indications of a conspiracy, no mention of the guns and ammo found at his apartment, or the 750 rounds of ammo in the trunk of his car.

Arresting officer Daniel Groth told Black he didn't remember the other suspects and that the arrest was only for a failure to signal a turn. When Black noted by phone to Groth that in the corner, there was a scribble on the top corner of the arrest report that said M-1 Rifle. Groth said there was nothing else involved; that scratch was nothing but a freak typo. Right.

In the end, 12 years later, Edwin Black researches his story, meticulously verifying available facts, and finds Thomas Arthur Vallee outside Houston. Under some tricky circumstances and the phone name of Eddie Brokaw, he meets and interviews him. Vallee admits the details of the Chicago incident but denies any plan to shoot the president.

Vegas and the Chicago Outfit

Yes, he admits he was anti-Kennedy. Yes, the CIA recruited him to train exiles to assassinate Castro. No, he was never called before the Warren Commission or contacted again by the Secret Service until 1966. He says he was a patsy, set up to take the fall if things went right for the other conspirators.

During their discussion outside of Houston, Chicago Secret Service agent Tom Hampton calls Black/Brokaw's employer – the offices of *Chicago Independent* magazine. He asks if there is an Eddie Brokaw employed there. When asked why the agent says, "Well, he's been asking a lot of sensitive questions, and we want to know why?"

How the hell did the Secret Service know? How did the Defense Intelligence Agency (DIA) know he had been commissioned to investigate the story? Why was he followed and harassed? Why was his apartment broken into? And what about Abraham Bolden, who provides background?

Abraham Bolden was a competent, engaging Secret Service agent. President Kennedy chose him to be part of his White House detail after he was temporarily transferred from Chicago to Washington D.C. He became the first African American assigned to protect the president.

However, after meeting with James Rowley, the head of the Secret Service, about "separate housing facilities for black agents on southern trips and the general laxity and the heavy drinking among the agents assigned to protect the President," Bolden was reassigned back to the Chicago office. Before the October 1963 warnings from the FBI about "a dissident Cuban group."

After the assassination and while working on anti-counterfeiting detail in the Chicago office, Bolden decided to offer testimony to the Warren Commission about the warnings from the FBI, Thomas Arthur Vallee, and the four men his Secret Service office surveilled in October and November of '63. He called Warren Commission General Counsel Lee Rankin and offered his help.

Word returned to Sam Giancana, who arranged for Johnny Roselli to intervein. One day before his trip to Washington, Bolden was arrested for trying to induce a bribe from Joseph Spagnoli and Frank Jones. They were two of ten counterfeiters under indictment for making bogus US Government Series E savings bonds and Bank of America traveler's checks. $450,000 worth of bad paper was involved. Bolden was too – he had arrested Frank Jones twice.

Bolden claimed he never offered confidential information for the $50,000 Spagnoli claimed. Still, upright citizen Mr. Joseph Spagnoli swore it all happened, and he was offering his testimony without any plea deal or offered from the government. We should always believe the ramblings of convicted felons.

Bolden was found guilty and sentenced to six years in prison. When he complained about the case, he was moved to solitary confinement.

In 2022, President Biden issued a pardon to Anthony Bolden.

J. Edgar Hoover between President JFK and brother RFK circa 1961 - U.S. National Archives and Records Administration / Public Domain

Chapter Nineteen

Chicago Crime Takes a Beating

In the light of the day after the Kennedy assassination, our country (and much of the world) mourned and questioned how it could happen. Then the boo birds arrived.

The whackos who questioned everything, insisting that no single man could have set up the crow's nest six stories above the presidential motor route, in a new job, and as an ex-marine who defected to Russia and then was inexplicably allowed back in the country with no handlers or oversight.

He got the gun with a phony name through a mail order ad and had it sent to a P. O. Box. Is that a joke?

Of course, it was all a defense mechanism. Certainly, the greatest country in the world with the most dedicated military and service personnel - the FBI, CIA, NSA, DEA, Marshall's Service, AFT (do I need to go on?), not to mention the Secret Service trained at great expense to be supremely prepared to protect the president couldn't be outthought and outmaneuvered by a single crackpot, a lone gunman, a crazy commie. Right?

Well, after nearly 60 years, we aren't much closer to knowing the truth than we were the day Kennedy's accused killer, Lee Harvey Oswald, was shot dead by another simpleton (according to the press then and now) – one Jack Ruby.

Ruby was just a local strip joint owner and friends with some of the police, so he managed to get at Oswald as he was being escorted through the basement of the Dallas Police Headquarters to an armored car set for the city jail. That's what we've been spoon-fed. It might even be true.

The Warren Commission was established on November 29, 1963, by President Lyndon B. Johnson and overseen by Chief Justice of the United States Earl Warren, who presented an 888-page report after listening to 552 witnesses.

They concluded that Oswald acted alone. They concluded there was no conspiracy. They never determined Oswald's motive. They concluded Jack Ruby acted alone.

Allen Dulles, former Director of Central Intelligence, was one of the committee's seven members. Later, according to a report by CIA Chief Historian David Robarge, acting CIA Director John McCone was "complicit" in a CIA "benign cover-up" for instructing CIA officers to give only "passive, reactive, and selective" assistance to the Warren

Commission.

They certainly didn't want the commission to know they had regular contact with Oswald. Or that the CIA knew he had caught a bus from Houston to New Orleans in late September, while the FBI didn't want to admit that Oswald had asked at their field office to talk to someone in charge but was denied. Or that they mostly ignored the specific warning in November that a team of four Cubans was coming to kill Kennedy.

Oswald arrived in Mexico City the next day and visited the Cuban consulate for a transit visa on his way to Russia. After five days of going back and forth between the Cuban and Russian consulates, he was denied entry to Cuba.

On 18 October, his visa was approved by the Cuban embassy. On 11 November, he wrote the Soviet embassy in Washington, D.C., and said, "Had I been able to reach the Soviet Embassy in Havana, as planned, the embassy there would have had time to complete our business."

The Warren Commission concluded they could not rule out the possibility that someone else had used his name in visiting the consulates. Likely Oswald was arranging the visas for an escape route after the assassination.

As for McCone's motivation at the CIA, it may have been to keep secret the CIA-Mob's efforts to kill Fidel Castro. According to well-known hitman turned informant Jimmy Fratianno, he asked Johnny Roselli about the assassination and was told, "I think Castro hit Kennedy because of the Bay of Pigs invasion. Mostly because I don't think Castro knew the CIA was trying to kill him."

"And I believe that because Santo Trafficante never did nothing but bullshit everybody. The plan failed because Santo flushed those fancy poisons the CIA designed down the toilet."

On the other hand, Chuck Giancana swears his brother Sam told him that he was part of the JFK assassination. Might be true too. And for the sake of more conspiracy argument, Johnny Roselli blaming Castro was an excellent way to hide any involvement the Outfit and Giancana may have had. And sending a tip that four Cubans were coming to kill Kennedy earlier in Chicago and New Orleans could have been disinformation.

As for Jack Ruby, please recall that he was born and worked in Chicago. He was a member of the International Brotherhood of Teamsters in the refuse and waste management end. Sam Giancana sent him and his brothers to Dallas after friend Benny Binion gave up his joints there and moved to Las Vegas.

On other high and low notes, Ruby worked with the FBI as a federal informant, meeting with agents eight times. He smuggled guns to pro-Castro rebels in the late '50s. He also was longtime friends of Sam Giancana, Joseph Campisi, and Joseph Civello, who took over the reins as Dallas crime boss in 1956.

It's likely Ruby ran a few routes as a money courier from time to time and worked as a bookie like Campisi, although Ruby was a low-level shop. Some say Campisi took over for Civello when he passed away in 1970.

There are also very credible accounts of Jack Ruby visiting Lewis McWillie at the Thunderbird Casino in Vegas, where he received "enough cash to pay off all the damn taxes" a week before he shot Lee Harvey Oswald.

Ruby repeatedly asked to speak to the Warren Commission, who showed little interest. Finally, in June 1964, Chief Justice Earl Warren went to Dallas to see Ruby. Who asked to be taken to Washington D.C. because "my life is in danger here" and "I want to tell the truth, and I can't tell it here." Warren declined, saying they had no way of protecting him since they had no police powers. Their conversation ended without additional statements.

Finally, in its final report, the House Select Committee on Assassinations stated:

There is also evidence that the Dallas Police Department withheld relevant information from the Warren Commission concerning Ruby's entry to the scene of the Oswald transfer. However, Ruby's shooting of Oswald was not a spontaneous act in that it involved at least some premeditation.

It is unlikely that Ruby entered the police basement without assistance, even though the assistance may have been provided with no knowledge of Ruby's intentions, and the committee was troubled by the unlocked doors along the stairway route and the removal of security guards from the area of the garage nearest the stairway shortly before the shooting.

Again, it's been sixty years, and you'll have to draw your own conclusions. I don't know!

On a final note, the attempted assassination of Castro by the CIA and the Giancanna/Roselli/Trafficante mix was hardly a new idea. It is the tip of the iceberg.

For some background, the CIA started as a military group called the OSS during World War II - Office of Strategic Services – and like its successor, including intelligence and special operations military functions.

OSS officers parachuted into China in the 1940s to train anti-government rebels. In the 1950s, the CIA worked with Tibetan rebels to help the Dalai Lama's escape to India. Then In the early 1950s, the CIA and Britain's Secret Intelligence Service worked together to overthrow the democratically elected government of Iran, Prime Minister Mohammed Mosaddeq, and re-install deposed Shah Mohammad Reza

Pahlavi.

Later came assassinations, overthrows, disinformation with paid media in places like Korea, Cuba, the Bay of Pigs, and the Castro assassination attempt. Then Bolivia, where Che Guevara was executed on October 9, 1967, by orders of CIA Paramilitary Operations Officer Félix Rodríguez. Plus, Vietnam, Laos, and a host of South American countries. All for the better good, we are sure. Again, draw your own conclusions, but who better to stage an assassination than the CIA?

And what of the changes that came after President Kennedy was assassinated? New President Lyndon Baines Johnson cranked up a series of successful social programs and ensured the industrial and defense industries were supercharged by escalating fighting in Vietnam. He would likely have handed over the presidency to Robert F. Kennedy had JFK's brother not also fallen to an assassin's bullets.

No matter the depth of any role by the Mob or the Outfit in JFK's demise, things didn't exactly go their way afterward. The FBI started what they called lock-step surveillance of Sam Giancana. The in-the-open, in-your-face surveilling caused annoyance and frustration for crime bosses, and FBI agents like William F. Roemer Jr. pushed their surveillance techniques to new heights, even goading Giancana into a verbal altercation at the airport after a long flight.

Giancana often remarked how smart he was and often got "That FBI prick's goat." And we know this because Roemer had placed listening devices in several of Giancana's favorite meeting places.

Roemer had a knack for turning desperate criminals into productive informants. While many bosses were known to use their influence as an informant (think Whitey Bulger) to their advantage, Roemer was still thriving.

His first significant flip was Richard Cain, a Chicago Police Department detective who handled local police payoffs through Outfit financier and political fixer Murray Humphreys' number one man.

In 1960 he took an absence from the CPD to work with Assistant US Attorney Richard Ogilvie in an investigation of Tony Accardo. During that time, he also helped train Cuban-Americans for the Bay of Pigs invasion in Mexico, where he was deported from in 1961.

Cain returned to Chicago and was appointed the chief investigator of the Cook County Sheriff's Office. He was later fired for lying to a grand jury about stolen drugs that went missing. At some point along the way, Roemer flipped him and gained valuable insight, some of which was used to solve investigations – practically a new idea for the FBI – perhaps because Cain's "tips" helped muscle in on his rivals and kept them under federal heat (again, think Whitey Bulger).

Also, about this time, Sam Giancana was told by multiple sources that the IRS was nearing a devastating tax fraud case against him (probably with the help of the exact US Attorney who pushed the screws on Tony Accardo). Giancana wasn't surprised, and since he had been buying land and ferrying cash into secure locations in Mexico, he stepped down from his position as head of the Outfit in 1966 and took up residence in Mexico.

Cain handled skimmed money from Giancana's casinos in Central America and Iran. He couriered cash from Chicago – until he was arrested for perjury, which came with a concurrent prison term of four years for being an accessory to bank robbery.

At about the same time, Marshall Caifano was serving time for trying to extort $60,000 from Indiana oilman Ray Ryan. His jail term and Cains ended in time for both to be on the streets of Chicago in the early '70s.

On 20 December 1973, Marshall Caifano had lunch in Rose's Sandwich Shop in downtown Chicago. An hour later, Richard Cain also had lunch, but his ended badly. Two of the four men he was dining with left the shop using the back door. A minute later, several men with black masks entered the restaurant.

Patrons were lined up against a far wall, and a man holding a shotgun and wearing gloves – one white, one black - asked, "Who's got the package?" They moved down the line of customers before stopping in front of Cain.

He was pulled away from the wall before the man with the shotgun blew his facial features away with a single, up-close shot. When he hit the floor, the second gunman blew another hole in his head with a handgun.

It seems that what goes around comes around, and the white/black gloves likely signified that the killers knew Cain was an informant working on both sides. Marshall Caifano bragged later about the killing.

Another of Bill Roemer's attempts at flipping a gangster ended similarly. He worked relentlessly on William Jackson, aka Action Jackson, a South Side of Chicago loan shark. Jackson was arrested with $70,000 in electrical appliances. His accomplices all fled, but Action got his name for the loan juice he collected for Sam DeStefano, not his speed (he weighed north of 300 pounds).

Roemer made inroads with Jackson, speaking with him several times, but he ultimately refused to help the FBI. Unfortunately, he was seen speaking with Roemer and had to be dealt with. There could be no maybes and no halfway measures.

Jackson was called to a meeting at Rover's, a pool hall with beer, and he and DeStefano stepped into an alley where he was knocked down, his gun taken, and helped into a panel truck.

The truck stopped at a meat plant a mile away on Lower Wacker Drive, and he was questioned by Mad Sam, who doubted his sincerity. Sam's henchmen stripped Jackson while beating him, eventually knocking him unconscious.

When he awoke, his torturers took a meat hook and jammed it into his anus before using ropes on his wrists and feet to hang him in the air. Then they systematically cut his body and stuck shards of glass and metal into sensitive areas.

When he refused to admit he was an informant, DeStefano brought out a cattle prod. Afterward, he was beaten with a bat. When he awoke from that session, a blow torch was used to scorch holes in areas all over his body.

The police found his body four days later. The medical examiner estimated he had lived three days after being abducted. His ribs were broken, his kneecaps shattered, and his head was swelled to the size of an overripe watermelon.

Years later, DeStefano went to his garage in the 1600 block of North Sayre Avenue to talk to his brother Mario and Tony Spilotro about some outstanding loans. Instead, when Spilotro walked inside, he blasted DeStefano twice with a shotgun, blowing his left arm off at the elbow and piercing his chest. Unlike Action Jackson, Mad Sam DeStefano died instantly. He was lucky.

Howard Hughes circa 1938 - Acme Newspictures / Public Domain

Chapter Twenty

Las Vegas in the '60s

The country's fascination with Las Vegas was piqued when they opened their papers and saw a photo of Bugsy Siegel sprawled across the floor, murdered in 1940s style.

The 1950s brought more casino names like the Dunes, Sahara, and Sands, each offering a continually updated and more extravagant array of shows and Hollywood stars in their showrooms.

By the 1960s, Las Vegas was a worldwide phenomenon, and

although local businessmen were confident, outside financial consultants insisted the town had been overbuilt and would collapse. Which do you think happened?

You're right. More elaborate casinos kept coming, contributing jobs, tax dollars, and pre-tax skim to Mob families around the country. The Tally Ho opened in 1962 and became the King's Crown but had no gaming because crime groups kept trying to get known agents on the gaming license. The Aladdin joined the Las Vegas Strip in 1964 with a respectable frontman and was soon operated by the Detroit Partnership and the St. Louis crime family.

But the big news in town was the opening of the lavish 700-room Caesars Palace on 5 August 1966 by Jay Sarno and Nate Jacobsen. To welcome guests (purloined high rollers from other casinos' Rolodexes), the partners spend over a million dollars on food, including 300 pounds of Maryland crabmeat and two tons of filet mignon, buckets of caviar, shrimp, pasta, and enough champagne to fill 50,000 glasses.

The Roman holiday feast was a financial drop in the bucket as the casino and hotel booked millions of dollars in room reservations for the year.

But how did Sarno and Nate Jacobsen pay for construction? With a $24 million loan from the Teamsters Union Central States Pension Fund, of course. Jimmy Hoffa got a cut equaling over 1% of the loan package as he had on Sarno's motel projects.

And since his projects, or at least all that loan money he got, gave him easy access to cash, Sarno became a degenerate gambler losing more than a million dollars in the early '60s at the Desert Inn and Riviera casinos. He needed the loans to keep the castles of sand upright. Besides, what better person to front a grand new casino?

Of course, the Mob never worried about finding money; it was all free and on someone else's back.

Caesars Palace was an immediate success, and high rollers flocked to the property losing untold amounts of money. Untold because the skim happened hard and heavy. Several families got a piece of the money that acted like disappearing ink for years. Meyer Lansky, semi-retired and living in Miami, never stopped finding cash leaks at Vegas casinos. At Caesars, "Jimmy Nap" Napoli and Zarowitz took care of the skim for "Fat Tony" Salerno who got it to Lansky.

The government finally made a case against the Teamster loans and sketchy financials and cut the cord on the New York and New England crime families. So, the Mob did what it always did; it brought in new front of people.

This time, it was Stuart and Clifford Perlman who started their business venture as Lums Inc. with a hot dog stand in Miami Beach in 1956. They were very successful, and by 1965 the brother's controlled 15 restaurants. The only change they instituted in Las Vegas was a name change to Caesars World for the $58 million dollar property that doubled in value in less than three years!

About that time, Allen Dorfman was indicted with several other Teamsters leaders for embezzling from the union pension fund. His sentence? One measly year in the pen.

Down at the Riviera, business was sizzling too, but pushy feds kept insisting the owners pay their correct tax bills. In 1967 partners Ross Miller, Frank Atol, and Joe Rosenberg were indicted by a federal grand jury for tax evasion estimated at over $130,000 from April to June of 1963 disappeared.

Miller's son, Robert, served as a well-liked and respected Governor of Nevada. He admitted his father was a bookie from the tough streets of Chicago before being licensed to run the casino at the Riviera. Good thing nobody held a grudge.

To handle that kind of money, only trusted couriers were used.

Often that included Hollywood stars who owed the Outfit a favor for getting them the right agent or movie role. In Sidney Roy Korshak's

case, he was a longtime mob fixer dating back to the Capone era. The FBI called him "the most powerful lawyer in the world." And he may have carried some cash over the years, but he was never indicted for any crime.

Anthony Manzo was never arrested either. Tony stayed in the background, invisible and quiet, and took trips from Las Vegas to Illinois and Indiana. He specialized in skim from the Riviera, Flamingo, and the Stardust that ran as high as $100,000 weekly.

Manzo was an insurance agent (according to his business card) from Indiana. Tall and prone to wearing a suit jacket even in warmer weather, he was a nobody, an absolute Joe with dark glasses, white shirts, and boring ties.

According to Manzo, he never knew how much cash he was carrying. He just took a bag from the casino manager or a subordinate at count time on a set weekly date. The bags were as nondescript as he was, lending to grey and dark brown. A boss told him to forget black bags, "You don't want nobody thinking you're a doctor."

According to Manzo, his first two jobs were freebies other than train fare, meals, and a chance to see Las Vegas. He had no idea he was carrying cash back with him to Indianapolis. Later, he was offered a steady gig: five-hundred bucks a week plus food and train tickets. He specifically wasn't offered free meals or rooms at the casinos he couriered for: "Don't be gambling, you putz." As an insurance agent, he made slightly over $4000 yearly in the '50s.

After several months he got a bagman's boost - $1200 a month plus $75 for expenses on each trip. Later his stipend jumped to $500 per week when he stopped selling insurance and was always available.

At one point, he didn't have a day off other than a one-day stop in

Gary, Indiana, for nearly six months. He didn't complain. By the 1960s, he was pocketing a flat $2,000 each week. " Man, I thought I was rich."

His delivery time and location got adjusted regularly to avoid detection and robbery. Sometimes he got off the train in Chicago, where a known contact immediately met him. Mostly, his train passed into Indiana, where he was met after leaving the station. He never bought a ticket; a handler gave it to him with orders to never miss the train or his stop.

His trips were mundane for several years until he was robbed at gunpoint in Indianapolis by two men in their twenties who knew he was a regular traveler. His contact took the information and told him to return to Las Vegas.

The train trip back was the longest and most frightening of his life. When he arrived at Union Station on Fremont Steet in Vegas, two men grabbed him, shoved him into a car, and drove him to a house in North Las Vegas. Then they threw him into a bare room where he sweated for several hours.

Eventually, he was joined by two men he recognized. One had a gun, the other, fists, and Manzo was beaten until the man with the gun finally said, "You got lucky. We found the guys in Cicero. You lose another bag; you're dead and buried. You protect that bag with your life. There's nowhere we won't find you."

Manzo was relieved of his duties and retired to Lake Tahoe, Nevada, after the dustup at the Riviera and Kirk Kerkorian's purchase of the Flamingo casino in 1967 that reduced skim runs considerably. He never believed he had the option to quit before that.

******

After Caesars hit big, Sarno built a new casino with an eye for money from the other end of the gambling spectrum, the working man.

209

And although he was a rich bastard on paper, but not at the bank, he finagled a $43 million loan from the Central States Pension Fund of the Teamsters Union. Jimmy Hoffa was happy to oblige and get another check of his own.

If you ever wondered how there could be so much money available from the Teamsters, follow this:

In 1959, Moe Dalitz built a community hospital, the 100-bed Sunrise Hospital, with a $1 million loan from the Teamsters Central States, Southeast, and Southwest Areas Pension Fund. Hoffa signed as one of the beneficiaries. When it was done, or nearly done, the hospital was permitted to open with a dozen building code violations and fourteen plumbing violations, but hey, it was just a hospital.

To ensure it was a good deal for everyone involved, Dalitz and Hoffa arranged for the hospital to keep five beds available for the primary medical care of the Teamsters and Culinary Workers union employees at just $6.50 per union member per month. How many union workers were there in Vegas at the time? A lot.

In fact, by 1963, there were nearly 8,000. So over $50,000 was coming in monthly! The paperwork and loan went through fast because no Teamster officials had to account for expenditures of pension funds that they loaned out, even to themselves.

Once the new funding source was proven, it was heavily used. The next beneficiaries were the Fremont Hotel owners, who got $850,000 in 1961 as part of their package of loans for expansion. The cool part was that the deal was assigned to Three-O-One Corporation. The president was Icepick Alderman, and the vice president was Allard Roen. The loan went through even though three days earlier, Roen was indicted in New York court on a stock-fraud charge in the United Dye and Chemical case. He later pleaded guilty to securities fraud.

Of course, by the time the Fremont Hotel had all their loans wrapped together, they got a total of $4 million from the Teamsters fund. Major Riddle, who owned nearly 40 percent of the Dunes by the late 1950s, got a similar amount, and Dalitz and Roen picked up a little over $1 million to build the Stardust Golf Course.

Things didn't end too well for Jimmy Hoffa. He was indicted on charges of fraudulently obtaining $20 million in loans from the Teamsters Pension Fund and taking $1.2 million of the loan for himself and his co-conspirators. He received a five-year prison sentence. He was head of the Teamsters Union at the time.

Later, in 1964, he was convicted of bribery and tampering with a grand jury. That sentence was for 13 years. He served 58 months before President Richard Nixon commuted his sentence to time served.

As the Teamsters Union's latest beneficiary, Circus, there were no high roller amenities like steak and lobster. Instead, Circus had a $2.95 dinner buffet. There was dollar blackjack and craps, 25-cent chip roulette, and lots of nickel slot machines ringing at all hours.

There was also a circus atmosphere with trapeze artists performing on a highwire, jugglers, the works. Serious gamblers hated it. Locals, too, especially the pink and white strips on the building. Male dealers had to explain to their children why they wore pink shirts and an apron at work.

Do you know who didn't hate it? A short, stocky guy introduced to Jay Sarno's manager as Anthony Stuart, who paid $70,000 for the gift shop concession. Gift shops were a gold mine in Vegas. 500% markup was standard. Jewelry was closer to 10x.

And where could a regular guy like this, Anthony Stuart get $70,000 in cash? From his heavy work in Chicago, he was known there as Tony Spilotro. Joseph Aiuppa sent him. He was now in charge (with Tony Accardo backing him) after Sam Giancana got bounced for bringing the heat on the Outfit and not sharing his outside casino profits - to take Johnny Roselli's job.

Vegas and the Chicago Outfit

That job was watching the skim at Outfit casinos. Specifically, he tailed and watched over the casinos Frank Rosenthal was managing: the Stardust, Fremont, Hacienda, and Marina. The Outfit loved Rosenthal's bluff but hated his blunder. He, too, was pompous, but he produced. How much? The Outfit wasn't sure.

Tony "The Ant" Spilotro found hanging with Rosenthal dull unless he could bust some heads (or bang his wife). FBI Agent Bill Rohmer in Chicago had fingered him to the police but little stuck. He called him a pipsqueak, a tiny pissant. When Rohmer was quoted, newspapers adopted 'The Ant."

Spilotro organized a band of merry men, dubbed the hole-in-the-wall gang. They pillaged and plundered businesses and residences and often sold stolen jewelry at their jewelry store.

Tony was the quintessential crime-figure family man. Lovely wife, kids, and a few babes on the side. Inferiority complex, quick temper, raging hormones, and an ego the size of a Buick. He was right; you are wrong. Get used to it.

During the first three years, Spilotro spent in Vegas; there were more gangland killings than there had been in the previous 25 years combined. Some of his "missing persons" are still being dredged out of Lake Mean near Vegas now that the water level has dropped. How many did he kill? As many as he wanted. And that was a problem.

Chicago, New York, Detroit, St. Louis, Miami, Philadelphia, Buffalo – hell, those families wanted things quiet, like that crazy millionaire Howard Hughes.

Early on Thanksgiving 1966, a special train pulled into Union Plaza, and a waiting ambulance picked up a single occupant, Howard Hughes. He hadn't been seen in eight years, but business deals and the sale of his TWA stock had made him one of the wealthiest men in the world.

After two plane crashes and a continuing addiction to a slew of drugs that started with Emperin Compound No. 4 (a modified form of morphine), Hughes' frame had fallen from a robust 180-pound 6 foot four inches to a 6'1 115 pounds.

He was easily agitated, delusional, and prone to sleep days and then be awake all night or longer. After first taking codeine tablets and Valium, Hughes switched to dissolving the codeine in water and injecting the liquid into his forearms. Often he would drift off with the needle still in his arm. When he rolled over, the needles broke off and were forever embedded under the skin.

Hank Greenspun, the owner of the Las Vegas Sun, got him rooms at the Desert Inn casino. When Hughes was asked to leave so the casino could use the rooms for New Year's high rollers, he refused.

Robert Maheu (the same FBI – CIA asset) was Howard's frontman since the good Mr. Hughes couldn't be seen with his inch-long nails or shoulder-length, unwashed hair. And it was easy for Maheu to manage talks with Johnny Roselli and Moe Dalitz, who wasn't interested in having the crazy rich guy upstairs.

But what if Hughes bought the place? Maheu, Roselli, and Dalitz saw the benefits of a deal like that, and they played Hughes like a fiddle. The property was worth at least ten million, but they pushed the price to $15 million. At the same time, Hughes told Maheu, "That damn Moe, I know about Kleinman, I know about Hoffa, I know about the Purple men (Purple Gang)," as he and Maheu talked over a phone line that stretched just 30 feet from Howard's private 250-foot bedroom and suites main room.

No matter how good a negotiator Moe thought he was, he had met his match in Howard Hughes. Not because Hughes drove a hard bargain but because Hughes second-guessed himself every ten minutes. Once the men got in the same ballpark, Howard demanded some concessions. Moe relinquished none initially but caved to later demands. Eventually, an agreement was ready for lawyers, so Howard changed the wording and transfer details. When Moe agreed, he demanded another dozen changes be made. Howard wanted the deal to be consummated at 7 pm, then at 6 pm, then midnight. Moe refused.

Howard sat up each night writing notes to Maheu, his aides, Jean Peters (yup, he was still married), and then changed them each afternoon. Once the lawyers got the papers, Howard still wanted to make more changes. Eventually, the paperwork was done and sent back to Howard.

On March 22, 1967, the D. I. negotiations ended with a purchase price of $13.2 million to be paid by Howard for the land and the buildings. Hughes's representatives at the meeting included Maheu and D. I. officials Moe Dalitz, Maurice Kleinman, and Jack Donnelley. The transfer of casino ownership in Nevada is long and arduous unless you are Howard Hughes.

In this case, Howard gave his power of attorney to Richard Gray and had the license put in the name of Hughes Tool Company to avoid ever coming face to face with any Gaming Control Board members. All anybody knew at that time was that Hughes was 61 years old, listed at six-foot-two, 150 pounds (a lie), and maybe self-employed. Of course, for all anybody knew, he could also be dead.

That was good enough for the Nevada Gaming Commission and the Clark County Licensing Board, which unanimously approved the necessary local license to become effective at 12:01 AM, April 1, 1967. No official count was done at the casino cage, and it is impossible to know how much cash walked out the door with Moe Dalitz. It is also impossible to know how much money was removed from Hughes's properties over the years through skim. Officials estimate a minimum of $50 million.

It was a fantastic deal for the crime families across the nation that had a piece of any number of Las Vegas clubs. They could sell their casinos at an inflated price and still take a rake-off from an unseen owner! Maheu, a former FBI agent, saw skeletons in every closet and set about improving security at the Hughes properties, but that didn't keep them from bleeding cash.

Still, Howard was happy, and a happy guy with all the money in the world likes to play with things, so the Howard Hughes buying spree was just beginning. In July of 1967, Maheu and his contacts in the Mob made a deal for the Sands. Frank Sinatra was less than happy with the sale.

He still appeared in the showroom, and he and his Rat Pack were a welcome sight at any casino they happened to wander into. Sammy Davis, Jr., Dean Martin, Peter Lawford, and Joey Bishop made quite a group. They drank, gambled, and drew stares, photos, and publicity. Sometimes the Rat Pack Mascots were in town, including Angie Dickinson, Juliet Prowse, and Shirley MacLaine. Outside on the Sands marquee, the headline read, "DEAN MARTIN - MAYBE FRANK - MAYBE SAMMY" Fans adored them.

When Frank was at the Sands gambling, he'd often get chips on the sleeve (no paperwork) to double down on a bet. If he won, he'd pay the bet back. He'd walk away, off the hook, for any cash if he lost. He also made plenty of demands at the cage. "Look," he'd say, "if I can't get another $50,000, I may have to consider doing my show elsewhere."

When that happened, a manager usually signed for the free loan, and Sinatra never paid a dime of it back. One evening he had been to the cage twice, and when he demanded more money, he was denied. He was playing 21 and pounded the table, so hard chips flew out of the tray and onto the floor.

He berated the dealer, pushed the cocktail server away, and told the pit boss, "Listen, you're never working in this town again." The pit boss had already been told that Mr. Sinatra was done, no more money, so he stood his ground. Sinatra screamed at him again and then grabbed the railing of the 21 table and nearly turned it over. Again, chips rained to the floor, but the pit boss never moved. Sinatra stormed across the casino, his face twitching, searching for Carl Cohen, the Casino Manager.

When he found him in the coffee shop, Sinatra grabbed his table but couldn't pick it up because it was bolted to the floor. He did manage to spill Cohen's coffee cup. The 55-year-old Cohen looked at Sinatra for a moment and then rose from his chair. When he got to his feet, he plastered Sinatra in the mouth, knocking out two front teeth and leaving him with a bloody nose.

Sinatra was later quoted saying, "They wouldn't give me any credit in the casino, and I don't know what the problem was." Sinatra was probably more concerned with the $14.6 million sale of the Sands to Howard Hughes.

Meyer Lansky and others would be getting their fair share of the sales price, but Sinatra had lost all his "juice."

The Sands did fine without Sinatra and the Rat Pack, but other changes weren't as popular with locals or tourists. Hughes sat in his room, ignored his three-inch fingernails, and made long lists of changes for Maheu to make at the casinos, one of which was to stop the use of call girls for "high-rollers." Chorus girls were no longer expected to sit around the lounges for an hour after their shows. Governor Laxalt stated, "You're never going to eliminate the girls," but it was the beginning of the upgrading of Las Vegas.

After that point, if a high roller wanted a girl sent to his room, he had to get his "host" to take care of it, or he could always check with the Bell Captain. Guys at the bell desk always seemed to know what was going on in town and how to score whatever was needed. The city now had what amounted to corporate ownership of several casinos. What a concept. If they could only have seen who owned the properties!

It was also the time of the Weekend Warriors, who showed up late Friday night and left Sunday evening. Most of the warriors were young ladies from Southern California. Imagine being a 26-year-old kindergarten teacher in Pasadena and trying to live on $4,800 a year in teacher pay.

Some warriors were so good at their jobs in Las Vegas that they went pro, tripling their annual income.

Others were happy with a few "dates" and maybe $50 for an all-nighter on Saturday evening because a girl's gotta do what a girl's gotta do, and why pay for your hotel room? All Howard's new rules did was open the chip hustling and whoring to a new band of ladies, and soon the best ones didn't have to drive; they flew into town on $19 flights!

As for Howard, he hadn't been on a plane for a decade. His toenails were growing to extraordinary lengths and twisted in impossible directions. His feet no longer fit in the Kleenex boxes he wore as slippers years earlier, but it wasn't necessary to ever leave his room, as far as he was concerned.

For meals, his aides brought him cooked strips of chicken that might have already been reheated four or five times during the evening before he managed to choke down a few ounces. He drank milk, and dishes of fruit from cans were extraordinarily prepared for him.

Hughes continued purchasing casinos at an astonishing rate. He had almost no input on how they were run, and each lost a substantial amount of money. Maheu retained his crew of old bosses at each property. The skim ratcheted up so high that most of the properties turned red.

Hughes made the nation think Las Vegas was now clean, but the skim never stopped. After buying the Sands, he purchased the Frontier Casino for $14 million. The boys back east got their cake and kept the couriers coming with weekly cash. Listed stockholders included Anthony

J. Zerilli, the President of Detroit's Hazel Park Racetrack, Attorney Pete Bellance, Jack Dean, and Louis Elias.

The $3 million Hughes paid for the 230-room Castaway's hotel casino must have sounded like nothing to him. He paid more for the Silver Slipper across the street from the Desert Inn ($5.3 million), but only because of the heavily lit "stupid revolving slipper" that was too bright for his room, even with the blackout curtains. Well, because he was confident, the FBI was taking pictures of him from the toe of the shoe. For some reason, it stopped each revolution while pointed right at his penthouse.

The price was high, but Hughes didn't care. Soon the Silver Slipper became a free ATM for Nevada politicians, as $858,500 was drawn from the cage of the small club and given away. Nothing was improper about the contributions, but the payments were always made in cash, and the politicians never signed a receipt. How much of this slush fund went to political campaigning costs is impossible to say, but the reader should think small.

Hughes also bought the Landmark construction site and competed with Kirk Kerkorian to build the tallest structure in Nevada in 1969. The crazy Space Needle-like property was an instant loser, far off the Strip and butt-ugly (as locals said).

Kerkorian's International property opened to fame and fortune with Barbra Streisand and Elvis Presley. The Elvis show sold out for all 30 days of his contract, and the property was filled with happy gamblers. The Landmark offered a live, local band.

Howard never visited a single casino he purchased or made a profit running them. He was also worried about "the damn government blowing off all those nuclear bombs at the Nevada Test Site."

He could feel the shock waves they produced out on the Strip and up in his tenth-floor penthouse. He was also concerned about the potential risk of radiation poisoning to the air and water supply. He wrote memo after memo to Maheu and William Gay to send to his Nevada representatives in Congress. When that didn't work, he told Maheu to offer President Nixon a $1 million bribe. Strangely, that didn't work.

The casino buying stopped, the nuclear tests continued, and Howard slipped out of the Desert Inn on Thanksgiving Day 1971 and made his way to the Bahamas.

Nuclear Test in background circa 1950s - National Nuclear Security
Administration - Nevada Site Office / Public Domain

Chapter Twenty-One

Other Outlets – More Killings

In 1955 the Nevada Legislature created the Gaming Control Board
within the Nevada Tax Commission to "eliminate the undesirable
elements in Nevada gaming and to provide regulations for the licensing
and the operation of gaming. The Board was also to establish rules and
regulations for all tax reports to be submitted to the state by gaming
licensees."

The original eleven names included three from Chicago, Marshall
Caifano, Murray Humphreys, and Sam Giancana. When Sam was found
in Frank Sinatra's Cal-Neva Lodge, he broke the law. His ownership was
hidden, and money skimmed went directly to him.

Several of his casinos in other countries were personal

investments, not Outfit businesses. As alluded to earlier, it irritated Tony Accardo. It forced the other bosses (especially after Accardo went to Mexico) to pay more cash from their skim and illegal businesses to grease the never-ending cash pump to police, politicians, and judges.

Far be it from me to say the Outfit was struggling financially, but several Las Vegas casinos had finally managed to stem the cash flow out the door. And that hurt.

Consequently, more emphasis was put on finding creative ways to make more cash. Of course, not everyone was on board. Giancana was done with most of his deals and living a quiet life in Cuernavaca, Mexico.

Teamsters loan king Allen Dorfman was in prison. Mad Sam DeStefano was dead. Richard Cain was dead. Felix "Milwaukee Phil" Alderisio was dead. Fiori (Fifi) Buccieri was dead. Marshal Caifano was out of prison and still a threat to a decent and not-so-decent society.

Caifano still carried weight and a grudge when he got out of the joint. According to a federal informant, in 1973, Ray Ryan, who had testified and sent him to prison for ten years, wanted to make amends so Caifano "wouldn't be too mad at him" and offered cash. Caifano said, "Sure, give me a million bucks."

Later, according to the informant, Caifano said, "let's take the million and kill the motherfucker anyway." Communication between Ryan and Caifano broke off.

In 1974, Ryan's business manager William Gorman died in a mysterious horse-riding accident. It could be a coincidental tragedy. What happened later certainly wasn't.

On October 18, 1977, Ryan exited his health club and turned the ignition of his new Lincoln Mark V, and the explosion was heard miles away. One piece of metal landed 377 feet from the parking spot where

Ryan's car was parked and was found by investigators on their second day of recovery. Ryan was killed instantly; the murder was never solved.

There were at least 96 Outfit-related deaths in the 1970s, from Carmen Trotta's on March 21, 1970, to Henry Lopez on December 12, 1979. As few as five were committed by Tony Spilotro, but as many as fifteen may have involved Cicero crew lieutenant Harry "The Hook" Aleman at the behest of his uncle Joe Ferriola, the Outfit boss from 1986 to 1989.

Las Vegas casinos had a track record of getting extensive Teamsters loans and occasionally paying them back by selling the property and retaining the casino operations. But between 1959 and 1969, most Central States Pension Fund Plan loans had gone unpaid, and nobody seemed too worried when loans went sideways.

In 1971, Irwin Weiner, a Chicago bail bondsman and Outfit confident and friend of Jack Ruby, registered Gaylur Products, Ltd. as a foreign profit corporation in New Mexico to produce 5-gallon plastic buckets and imitation magnesium mag wheels.

Weiner and partners Tony Spilotro and Joseph "Joey the Clown" Lombardo met with Allen Dorfman to get a loan from the Teamsters.

No problem said Dorfman, and in exchange for $906,004, the Central States, Southeast, and Southwest areas pension fund got a $7,000 deposit. The loan was due and payable on February 1, 1974, bearing interest at 6% until maturity and 9% after that. Weiner slipped $22,000 directly to Dorfman.

The company contracted with Linda DeAngeles and R&D Engineering in New Mexico for pumps, presses, and vacuum-forming hubcap molds. She bought a house, put in a pool, and then purchased a plane.

Within a year, DeAngeles agreed to give Gaylur Products a quit-claim deed to her house and submit paperwork that she was "maintaining the plane" for the company. Certainly, no pressure was applied on DeAngeles to make these wonderful concessions. But even with this windfall, Gaylur needed more cash!

So, even though no products had been made yet, the principles returned to the well and drew another promissory note for a $500,000 loan at 8 ½ interest on October 3, 1972, which was payable on demand. The "land value and buildings secured the note at the factory site.

The first loan was due on February 1st. Since the company was in operation but ready to go bankrupt, Allen Dorman (and others) was indicted for fraud regarding the $1.4 million loans to Gaylur Products/American Pail Company from the Teamsters union.

Although there was a company, and it was producing a product, it was a sham and a front. The money was gone, the products were inferior, and even the factory manager, Daniel Seifert, knew it was a bust.

In Bensenville, Illinois, Seifert opened a new plastics factory with his wife and son, named after "Joey" Lombardo. Seifert was scheduled to testify about what he saw in New Mexico and the fraudulent loan package use, but Spilotro and The Clown had their plan.

Seifert had been a partner of Lombardo and Spilotro's in a work-pail manufacturing company and was on the verge of testifying against them in a Teamsters union pension fund fraud case tied to their business dealings. The murder was carried out at Seifert's new Bensenville, Illinois, plastics factory and witnessed by his widow Emma and their son, Joey, named after Lombardo himself.

Lombardo knew the 29-year-old kid had to be hit, so he arrived with the hit squad but placed Emma and Joey Seifert in a public restroom in Danny's factory and guarded them while his soldiers chased Seifert down and shot him dead in the factory's courtyard.

Vegas and the Chicago Outfit

The idea that mob hits should be private certainly wasn't the Chicago norm. Still, Seifert's very open execution, especially with his wife and child nearby, knocked Tony Accardo and Joey Aiuppa for a loop. Didn't The Clown know any better?

According to a government source, "Joe B (Accardo), who loved Joey, lost his mind. He saw news of the Seifert thing come on television and almost had a heart attack. He got so angry. Aiuppa wanted to take him down. Lump (Lombardo) had to come in, hat in hand. Joe Batters used it as a teaching moment."

Public or not, Seifert's death left no witness to the $1.4 million fraud case, and Allen Dorman walked.

In the meantime, it was 1975, and Tony Spilotro and his wife Nancy, and son Vincent were enjoying their comfortable 2,400-square-foot house at 4675 Balfour Drive near McLeod Drive and Tropicana Avenue.

He didn't bring his problems home, but everywhere else he went, they came right with him. Tax questions, problems with Tony Accardo and Joey Aiuppa over the Seifert killing, questions from Lefty Rosenthal, who was handling the skim at the Stardust and other properties (and taking a massive chunk for himself), and then things got weird.

In the aftermath of a New York Times article exposing clandestine and questionable operations perpetrated by the CIA, the United States senate decided they should get to the bottom of these alleged abuses. Chaired by Idaho Senator Frank Church, the investigation became known as the Church Committee.

Not to be overlooked, the House of Representatives also initiated committees to investigate US Government Intelligence issues, including the Pike Committee and the presidential Rockefeller Commission. Thank goodness, after nearly 15 years, our government suddenly felt like working – with three groups prodding along the same lines. Those led to the US Senate Select Committee on Intelligence. (a bit more on that later).

The Church Committee learned several vital things starting with the fact that the CIA/US Government/Mafia had worked together to try and assassinate Fidel Castro. That was shocking.

Even more shocking was that backlash from the attempt may have led to the killing of JFK and even the Mob's role in the assassination. More than 50,000 documents have been declassified regarding both issues, but not all of those are available. What could be so important about documents from the 1960s and 1970s? Perhaps something about the death of three individuals scheduled to appear before the Committee.

On June 19, 1975, his police protection was called off. As Jimmy Fratianno put it, "He was bed-ridden for three weeks and only left the hospital in Houston because the cops was hassling him. He can't even walk up the stairs his heart's so bad."

Giancana's heart condition meant he couldn't eat spicy foods but was frying sausage and peppers at his stove, perhaps for a friend who had come to dine. That was when a gunman shot him in the back of the head. He pitched forward onto the stove, spilling hot grease and sausages across the kitchen floor, and then fell to the ground. The shooter rolled him over and pumped six more shots into his head and neck. He never testified.

Johnny Roselli did testify before the Committee on June 24, 1975. His testimony included his involvement in Operation Mongoose, the CIA plot to kill Castro. Shortly after Giancana's murder, Roselli moved from Los Angeles to Miami, Florida.

The committee recalled Roselli to testify about the conspiracy to kill President Kennedy, but he disappeared. On August 9, 1976, his body washed up inside a 55-gallon steel drum in Biscayne Bay. He had been stabbed and strangled. His legs were cut off because rigor mortis had set in, and he couldn't be bent into the drum.

Jimmy "The Weasel" Frattiano was certain the sloppy job could only have been orchestrated by: "A family bossed by a creep like Aiuppa."

Then Jimmy Hoffa disappeared. The former Teamsters Union boss just vanished from the Machus Red Fox restaurant parking lot in Bloomfield Township, Michigan, on July 30, 1975. What happened to him and exactly why? Nobody knows – it's like the JFK assassination.

Fratianno said, "It took them guys long enough. He was a good man, but he was hard of hearing. Detroit told him to cool it, and he couldn't do it." Tony Delsanter added," It wasn't no outside help. Detroit don't need nobody to clip their own fucking guy. Tony Zerilli and Mike Polizzi gave the order and that was all she wrote."

Common sense is clouded by outrageous claims and attention-whoring know-it-all wannabes. In the end, they're both gone. Hoffa's disappearance is still a mystery to this day. He never testified.

All those government committees didn't get enough people killed off, so the House of Representatives came up with the House Select Committee on Assassinations. Cool.

On March 29, 1977, Charles "Chuckie the Typewriter" Nicoletti caught three bullets in the back of his head was sitting in his car parked at the Golden Horns Restaurant in suburban Northlake, Illinois. He was a known hitman who worked on the M&M Murders with Spilotro and as many as 19 other killings. He was scheduled to testify before the House Select Committee on Assassinations at the time of his death.

George de Mohrenschildt, a petroleum geologist, CIA informant, and a Lee Harvey Oswald intermediary whom the CIA had introduced him, was considered a "crucial witness" by the HSCA.

On the same day Nicoletti died, author Edward Jay Epstein

interviewed de Mohrenschildt, who told of his friendship with Oswald.

"I would never have contacted Oswald in a million years if Moore {CIA Agent J. Walton Moore} had not sanctioned it," de Mohrenschildt said. "Too much was at stake."

Later that day, an investigator for the House Select Committee on Assassinations sent de Mohrenschildt a business card from investigator Gaeton Fonzi, asking de Mohrenschildt to contact him because they considered him a "crucial witness."

That evening, again, March 29, 1977, de Mohrenschildt was found dead from a shotgun wound to the head. The coroner's verdict was suicide.

Strange things happen, and some don't make much sense, but most of us survive. Does it make sense that it took the FBI 20 years to investigate Allen Dorfman's non-repaid $100 million in questionable loans to Mob recipients? No, but it finally happened.

The FBI went right to work with Operation Pendorf (Penetrate Dorfman). His insurance offices were bugged, the FBI got lots of dirt, and two years later, a Chicago federal grand jury indicted Dorfman and was convicted in December 1982.

Also convicted were Joey Lombardo and Teamsters president Roy Lee Williams for trying to bribe Nevada Senator Howard Cannon to oppose the deregulation of the trucking industry.

Dorfman was considered a risk to spill his guts in open court to avoid a lengthy prison sentencing, especially with two additional trials.

Three days before his scheduled sentencing on January 23rd, 1983, Dorfman walked with Irwin Weiner outside the Lincolnwood Hyatt in Illinois after a nice meal. It was his last.

According to witnesses, a car pulled up nearby, and a man with a gun exited the passenger's side. He yelled, "This is a robbery, turn around." When Allen and Irwin turned, the gunman shot Allen in the head, crippling Dorfman and sending him to the pavement. The gunman emptied his magazine, leaving the body riddled with bullets and the ground pooled with blood.

Weiner was ignored, nothing was taken from either man, and the shooter climbed back into the waiting car and it drove away. Nobody saw the license plate. Descriptions of the men conflicted. The case was never solved.

Chapter Twenty-Two

The FBI Ends the '70s with Miracles

Las Vegas, for all its casinos and twinkling lights, may look happy and bright, but there are more heartbreaks in Vegas than in any other town in the US. It's a tough go, even when the Mob isn't directly involved.

According to police, in 1967, cab driver Marvin Shumate and a buddy dreamed up a plot to kidnap Benny Binion's younger son, Teddy, who was a friend of Shumate's son. They figured it would be easy to snatch Teddy, hold him for $100,000 in ransom money, and then turn him loose. Shumate's fellow cab driver was okay with the idea until the plan was changed to kill Teddy to keep him from being a witness.

Unfortunately for Shumate, his buddy got cold feet, went to Benny, and spilled the whole plot. He was allowed to leave town alive. Shumate wasn't so lucky. Tom Hanley and his son, Gramby, took Shumate up to Sunrise Mountain and blew half his face away with a shotgun blast and a few stray bullets from a .38 revolver.

After the body was found, evidence pointed to the Hanleys, so Alphonse Bass, a friend, and bodyguard were picked up for questioning. He intimated that the Hanleys might have been involved, but he could never testify. His body was found in a torched house, tied to a chair.

Tom Hanley was suspected in several other murders, including the killing of union agent James Hartley, found shot in the head and dumped in the desert. Hanley also was a suspect in several bombings, including a dynamite blast in 1972.

William Coulthard ran the Las Vegas FBI office from 1939 to 1945. He married Lena Silvagni, daughter of P.O. Silvagni, who built and owned the Apache Hotel, the first air-conditioned hotel in Las Vegas. When Lena passed away in 1955, she left her husband her share of the Apache land, 37 percent of the property where Binion's Horseshoe stood.

Coulthard was involved in lease negotiations with Benny Binion, where the land lease hadn't increased in 10 years. The negotiations were later described as "heated," as Binion accused Coulthard of trying to "Jack up the rent to improve your casino" because Coulthard was a corporate officer and stockholder of the Four Queens casino across the street.

On July 25, 1972, Coulthard went to his parked Cadillac on the 3rd floor of the parking terrace adjacent to his office in the Bank of Nevada building. He climbed into the car and turned the ignition, which tripped a clothespin trigger that ignited three sticks of dynamite planted beneath the engine near the steering column.

The explosion demolished the Cadillac, and the fire spread to five other vehicles. Another 20 cars were damaged. The force of the blast blew a hole in the concrete floor of the parking garage down to the second floor and shattered light fixtures in the Bank of Nevada. Coulthard's body was so badly charred that the only way for investigators to confirm his identity was through his dental charts.

In 1976, Culinary Union boss Al Bramlet contracted with Tom and Gramby Hanley to help him convince local restaurants that they should be union shops. Some resisted. Bramlet told Hanley to bomb the restaurants, and one was. Two others, the Village Pub and Starboard Tack were targeted, but the car bombs there were duds, and neither exploded.

According to later court testimony, the Hanleys wanted to be paid for all three bombs, but Bramlet refused to pay for the two that did not ignite, only the one at David's Place on West Charleston, where the bomb exploded. When Bramlet returned from a trip to Reno on February 24, 1977, he was in for an ugly surprise when the Hanleys and Eugene Vaughan met him at McCarran Airport.

They cornered him when he exited the plane and forced him to the parking lot, where they had a van waiting. Tom quickly punched him to the side of the head, knocking him down. As his eye swelled, Bramlet's wrists were handcuffed behind his back. "All we want is to get paid; you don't want to die for ten grand, do you?" Tom asked. Bramlet said, "No, I'll get the cash," so the group stopped at a pay phone, and Bramlet called Syd Wyman at the Dunes Hotel and told him he needed $10,000 for a personal matter. "Take it to Benny Binion down at the Horseshoe," Bramlet said. Wyman agreed.

Bramlet was then gagged and driven into the nearby desert, where he was repeatedly shot and dumped in a shallow grave. The case unraveled quickly after that, and the Hanleys were tried for murder and attempted murder for the car bombings. They were both sentenced to life in prison without parole. Tom Hanley lasted only months in prison before he died of natural causes.▢

Inside the casinos, the Nevada Gaming Control Board and its agents did their best to keep managers on the straight and narrow. Chips, dice, slot machines, playing cards, and even roulette balls were checked regularly. Unfortunately, the number of agents wasn't close to what was needed to enforce things. Catching a club with bad gaming equipment rarely happened.

In most cases, counterfeit chips or tampered slot machines were the work of outside cheats. In the late '70s, as jackpots got larger, casinos spent more time and money trying to stop the loss of cash to crooks who spent their lifetime perfecting penetration skills.

At the craps tables, bad dice were occasionally slipped into a game. In Reno, at the Riverside, bad dice were alleged two times. The first time a player contended, the dice were switched on him by the casino. He sued, but the case was thrown out since, under state law, gaming losses could not be recovered. Interesting.

The next time the dice were switched, gaming agents were surveilling the game, and the casino was shut down, forcing a property sale. That's a better outcome. It was similar to the closure at the Silver Slipper across from the Desert Inn.

Good enough! At the Silver Slipper, the same defense was used after the club was closed on the spot when crooked dice were found on one of the craps games. The owners claimed ignorance and floated the possibility that they had been planted there by an employee. Well, of course, they were put there by an employee, geez.

An employee was caught cheating two months later, too, when a blackjack dealer was repeatedly seen dealing "seconds," The Gaming Commission shut the casino down for good, license gone.

Other times the dealers were much too good to be caught. Several casinos, including the North Shore Club and the Cal-Neva Lodge, had dealers that specialized in card manipulation to take down players on a heavy win streak.

Of course, everyone was stealing at the King's Castle. Nate Jacobsen was a fireball with a twinkle in his eye. The former insurance salesman parlayed his winning smile and glib patter into ownership of the Baltimore Bullets before moving to Nevada and the casino industry.

With pressure on Caesars Palace in the late '60s, Jacobsen sold his interest and moved to Incline Village at Lake Tahoe, where he took a Teamsters Union loan and opened the King's Castle Casino.

Lake Tahoe was seasonal then, and the small casino struggled to get a foothold in the resort community. When the snow flew, so did most of the tourists.

Jacobson mimicked the statues and opulence of Caesars Palace with a medieval castle motif, including walls, turrets, and an indoor dinner theater named Camelot. Outside, a courtyard included a full-size Lady Godiva on a horse and four palace guards.

Unfortunately, the guards inside the casino weren't to be trusted. At least two of them had keys to the drop boxes from the blackjack tables, and when the boxes went to the soft-count room in an elevator, the guards would help themselves to a few hundred dollars each night. They got caught because one of them accidentally took the "fill-slip" table information along with his nightly cut.

In the food and beverage department, bartenders and cocktail servers took $100 and $50 nightly from drinks the tenders never rang up on the cash registers. Jacobsen read the handwriting on the wall and his bottom line and sold out.

There were similar issues at the Aladdin casino in Las Vegas. The property went through two transformations (Tallyho and Kings Crown) before it finally got off the ground as a casino. Then, it struggled to show a profit because of its cash leakage.

Milton Prell had the reins from '66 to '68. Still, he made no profit, so in 1969 Parvin-Dohrmann of Los Angeles took over the property. But who was Albert Parvin?

Well, Parvin was a Chicago (yeah, big surprise) businessman who managed the interior fixtures for the Flamingo. Things like tables, chairs, beds, and carpeting, and he did it at below cost. Bugsy was so broke that Parvin took points in the property instead of cash, and he was lucky to get that. When Gus Greenbaum got whacked, Parvin was the perfect front, taking a stake and moving up to president of the Flamingo.

In 1960, Parvin sold his shares to the Florida group headed by Morris Lansburgh for $10.5 million. Meyer Lansky got a $200,000 finder's fee. Later, Lansburgh got a short prison sentence for that transaction. Parvin walked. They must have had powerful friends!

He did. Supreme Court Justice William O. Douglas held a seat on the board of Parvin-Dorhmann, now one of the world's largest hotel, restaurant, and hospital furnishing companies. And as a company with friends, they bought the Fremont Hotel for $16 million and the Aladdin Hotel for $12.

And during the casino buying, a curious thing happened. Four conspirators embezzled nearly $7 million from the Cosmopolitan National Bank of Chicago. They were caught. They were charged. And in the ensuing 30-count indictment were the notes that $550,000 of the embezzled money got deposited into Albert Parvin's account. Hmm, that's interesting.

Parvin feigned ignorance, the four conspirators were jailed, and Parvin was never indicted. I'm not even sure he was investigated. The government did confiscate the cash, however. Bummer.

Next, the casino-collecting company took a shot at the Rivera property, but the Nevada Gaming Control Board nixed the deal. So, they dumped the plan and worked a few other deals to boost their stock value with Delbert W. Coleman, owner of the J.P. Seeburg Corporation (jukeboxes, cash business, out of Chicago), to purchase 300,000 shares of the casino and furniture company.

That gave Coleman 22% of the stock, so Albert Parvin signed paperwork with the Gaming Commission saying approval of a license would take effect after the first of the year. It seemed weird but all right.

Then Coleman and Sidney Korshak went to work to pump the stock. Shares were purchased over a period of weeks while Korshak got a boiler-room stock sales office working and managed outrageous articles about profitability and overall worth to Outfit-controlled media, and viola, the stock doubled from $35 to nearly $80.

Backroom contributor Bernie Cornfeld's FOF Propriety Fund in Switzerland sold slowly, taking more than $4 million in profits, then bought back in to keep the price rising to $141. Then the freefall came while Parvin was enjoying a safari in Africa.

Amazingly, by the time he returned to Los Angeles, the stock had catered to $12.50, so he bought out Coleman. The ensuing bad press, a congressional fight between representative Gerald Ford and Douglas, and an SEC investigation soured the public on Parvin Dohrmann and the Parvin Foundation, where Douglas was appointed a lifetime seat and $12,000 annual salary.

The scandal led to Albert Parvin getting placed on the US Justice Department's list of organized crime figures. In response, Parvin-Dohrmann changed its name to Recrion and consummated the purchase of the Stardust. Korshak was issued a $500,000 finder's fee.

Those fees seemed to be popular, and when Recrion sold the Aladdin to Morris Shenker's partners in St. Louis. He also got a $500,000 finder's fee.

Vegas and the Chicago Outfit

After selling the Aladdin to Sam Diamond, Richard Daly, St. Louis politician Peter Webbe, and well-known mob attorney Sorkis Webbe, the resort was upgraded at the cost of $60 million. The property struggled financially while those around it prospered. Strange.

Recrion's adverse publicity and detrimental government actions caused the Nevada Gaming Control Board to send damning reports to the Gaming Commission, who suggested to Recrion that they leave the Nevada gaming scene permanently.

So, Recrion and their Chicago friends worked for months engineering the perfect scenario for a lock, stock, and barrel purchase that eventually included the Fremont, Marina, Hacienda, and the Stardust. And the deal introduced Las Vegas and eventually the whole world to Allen R. Glick of Argent Corporation, a 32-year-old real estate investor from San Diego, California. It was a match made slightly lower than heaven.

In August 1979 at the Aladdin, four men were convicted by a federal grand jury in Detroit for conspiring to allow hidden owners to exert control over the Aladdin, prompting the Nevada Gaming Commission to close the hotel.

In September, the Aladdin Hotel Corp., Sorkis Webbe, and Del Webb Corp. were indicted on conspiracy charges to defraud the Teamsters Union during the 1975-76 Aladdin remodeling. The indictment alleged subcontractors were forced to pay kickbacks during construction totaling $2.5 million. Del Webb Corp. owned the Sahara Tahoe, Sahara Reno, and the Sahara Las Vegas at the time. The casinos changed hands quickly afterward.

Casino Ownership Headaches

Not every casino was a genuine money maker and some that cried poor over the years were only broke because the skim stunted their growth and contributed to an impoverished look that kept visitors away. Still, the Mob taking skim never bothered the average Joe who says,

"Hey, they're just stealing from themselves."

They were like Bonnie and Clyde during the depression, who robbed banks. The world was in financial turmoil. Thousands of people had their homes and farms foreclosed on by banks, their lives turned upside down - and were left homeless and penniless – it must be the bank's fault. Bonnie and Clyde were seen as vigilantes and heroes. So was the Mob when they escaped federal taxes. Big deal, right?

Well, the Mob stole cash before some legitimate casino owners got their fair share; and the IRS lost out on what everyone thinks is an unfair share. Because everyone hates the IRS. It's in our DNA.

But of course, the loss of skim meant the clubs didn't get the new towers and showroom attractions. That's why a few casinos that were super earners for the Outfit didn't join in the power-hungry bidding wars for Hollywood talent in the 1970s. They couldn't afford to.

At the Hacienda Casino, there were never any superstar shows. It was a nice place, and Doc Bayley ran the resort at near break-even until he passed away in 1964. The cash going out the door was limited, mainly because the cash coming in was limited too. The casino sat at the far end of the Strip, isolated, referred to as the bus station casino.

After Doc died, Judy Bayley took over and ran the business until 1971, when she passed away. She didn't run the casino. Experts did.

So the following year, Paul W. Lowden purchased 15% of the Hacienda with some partners and made himself the entertainment director. Others before him had done similar things while finagling a casino license. And one of his partners brought in Allen Glick, a young land developer from San Diego who took a controlling interest. Hmm. Just another scam? Not exactly.

Lowden was doing things differently during the FBI and Nevada Gaming Control Board's busiest, most successful decade of enforcement and change. So, before we get to Glick, Operation Strawman, and the massive skim going on, let's look at Lowden.

He was a trained musician and played in a band at Harold's Club in Reno in 1961 before arriving in Las Vegas to play keyboards in the Fremont's Carnival Lounge. Wayne Newton and his brother were the headliners. He was also the accompanist to Ann Margret when she hit Vegas, but Paul had a head for stocks and business—sometimes playing the organ with a copy of the Wall Street Journal next to him.

His musical talents brought him to the Flamingo casino, where he was hired as the musical director, but his stock acumen took his initial $7,500 investment to extraordinary financial heights. Enough to invest $125,000 with a matching loan from Valley Bank of Nevada to get that 15% piece of the Hacienda.

The Hacienda turned profitable, and Vegas was jumping, so Lowden parlayed his good fortune into a piece of the Tropicana in 1975, but there were pressures that hadn't surfaced yet at the Hacienda.

Sad Days for the Tropicana Casino

The pressure came from Joseph Agosto, the Trop's entertainment director. But he wasn't worried about "Les Folies Bergere," the topless revue at the Tropicana that had been running since 1959. Instead, Agosto was worried about the casino and the skim. He had been entrusted with skimming the daily table game win and getting the cash to Chicago and Kansas City. Lowden knew the score.

He tried to get Mitzi Stauffer Briggs, a significant owner, to buy him out (he was in for $500,000), but they refused, so he told her, "My license means more to me than the money; pay me when you can," and he walked out.

In 1977, Lowden arranged a $22-million buyout of Glick and the other owners at the Hacienda, with Valley Bank holding a first mortgage and First American National Bank taking a second.

Two years later, he was awarded $250,000 from the Tropicana. The rest went up in smoke. Later, he devised time-shares for one-week stays at the Hacienda and the Imperial Hotel in Hawaii.

Those mortgages allowed Lowden to purchase the Sahara casino from the Del E. Webb Corp. after their debacle at the Aladdin. He continued to flourish into the 1980s.

Unfortunately, Mitzi Stauffer Briggs didn't have so much luck. Her story in a minute, but first, here's how the Tropicana became one of the leading skim machines in Las Vegas!

Frank Costello footed a sizable portion of the Mob's investment at the Flamingo in 1946, along with a host of stockholders who came away with zippo.

The Chicago Outfit also held a big piece of the Flamingo since the Mob loved to have front men foot the bills. And while the casino earned cash like the Thunderbird, Riviera, Sands, Sahara, Dunes (the list goes on), the Mob always wanted more. Costello's slot machine partners in New Orleans, Phil Kastel and Carlos Marcello, suggested Ben Jaffe, owner of the Fontainebleau Hotel in Florida, was the perfect builder for a new Vegas casino.

Kastel fronted a half million dollars and contracted with the Taylor Construction Company of Miami after they finished the final touches on the Riviera to build the new resort. Once his cash was committed, the forty-acre project styled on the Mob's casinos in Havana began to take form. That's when Jaffe fell right into the quicksand of the desert that had swallowed Ben Siegel ten years earlier.

As building costs ballooned, Ben Jaffe was forced to sell his interest in the Fontainebleau for $3 million. He was beside himself; he loved that property. He wondered how he got himself mixed up in the desert of Las Vegas. But wait, there's more. Now how much would you pay?

The fees and equipment costs continued unabated, so next came $3 million from his insurance company holdings. By the time the club was ready to open on April 4, 1957, the total investment was $10 million, much of it from Jaffe. Louis Lederer and J. Kell Houssels, Sr. were licensed to run the casino, and later Houssels bought out Jaffe's share of the resort facilities and the casino but retained ownership of the land.

Back then and through the 1970s, slot machines and table games pulled all the weight. Restaurants, showrooms, and hotel rooms didn't have to make money. Those amenities were complimentary to decent players. Big players got gold treatment with limos, stage-front seating, and women in their rooms. Low-limit players paid for their stay, but with $9 rooms and $5 steak dinners, Vegas was a dream come true. The drinks were 50 cents. Property owners who leased the casino rarely gained much back in profits.

The Tropicana rivaled its predecessors in skim flowing east. Thirty, forty, fifty thousand a week got carried by trusted bagmen and women to safe havens before Meyer Lansky directed the split. Not a hitch for years, and then things went south. The property may have even gone legit, the horror! And then, ownership changes came fast and furious.

In 1970, the property was sold by the Houssels family and partners to Trans-Texas Airways. That didn't work to get the Mob back in the count room, so the Trop got sold to Deil Gustafson from Minnesota. In the coming years, Gustafson's company, Hotel Conquistador Inc., was charged with marker fraud (a table-side loan of chips not paid back) to known Detroit criminals. Gustafson was ordered to sell his controlling interest in the hotel. And then came Ed and Fred Doumani and the nicest casino owner ever, Mitzi Stauffer Briggs, the wealthy niece of a former Stauffer chemical company owner.

Sweet and undemanding, she took people at their word. And when a friend suggested she consider an investment at the Tropicana, she got roped into the back end of the gaming business. Friends told her an investment might be risky, "But the people I met, to me, seemed very nice. And I thought, 'Maybe this is just sour grapes on the part of some people.'"

She had no experience in gaming but had heard casinos made serious cash. So, she took a flyer and invested $6 million for 15% of the resort's stock. She could afford it, and although Nevada gaming regulators worried about Briggs's lack of experience, she was issued a temporary license while counseled by Gaming Control Board agents about the characters she'd be doing business with.

Then came some new investors called the Associates of the Tropicana, with Joe Agosto as head of the Folies Bergere show. Agosto had a criminal background and Mob connections but was still allowed a director's license. Although he worked for Ed and Fred Doumani, Joe went to work feasting on skim and sending it to Chicago and Kansas City. And even after being arrested by U.S. Immigration Services as an illegal immigrant, he prevailed – or more accurately, his high-priced superstar (and future Las Vegas Mayor) Oscar Goodman did - beating the immigration charge.

And with all the questions, Mitzi Briggs loved Joe and believed every lie he told her, pumping another $11 million into the resort for 51.2% of the company's stock. But that wasn't enough because the property was bleeding cash from the skim and unpaid markers due to bad credit.

Those issues fell on the credit office, where players claim the ability to pay by check at the end of their stay. When they don't, or can't, because they don't really exist, that's a problem.

So, Mitzi had a chance to shore up the property and be nearly the sole owner for just another $27 million (including a new twenty-two-story hotel tower). Although it took her investment accounts down to the nubs, she trusted Agosto. She jumped. And then came operation strawman.

Although the FBI was making considerable headway against the Mob in the 1970s, their first significant bust that tied family bosses to money skimmed in Las Vegas came about because of a fluke.

On a tip about a coming Mob hit, the FBI got a federal judge's permission for wiretaps and microphones to be installed inside the Villa Capri tavern, the home of Josephine Marlo, and the law office of John Patrick Quinn in Kansas City, Missouri.

Installation was easy at the businesses. The FBI agents broke into the closed restaurants and had all the time they needed to set things in motion. The job at Marlo's home was a bit trickier. FBI Special Agent H. Edward Tickel, a top "quiet entry" expert and 14-year veteran of black bag operations, created a telephone line break and responded to the service interruption dressed as a telephone repairman. Once invited inside the home, he placed a microphone inside the telephone.

The information gleaned from the wiretaps didn't stop the mob hit. Still, agents reported several conversations at the Villa Capri that seemed to involve Kansas City mob boss Nick Civella, Carl Civella, and someone named Joey A, or Gusto.

The local Special Agent in charge tasked his officers with tapping more locations, and Tickel went back to work. Eventually, Gusto turned into Joe Agosto, and "out west" became the Tropicana in Vegas. When things looked promising, Operation Strawman came to life.

During a five-year investigation, local FBI agents entrenched themselves in the local community (think about the movie Donnie Brasco, FBI in Milwaukee) and fired-up dozens of phones. They planted devices in homes, insurance companies, and even garages where people sat and talked. They started businesses to attract shady deals and stole cars to plant microphones in them.

The man hours, dollars spent, and coordination with agents,

agencies, and judges for wiretaps, lawyers, and bosses was enormous. Individual agents turned their lives inside out to become interconnecting pieces of sometimes illegal activities and get accepted by local criminals, even if those people weren't specifically a part of a crime family. You had to not just look and sound the part, you had to be the part – or you were never trusted.

Years dragged on, but eventually, the FBI knew everything: names, dates, pickups, delivery times, amounts, splits, and plenty of side deals they never knew were happening. They had a case they could prosecute.

The FBI moved in on February 14, 1979 (affectionately known by many as the second coming of the St. Valentine's Day massacre). Conversations verified that the latest skim of $80,000 would be on its way to Chicago to be chopped and distributed by armed couriers to crime families in Chicago, Kansas City, Cleveland, and Milwaukee.

On-site surveillance captured the cash leaving the casino and moving on. In Chicago, one of the couriers involved was police officer Anthony Chiavola Sr. He was later indicted along with nine other crime figures.

Two years later, a Kansas City grand jury indicted Joe Agosto, Kansas City boss Nick Civella, his brother Carl, operations expert Carl DeLuna, and Carl Thomas of skimming cash at the Tropicana. Four were convicted in 1983; Agosto turned state evidence to avoid prosecution but died in prison beforehand. Nick Civella died in 1983.

Also indicted was FBI Special Agent Tickel, who was caught in the act of breaking into the FBI headquarters credit union and magically opening a locked safe containing $260,000 in cash. He pleaded not guilty to other charges, including income tax evasion, theft, and selling $37,000 worth of stolen jewelry. He was sentenced to eight years in prison.

In the aftermath of the Tropicana's organized crime problems, all investors were considered independent contractors. Mitzi Briggs and her partners sold their holdings to Ramada Corp., which dragged its feet, filed injunctions against discovery, and was eventually forced by a Nevada court to reach a payoff settlement.

Somehow, little Mitzi was left holding an empty bag. Nobody did well, but Mitzi's $44 million investment vanished in the air like a gambler's dreams. As longtime casino owner Jackie Gaughan put it, "They beat her like a drum."

As Joe Agosto put it while the cash disappeared from the house of cards, "Mitzi, I couldn't help it. They had a gun to my head."

She believed him, and years later, after struggling financially and moving to a small apartment and working at the Most Holy Redeemer church, she never complained or blamed anyone. "Poor Joe Agosto," she would say. What a sweetheart.

Agosto engineered a check floating scheme while working at the Tropicana that had bad paper being held up for weeks before new bad paper (checks) replaced others. He was convicted in Minneapolis of using several local banks in the process and sentenced to 20 years. "Poor Joe Agosto."

Chapter Twenty-Three

A Crushing End to Vegas Skim

Frank "Lefty" Rosenthal was Chicago born and bred from his head to his toes. He enjoyed a comfortable upbringing without the beatings and bullshit so many inner-city kids attributed to their life of crime while growing up on the dirty streets of the Windy City.

Instead, Lefty spent his youth at the track with his dad, who owned several racehorses. Good or bad, misspent youth or not, walking the stands, the training facilities, the stables, and the betting isles of the track gave him an intimate knowledge about the sport. He absorbed, almost through osmosis, what was important when owning horses or betting on them.

He said later that much of his education was in psychology; how betters thought, and more decidedly, why they lost. He avidly watched boxers when they fought locally and when they appeared in grainy black and white TV of the '50s, but again, he understood their drive, motivation, and greed.

And while he loved basketball and football, he had an affinity for baseball. "Every pitch, every swing, everything had a price," he said. By 18, he had already worked in several bookie joints, taking bets, offering advice, watching the players, and how the odds moved with their bets.

He knew if he was booking the Cubs, he could find the sweet spot, that exact line where the bettors who lived and died to follow and wager on the team would finally give up and skip a bet that day, and how to back just off that number. He pushed them as favorites even when the odds in his mind made them obvious dogs.

Chicago had several sports experts in town and across the country who set the lines. Lefty didn't always agree, and his bosses took notice after a few sports seasons. Bookies make their money by setting the lines, so the wagering is evenly split and paying ten units for an 11-unit wager. Then they earn half of the 9% left over.

When Rosenthal was strong on a side, he'd set the money line to split the wagers but lean the line in his chosen direction. His picks earned more than national handicappers, more than the 4.5% on straight bets. Often 10%. The kid was amazing.

His primary talent was missing sleep. He had stooges at tracks and games everywhere, calling to tell him when a horse pulled-up lame training or a pitcher had a tired arm. And, since Chicago had national newsstands, he read papers from two-dozen major cities. That, and he had the ability to calculate odds in seconds, giving him a knowledgeable, uncanny edge.

By twenty-one, he was setting lines out of the largest bookmaking office in the country, an Outfit operation called Cicero Home Improvement. When he was able (reasonably often), Lefty bribed players to throw games and boxing matches and shave points, so the point spread was just right for the Chicago Outfit to win in high school games to major professional sports.

Sonny Liston fought Floyd Patterson, the reigning heavyweight champion of the world, at Comiskey Park in Chicago on September 25, 1962. Patterson was quiet in interviews, confident, but still surprised he was the champ. Many boxing fans felt he was untested, although his record was 38-2 with 29 by knockout.

Liston, quieter still because he felt inarticulate and was stung by a media that Sonny. He sported an impressive record of 33-1, 23 by knockout. Compared to Patterson, his road to the title fight was filled will more impressive opponents.

In an article by James Baldwin, Liston said, "Colored people say they don't want their children to look up to me. Well, they ain't teaching their children to look up to Martin Luther King, either." There was a pause. "I wouldn't be no bad example if I was up there. I could tell a lot of those children what they need to know—because—I passed that way. I could make them listen." His comments were introspective and extroverted at the same time.

Liston weighed 213 pounds to Patterson's 189. The local newspapers (paid columnists) pushed Patterson as an obvious choice. He was the champ, they said; Liston was too heavy. Really?

The bookies wanted to get bets on Patterson in the worst way and did everything they could to keep the odds down, but all the late money in Chicago went on Liston with the opening line close to pick-em; the final countrywide line closed at 7.5 to 5. Jimmie (The Greek) Snyder's final line in Las Vegas was 9 to 5.

The bookies admitted, "Yeah, we let some heavy money come in late when we had enough on Patterson." Ever feel like a sucker? The fight lasted until 2:06 of the first round before Liston knocked out

Patterson with a vicious uppercut that staggered the champ and three fight-ending thunderous blows that could be heard in the cheap seats.

As Gilbert Rogin of **Sports Illustrated** put it, "that final left hook crashed into Patterson's cheek like a diesel rig going downhill, no brakes." The fight wasn't fixed. Nobody took a dive. Only the early bettors got beat worse than Patterson. Bookies in most cities took a beating too, but not in Chicago.

Rosenthal moved to Florida, given free reign from the Outfit to spread his gift to new players if he shared the wealth. His reputation as a handicapper and oddsmaker was international, and he was often seen in the company of prominent Outfit members Jackie Cerone and Fiore Buccieri.

But those friends brought the heat, and he was issued a subpoena to appear at U.S. Senator John McClellan's subcommittee on Gambling and Organized Crime. He invoked the Fifth Amendment 37 times regarding a charge of match-fixing. Lefty was never charged. Still, he was barred from all racetracks in Florida. BFD, right?

The following year he wasn't so lucky after making the Outfit, a few close friends, and himself even richer with a point-shaving scheme. He pleaded no contest in '63 to bribing New York University player Ray Paprocky to shave points at a basketball game in North Carolina and was convicted – he paid a fine and went on his way.

In 1964, Sonny Liston fought Cassius Clay in Miami, and Rosenthal was at ringside. According to FBI documents, Mob guys Frankie Carbo and Blinky Palermo secretly owned Sonny Liston's contract. Liston was a 7-1 favorite but had to quit during the fight because of a sore shoulder. In a rematch, Listen was knocked out by what became known as the "Phantom Punch," and Listens' loss, once again, won guys in the know a bundle of cash. Rosenthal knew everything that was coming.

When he had problems, he had friends do the dirty work. The FBI opened an ongoing case file on him that grew to more than 300 pages, detailing point-fixing, shaving, influence peddling, extortion, and a series of car bombings in Miami. He was never charged, and when the heat got too intense in 1968, he moved to Las Vegas.

Rosenthal didn't have a trunkful of cash upon reaching Las Vegas like Benny Binion, but he had enough bread to buy a house at 972 Vegas Valley Drive. The house was spacious, 3,200 square feet, with a pool that overlooked the golf course.

What he did have was the Outfit's blessing to go about business at their casinos and improve profits – and the skim. Johnny Roselli was busy selling casinos to Howard Hughes at the time and rearranging drop teams to keep the skim coming. The Parvin-Dohrmann group was about to rise and fall so fast in value that it had to become Recrion and attract an eager, fairly sharp Allen R. Glick, as mentioned earlier.

With a little piece of the Hacienda and the Tropicana, Glick figured he had found the golden goose and was scouting for another casino to invest in. Now he was interested in the Stardust and talked with Marty Buccieri, a pit boss at Caesars Palace. Buccieri told Glick he could help with a loan connection, and the next thing Glick knew, he was talking to a fellow named Frank Balistrieri, who promised to put in a good word with the Teamsters Central States Pension Fund. In short order, Glick owned the Stardust casino. He also owed nearly $140 million but was happy with his new Argent Corporation.

After purchasing the Stardust, Glick was called to a meeting in Kansas City, Missouri, with Nick Civella. Nick told Glick in no uncertain terms that he owed a $1.2 million fee for the family's assistance in getting his first $23 million Teamsters Central States Pension Fund loan. Five percent juice, turkey.

He was also told that Frank Rosenthal would be his director at the Stardust and that whatever Lefty said was the law of God. Glick gave a shaky smile and returned to Las Vegas.

Meantime, Tony Spilotro has found Las Vegas to be a goldmine. Even with his stipend for watching the skim at the Outfit's four significant casinos, he was doing some sports betting (you paid him if he won, he ignored you if he lost), some loansharking at the Dunes under the worried eye of owner Major Riddle, and helping himself to the proceeds of burglaries.

On June 23, 1973, William "Red" Klimm was murdered in Las Vegas in the Churchill Downs Race Book parking lot. Spilotro's first Las Vegas murder. He must have been so proud. Or he would have if he had a conscience that matched his ego. When people met him, they came away with an eerie feeling that he was reptilian, cold-blooded. There was nothing behind the eyes, just disrespect, and disdain. He was a sociopath. If you know about Theranos, think of Elizabeth Holmes.

More killings were to come, even though the Mob always said, "You gotta get 'em out of town," but this Joey Red (Klimm) wasn't feeding Spilotro any juice from his bookmaking, so he had to go. Spilotro was suspected, but no case was made.

Knowing he was on the hook for $1.2 million, Glick still signed on for more heat by buying (with Teamster loans) the Fremont and Marina casinos. Las Vegas newspapers called him "The Golden Boy of Gaming." The Outfit just called him, "Our boy."

While Spilotro ran wild in Las Vegas, even staffing a crew of burglars called the "Hole in the Wall Gang," the Chicago family (as well as those in Milwaukee, St. Louis, and Kansas City) stayed mum. At the same time, their casinos continued to skim enormous amounts of money.

Getting Lefty licensed wasn't as easy as getting Nick Civella paid. The Gaming Control Board rejected Rosenthal for the position of General Manager and then rejected him as the Poker room coordinator. After that, they rejected him as the assistant entertainment director too, but not until after he oversaw the construction of the new showroom that included several dozen tables not on the floor plans or the books so that tickets purchased for those seats could go directly into his pocket.

He also orchestrated several colorful ideas, such as the "scales skim." In the early '70s, the Stardust had 2000 slot machines. $1 slots were trendy, and because of the significant number of $1 tokens in use, coins were weighed in bags instead of being counted. Then, the scales in the "hard count" room where all the buckets of coins were taken each morning at 4:00 am were rigged.

Instead of each bag containing 500-dollar tokens, each bag had 510. And, to ensure the most could be made from the new scam, the hard count room at the Stardust was used for quarters and dollar tokens from the Fremont, Marina, and the Hacienda. It all looked like cost-cutting measures, using one facility, but it was all done to get more money to the Mob.

The scheme only had one problem. What to do with thousands of extra $1 tokens each night? Lefty Rosenthal to the rescue! He just had the casino's slot personnel buy them. Like the extra seats in the showroom, Lefty had two extra coin cabinets installed up on the casino floor that wasn't part of any financial accounting.

Then, the bags delivered from hard count were opened, and the $1 tokens were put into racks of 100. The employees never knew what was going on. A boss would sign in 100 bags totaling $50,000 and later sign out $50,000 in cash, which was taken to the soft count room. Another fellow came by and picked up the extra $1,000 in cash that had been produced.

Over several years, the dollar token skim amounted to over $5 million. Pretty good for a few extra dollars a bag and never suspecting slot attendants are doing all the work for you!

In 1975, Marty Buccieri, the Caesar's Palace pit boss, dropped by

Glick's office and reminded him what he had done for him. "Where's the love, Allan? Where's my end? I deserve at least a $30,000 finder's fee for getting you those huge loans from the Teamsters, right?"

Glick went to Rosenthal; Rosenthal went to Spilotro. Marty Buccieri was killed in Caesars' parking lot. Spilotro was suspected, but local officers couldn't come up with a motive. The crime was never solved.

Tamara Rand, a friend and business partner of Allen Glick's in San Diego who invested $2 million in his Vegas casinos, was hired as a consultant at the Hacienda. She asked what her 5% of the Hacienda would get her now that the property was profitable. Glick denied he owed her anything for her investment.

She was killed in her beautiful Mission Hills home in San Diego on November 9, 1975. The police were perplexed. They knew the wealthy 54-year-old was tied to Glick and organized crime from her $560,000 suit against him alleging fraud and misrepresentation. And the crime scene was brutal. She was shot first through the back, then once in the ear, and finally three times under the chin. Police found five .22 casings on the rug. Spilotro (and Glick) both professed their innocence. The crime was never solved.

LA's Frank "Bomp" Bompensiero swore he wasn't involved, "I just took Tony Spilotro and showed him her house. Bomp got clipped on February 10, 1977, shortly after it was confirmed he'd been sharing information with the FBI.

Meanwhile, the four casinos under Glick's name and the Outfit's control skimmed millions and millions of dollars while making very little for Glick. He was relegated to overseeing departments that were never intended to make a profit, like housekeeping.

On August 1, 1976, Jay Vandermark, who physically managed the skim removal at the Stardust, disappeared. He was wanted for questioning by the FBI after they raided the Stardust in May of 1976. He was seen in Phoenix with Spilotro's Arizona crew and was likely killed in

Mexico later.

In Phoenix, **Arizona Republic** reporter Don Bolles wrote a series of stories documenting Arizona Racing Commission member Kemper Marley and his ties to the racetrack concessionaire company, Emprise. They highlighted the federal investigation of Emprise, located in Buffalo, New York, and their association with prominent organized crime figures. The company was convicted and fined $10,000 in U.S. District Court in Los Angeles for its hidden ownership in the Frontier casino in Las Vegas.

On June 2, 1976, Bolles started his car in a Phoenix hotel parking lot, and a bomb exploded, mortally wounding him. He did mutter several words before lapsing into unconsciousness, including "Adamson, Emprise, Mafia." After his death, John Harvey Adamson pleaded guilty to second-degree murder.

Spilotro wasn't through with Jay Vandermark in 1977, but he found his son, Jeff, in a cheap Las Vegas apartment. Jeff swore he didn't know where "dad" was, so Tony beat him to death.

Back in Chicago, the skim killings continued. On July 24, 1977, Joey Auippa sent a squad to his alarm company offices in Park Ridge, where his associates secretly managed the affairs of getting the skim cash into new hands – washing it, if you will. Joey Doves had heard that Joe LaRose, John Viache, Malcolm Russell, and Don Marchbanks were skimming some of the skim – a stupid move with the records kept by the Vegas bosses. When confronted, one man nodded in understanding. All four men were executed.

It wasn't until June of 1978 that the Nevada Gaming Commission told Rosenthal that his duties, regardless of his job title, required him to obtain a gaming license. Chairman Harry Reid took offense to the verbally abusive Rosenthal during the hearing. Lefty was refused any license at the Stardust.

Harry Reid didn't make too many friends as head of the Gaming

Control Board. One evening his wife checked under the hood of their car because the engine had been running rough for several days. When Landra Reid popped the hood, she was amazed to find an unexploded bomb. Lady Luck!

Still, things weren't going so well for Spilotro by the close of the '70s. His income from the Stardust, Fremont, and Marina had dwindled to nearly nothing, and in 1979, an FBI raid on Gold Rush Ltd. at 228 W. Sahara Avenue produced $200,000 worth of stolen jewelry and gems. Spilotro, his brother Jon, Herbert Blitzstein, and Joseph Blasko, a recently fired Metro Police detective, were arrested.

As usual, the FBI had trouble with the court system. A judge later dismissed the racketeering case, stating that FBI agents had overstepped their authority.

As for the Las Vegas car bombings, Bugsy's old warning that "We only kill our own" seemed weak in the face of many other bombings, mostly with dynamite.

Chicago survived massive hits in the '80s to face a new future

Chapter Twenty-Four

Allen Glick Goes All In, Folds, and Still Wins

In 1979, the Nevada Gaming Control Board's audit group revealed that $7,200 in quarters were placed in the Stardust's auxiliary vault without being recorded. Further reviews at the Fremont showed that $3,500 was hidden from taxes by using rigged scales to send all coin bags used to fill slot machines short by several dollars. With thousands of slots, the skim was large.

The Audit division estimated that the diversion of cash out of the casino (just from slots) likely topped $12 million in the past year.

Vegas and the Chicago Outfit

Finally, the Nevada Gaming Control Board told Allen Glick that his time in the industry was over. Glick sold Argent Corp. to Trans-Sterling Corp., which was heralded in the newspapers as a final death blow to organized crime's control of the casinos in Nevada. For visitors to Las Vegas, the news was exciting but not earth-shattering. So, the Mob was being pushed out of Nevada's casinos, yeah, whatever.

Of course, it wasn't as easy as all that. Not every mob guy just up and left town. Plenty of Wise Guys were still roaming the casinos and looking to make money. Las Vegas has a worldwide appeal. It's a 24-hour town where you won't be denied anything if you have the money. It doesn't matter if you're a gambler who gets lucky, a poker player who has talent, or a Mob guy who loves the nightlife. Why leave?

The Outfit in Vegas joined the corruption party late, stayed up all night for years, bled casino properties dry, and just couldn't stay off the skim, the Mob's candy, long enough to do any actual renovations and prepare for the 1980s. A few mobsters, most notably Moe Dalitz, were able to transition from a life devoted to crime to one that gave up most of the hard stuff. After selling the Desert Inn to Howard Hughes, Dalitz owned the Sundance Casino downtown. Afterward, he devoted his time to playing golf and contributed money to local charities.

Dalitz teamed with friends Allard Roen, Mervyn Adelson, and Irwin Molasky in the 1970s to build the La Costa Resort in San Diego - financing the property with Teamsters' pension fund loans. In 1975, a *Penthouse* magazine's article, *The Hundred-Million-Dollar Resort with Criminal Clientele,* headlined La Costa in an honest, unflattering light. In response, the builders and owners sued for $522 million. The case dragged on for years, but a jury upheld Penthouse's right to print the article and found their reporting accurate. A judge threw the case out.

In 1985, a state appellate court reinstated the 10-year-old libel case by Dalitz, Roen, and the others. At that time, the two sides settled. No money changed hands, although the lawyers for both groups must have done quite well.

Records show that in '75, the FBI investigated twelve personal loans made by United States National Bank - which handled the cash for Rancho La Costa through the Teamsters Pension Fund – made out to Morris Barney Dalitz. According to the report, "loans were 'written off' at USNB as financial fees for Dalitz's influence to get the Central States Teamster Pension Fund to deposit millions of dollars with USNB at a time the bank badly needed the deposits."

The FBI report also states, "The Register of loans made by USNB for 1969 and 1970 was searched for loans obtained by the subject, and no loans in the name of Moe Dalitz as borrower were found." However, a list of loans written-off, issued to another named individual, is listed directly below this statement. Unfortunately, the name of the recipient is redacted (crossed out).

As for other owners and casino properties, Howard Hughes purchased most of the previously Mob-controlled casinos in the 1960s. Several of them were closed over the years. The ones that stayed open were sold to companies instead of individual owners. Hughes also purchased Harold's Club in Reno in 1970. He was impressed by the casino's ability to win so much money in Reno compared with much larger properties in Las Vegas, but that was also a Las Vegas illusion.

By the time Hughes got his hands on the casino, it was in decline – as was Reno, and finally, the truth came out. Many of the larger properties in Vegas had been reporting much lower earnings due to the heavy skim of the profits. And that continued even into the 1980s.

Sachs and Tobman had long careers in the gaming industry. Sachs worked his way up from a dealer position in illegal Chicago clubs to pit boss in Cuban casinos. He opened Royal Nevada in 1955 and held an interest in the Tropicana. In the 1970s, he became president of the Stardust.

Tobman's gaming career started in the 1950s when he was general manager of the Moulin Rouge, which had severe financial problems. He had worked for two other clubs before he became the general manager of the Aladdin, which went into bankruptcy. Sachs was president of the Stardust in 1974 when he promoted Tobman to vice president. Long story short, they were both working or managing properties that had skim money going out the door. Who would license them?

But when the Stardust owners were forced to sell their holdings to Trans-Sterling, Allan Sachs and Herb Tobman were licensed to take over the casino on the Strip and the Fremont casino in downtown Las Vegas based on their "sterling character." Perfect for the new owners of the Stardust and Fremont. Way to go, Nevada Gaming Control Board!

Five years later, in 1984, Sachs and Tobman were fined $3 million and had their licenses rescinded for again failing to take "appropriate action" to prevent skimming from the two casinos. Both men professed their innocence of taking any skim or working with the Mob. Of course, if that was true then they were both grossly incompetent.

Frank Rosenthal was still in Vegas in the 1980s, hanging around the casino periphery and fighting the Gaming Control Board over his exclusion from the Stardust. In 1982 he had dinner at Marie Callender's restaurant at 600 E. Sahara Avenue with three friends, Ruby Goldstein, Stanley Green, and Marty Kane. He walked to his car, got in, and turned the key. The resulting explosion demolished his car.

The blast was so strong that it blew the windows out of the back of the restaurant. Luckily for Lefty, a metal plate below the vehicle deflected much of the bomb's force. Local ATF Special Agent John Rice said the high explosive went up and back toward the restaurant.

Rosenthal refused to sign a crime report and was transported to Sunrise Hospital, the same hospital the Teamsters' money paid for with loans through Jimmy Hoffa. Lefty was released from the hospital several days later with nothing to show from the blast but some hearing damage and burns to his legs, left arm, and the left side of his face. He moved to Laguna Niguel, California, shortly after that. He was placed in Nevada's Black Book of undesirables in 1988, 12 years after the first Stardust investigation, and showing that the Gaming Control Board was on top of things.

Although the case was never solved, Milwaukee crime boss Frank Balistrieri was heard on FBI wiretaps saying he blamed Lefty for the Mob's problems in Las Vegas and "was going to get full satisfaction from him."

Balistrieri, sometimes called the "Mad Bomber," became Milwaukee's family boss in 1961. He was college educated but learned the business from his father-in-law, crime boss Joe Alioto. Balistrieri arranged the Teamster loans for Allen Glick and took the skim from the Stardust and Fremont for distribution to Kansas City, Chicago, Milwaukee, and Cleveland families.

In 1977, during an FBI sting operation, Special Agent Joseph Pistone worked undercover in New York under the name Donnie Brasco (yeah, there's a movie called that). Then he went to Milwaukee and set up a vending machine business to antagonize Balistrieri, trying to get him to make a move for which the FBI could prosecute him. When the men finally met, Balistrieri told him, "It's a good thing you came to see me and show me some respect. I was getting ready to kill you."

As for the Las Vegas skim, Balistrieri and Civella feuded over how much each family should get. They were so antagonistic that the only thing they could agree on was to go to arbitration presided by the Chicago Outfit. They both lost. Outfit leader Joseph Aiuppa and underboss John Cerone demanded that The Outfit receive an additional 25% of the cut Kansas City and Milwaukee were getting. Now that's funny.

Eventually, the FBI, Nevada Gaming Control, and a host of Department of Justice teams joined to try and finally convict known crime figures for stealing pre-tax casino income. The results were excellent.

There were many witnesses, including Joe Agosto and inside star Allen Glick, who said, "I never was a frontman; I was caught in a vise between people who had infiltrated the casino and the government's agents.

He testified that he was a terrified victim of the mob figures who influenced the Teamsters Union leadership to finance his purchase of the Stardust and Fremont and was forced to do the Outfit's bidding.

In 1983, Balistrieri and his two sons were indicted on charges of skimming at the Stardust and Fremont casinos. Balistrieri was convicted on five charges and won the grand prize of 13 years in prison. His sons were convicted of extorting a local vending machine route operator and received two-year prison sentences.

Also indicted were Chicago mob bosses Joey Aiuppa, 75, Jackie Cerone, 69, and Angelo LaPietra, 62.

Tony Spilotro was indicted along with Joseph Lombardo, 54, for trying to bribe a U.S. senator. Spilotro was also the subject of a series of FBI raids that targeted homes, offices, businesses, and even cars owned by him, Glick, Rosenthal, and brothers Michael and John.

The raids turned up police scanners, loan shark details, confidential police records about the Chicago family in Las Vegas, and $200,000 in cash – wrapped in bright blue Dunes casino wrappers.

Others indicted were Milton Rockman, 75, connected to Cleveland; Carl DeLuna, 55, number two Kansas City boss; Carl Civella, 72, the big man; Peter Tamburello, 51, and Carl Thomas, 51, a former Las Vegas casino operator. All did jail time.

Tony Spilotro wasn't so lucky; he never made it to prison. Tony and his brother Michael left for a meeting on June 14, 1986, two days before the second "Hole in the Wall Gang" burglary and fencing trial in Las Vegas.

They were never seen alive again, but their battered bodies were found buried in an Indiana cornfield. Sand found in their lungs during an autopsy indicated they were buried alive. Tony Spilotro was 48 years old at the time of his death. He wasn't responsible for all of his associates' deaths, but the list of Vegas hits grew exponentially in the years he was in town.

Ironically, Spilotro had a hand (kind of) in the September 14, 1986, killing of Chicago mob enforcer Giovanni Fecoratta who got whacked for screwing up the Spilotro brother's "final resting place." Tony and Michael's graves were quickly discovered because his crew got disoriented and thought they were under attack – leaving the graves easy to find. Oops.

One year later, Steve Wynn reinvented the Las Vegas Strip. He made millions with his Golden Nugget Casinos and envisioned what would come. By then, he had refurbished the downtown Las Vegas facility and built the Atlantic City Golden Nugget Hotel & Casino. The New Jersey resort was a 1980 partnership of Golden Nugget Companies and Michael R. Milken worth $140 million. Milken was a wheeler-dealer and junk-bond king. His activities attracted the attention of the SEC, but not before he was able to raise $630 million to fund the building of Wynn's Mirage.

The Mirage was considered extremely high-risk because Las Vegas was in a gaming slump characterized by older properties, smaller conventions, and a drop in gaming revenues. The new resort featured a South Sea theme and an erupting volcano leading to the main entrance. The property's high cost and emphasis on luxury were cited as reasons the property would fail. Steve Wynn, of course, had the last laugh, as the property was enormously profitable.

Vegas and the Chicago Outfit

With the success of the Mirage, Wynn continued to expand on the Strip with Treasure Island and the Bellagio. Milken also helped obtain financing for Harrah's Entertainment, Mandalay Resorts, MGM, and Park Place. He fell from grace in 1989 when indicted for racketeering and securities fraud. He eventually pleaded guilty to securities and reporting violations and was sentenced to ten years in prison.

He was also fined $600 million (probably close to what the Mob skimmed in 40 years) and permanently barred from the securities industry. His sentence was then reduced to just two years for good behavior and cooperating with testimony against his former colleagues. The charges and prison term didn't stop his income, and currently, Mr. Milken is worth approximately $2.5 billion.

I've no idea who the real crooks and good guys are anymore.

In the 1980s, the Nevada Gaming Control Board changed its internal control policies for casinos. Minimum Internal Control procedures were implemented, and new audit directives emerged. Today, the Audit Division has a professional staff of 89 employees and is run like a CPA firm.

According to the NGCB, "The Audit Division is primarily responsible for auditing Group 1 casino throughout the state (i.e., those casinos with annual gaming revenue of approximately $5.87 million or more). There are approximately 148 such casinos, and the audit cycle is about 2.3 years."

Also, audit personnel can request paperwork, view actual procedures of departments like the cage's "soft count," where the cash is counted, and review transaction logs. Skimming profits, as was often the norm in the days leading up to the 1980s, certainly wouldn't be an easy task today. Beyond the tax benefits to the state of the Board's new procedures, keeping the money visible and the owners accountable also tends to increase reinvestment in the state's gaming establishments.

The Mob has been evicted from Las Vegas, but the legends remain for their crimes, tenacity, and foresight.

On September 27, 2007, a federal grand jury in Chicago found three mobsters, Frank Calabrese, Sr., Joseph Lombardo, and James Marcello, guilty of killing the Spilotro brothers. Las Vegas didn't notice.

Strangely enough, Allen Glick outlived everyone. He fared better than any Outfit boss, plundering a $70 million pre-tax profit from his Las Vegas casinos.

Later, he owned casinos in Costa Rica and a floating entertainment center in Cebu, Mactan, Philippines, called the Philippine Dream. Every indication is that he lived long enough to enjoy good and bad dreams. He passed away in San Diego at age 79 on August 9, 2021.

The Skim Stops

For many organized crime families, the successful FBI and Nevada Gaming Control Board investigations and federal trials for hidden interest and skim of profits of the 1970s were a crushing blow. Not just because of the loss of highly lucrative skim cash but because their top echelon of bosses was decimated by killings and prison sentences.

How organized crime fared afterward is up to interpretation. Although avoiding most of the Las Vegas allegations, New Orleans boss Carlos Marcello ruled from 1947 to 1983 and was imprisoned from 1983–1991. He died in 1993.

Kansas City: Nicholas Civella ruled from 1953 until 1983. He was convicted in 1977 and then in 1980. He died in 1983.

Milwaukee: Family boss Frank Balistrieri was imprisoned from 1967 until 1971 and from 1983 through 1991. He died in 1993. His sons Joseph and Peter managed things when he was in prison.

Detroit: The Partnership remained much as they were, with Joseph Zerilli managing the family business from 1936 until 1977. His son

Vegas and the Chicago Outfit

Anthony "Tony Z" Zerilli was acting boss from 1970 to 1974 when he was imprisoned.

Buffalo: The Magaddino crime family headed by Stefano "The Undertaker" Magaddino from 1922 through 1974 came through the Las Vegas skim years completely unscathed. Although they never held a significant position in a Nevada casino, there was always some juice flowing to upstate New York and some cocaine flowing from their drug ring in Las Vegas to Niagara Falls.

New York: Downstate, the Five Families, held sway over Las Vegas, funding and operating casinos starting with Meyer Lansky's advice, Bugsy Siegel's innovations, and Gus Greenbaum and Davie Berman's management. Berman was from Minneapolis, but the family there didn't benefit from Las Vegas operations after the 1940s.

Charles "Lucky" Luciano ran what many considered the Mob from 1931 until 1946. He had the brains and the power. Frank "The Prime Minster" Costello was the acting boss from 1937 through 1946 and became the official boss after Luciano's deportation until 1957, when he resigned after the Genovese – Gigante assassination attempt.

Vito "Don Vito" Genovese ran the family from 1957 until 1969, when he died in prison. The family's hold in Vegas changed dramatically after the Bugsy Siegel hit, and although skim flowed to Meyer Lansky for distribution to New York and Florida, dynamics were different.

Instead of investing in new casinos or finding fronts for old ones, New York took a comfortable back seat role— taking skim like a patent holder drawing monthly royalties.

In Cleveland, the money Moe Dalitz and his partners made transformed Wilbur Clark's stalled Desert Inn casino into one of the most popular, skimmable Las Vegas gold mines. Dalitz made a break from Ohio and moved to Vegas in 1947.

Taking the reins in town was John T. Scalise, who believed in earning money and keeping most of it instead of spending it trying to be ostentatious or fierce. It worked for decades as he ran his family from 1945 until 1976.

He kept his ties with Dalitz, added Meyer Lansky and Tony Accardo, and worked amicably with the Genovese crime family of New York. Scalise watched over a slow burn of expansion to St. Louis, Florida, and California.

Dalitz provided monthly skim from the Desert Inn with Scalish, and the Cleveland group also held a piece of the Stardust casino's skim that arrived bi-weekly.

When Scalish died during open-heart surgery in '76, James T. Licavoli moved into the top-man position. He was a colorful crime wave all to himself.

Born in St. Louis, he learned early to hustle pool, sell bathtub gin, and burglarize groceries. After a shootout with the police, Licavoli was left for dead in a pool of blood below his waist. "It's a scratch," he said. The gunshot put him in the hospital for ten days, but he pulled through and was only charged with carrying a concealed weapon. Later, those charges were dropped.

Afterward, Licavoli fled to Chicago, where he tried to sell bootleg liquor in Outfit territory and was taken on what was planned as a one-way ride. He got lucky; two partners were killed, but he escaped to Detroit, where he and his cousins helped tear down the Purple Gang. But instead of moving up in the Detroit Partnership, Licavoli was convicted of bootlegging and sent to Leavenworth prison.

While he served time, his cousins moved to Toledo, where he joined them after a successful parole hearing.

A short time later, his cousin's gang was suspected of the murder of Leo Lips" Moceri. James was a mover and a shaker, going into hiding in Pittsburg this time before moving to Cleveland.

In Ohio, he worked with Jimmy Fratianno and Tony "Dope" Delsanter robbing northeast Ohio gambling clubs and squeezing their way into illegal gambling. Licavoli disposed of Jim "Mancene" Mancini and slot machine king Nate Weisenberg to keep their spot.

After Scalish died, Licavoli took his spot. In 1977, his guys bombed John Nardi in his car and did the same with Danny Greene, ending the Cleveland Mob Wars.

In a brazen move, the Cleveland syndicate bribed Geraldine Rabinowitz, a clerk at the FBI's Cleveland branch. She gave them intel on organized crime investigations and the names of government informants.

When word of the successful breach of FBI files hit the street, Licavoli talked to Jimmy Frattiano and said, "Jimmy, sometimes, you know, I think this fucking outfit of ours is like the old Communist party in this country. It's getting so that there's more fucking spies in it than members."

Strangely enough, Ray Ferritto was charged with killing Danny Greene, a secret FBI informant. Licavoli put an immediate contract on Ferritto's life to silence him, and the opposite happened. He became a cooperating witness in a 1978 trial where Licavoli and 18 other Cleveland crime family members were indicted.

Most of those indicted were convicted. Licavoli got 17 years and died during his prison term.

Fratianno was also indicted, but he turned sides in 1977, making his lifetime handle of "The Weasel" apropos. He appeared regularly as a government witness in Mob cases and entered the Witness Protection system before working with Ovid Demaris on *The Last Mafioso*.

As for the FBI clerk, she and her husband Jeffrey pleaded guilty to accepting $15,900 in bribes for confidential information that they turned over to Kenneth Ciarcia. They got five-year prison sentences.

New England: The crime family thrived with unique organizations, one faction in Providence, Rhode Island, and the other in Boston, Massachusetts. From 1954 to 1984, when he passed away, Raymond L.S. Patriarca, Sr. ran the show, except for five years, he was in prison for killing Providence bookmaker Willie Marfeo.

Patriarca formed lasting relationships with the New York-based Genovese and Colombo crime families. Still, he didn't allow other Mob groups to operate in New England. His low profile and disdain for narcotics deals kept the law at bay.

Although the family never financed a Nevada casino or sent frontmen, slick as silk Joe Sullivan got them a chunk of the Dunes casino with help from Meyer Lansky.

Later, through Lansky and the Outfit, they scored points in other casinos but took no heat in the '70s since their skim deals had ended by then.

Chicago: And finally, the Outfit in Chicago took the heaviest hit of all crime families in the 1970s and '80s. Over the years, Tony Accardo, Sam Giancana, and Joey "Doves" Aiuppa had mountains of cash arriving daily from the swankiest casinos in Nevada. They started in the 1940s in Reno at the Bank Club. In Vegas, they profited at the Golden Nugget, Las Vegas Club, El Cortez, Turf Club, El Rancho, Flamingo, Boulder Club, Frontier, Stardust, Riviera, Caesars Palace, Fremont, Marina, and the Hacienda.

They also got a bite out of the Aladdin, the Sands, and the Desert Inn. And for decades, the big bosses were swimming in cash. So much cash that competitors went missing or were openly murdered. Chicago held an image in other countries (and places in the US, too) that never changed from the days of Al Capone, with gang wars in the streets and

Vegas and the Chicago Outfit

mobsters firing Tommy guns.

If you've never heard of a Tommy Gun, it's another way of saying Thompson submachine gun, the survival weapon of choice for marauding Prohibition killers. It's also known as the "Chicago Typewriter."

When the Outfit lost their Vegas skim, everyone suffered, from street soldiers to their capos to the bosses. There wasn't enough cash to go around. A mob of workers, safe houses, cars, delivery trucks, lawyers, financial analysts, real estate, and infrastructure costs a ton of cash.

With the flood of cash dammed up, Chicago lost the power to fund its valuable assets: judges, politicians, and police protection. They all slowly disappeared, especially after a series of local FBI stings.

First came Operation Safebet. In 1984, 300 FBI and IRS agents, with the cooperation of Cook County State's Attorney investigators, executed 14 search warrants targeting political corruption and the control of prostitution operations by organized crime. More than 75 defendants were indicted and convicted.

Next came Operation Incubator in 1986, which involved four aldermen, a deputy water commissioner, a former mayoral aide, and a Cook County clerk, followed by the arrest of 46 traders and brokers of the Chicago Mercantile Exchange.

Finally, in 1989, Operation GAMBAT targeted corrupt businesspeople and politicians. The sweep snared two clerks, an alderman, a judge, and a state senator. Chicago was turning itself inside out with the FBI doing the dirty work.

The actual end came with the end of Las Vegas skim, but Tony Accardo, the Outfit boss and advisor for nearly forty years, saw it all. The ups and downs, the flood of cash, and the endless river of bloodshed.

He preached moderation in everything while keeping a low profile and showing empathy for people in public view. In private, empathy was for suckers. So was the moderation.

As mentioned before, his estate had twenty-one rooms, an indoor pool, and a bowling alley. And according to FBI S.A. Bill Roemer, it had a black onyx bathtub that cost $10,000 to install in the fifties. All the baths had gold inlaid fixtures. But that was just to impress the people he knew and trusted.

Accardo died in 1992 after living 86 years of murder and mayhem but spending just a day in jail. He lived and died at the right time and according to his rules.

Las Vegas survived 40 years of Outfit skim and grew to new heights

Bibliography

Interviews for this work were done over many years by the author. Those contributing important information include:

Karl Berge, Ty Cobb, Sammy Davis, Jr., Jim Dotson, "Pick" Hobson, Johnny Moss, Warren Nelson, Sil Petricciani, Bill Pettite, Fran Pettite, Robert Ring, Harold Smith, Sr, Richard Taylor, and Anthony Manzo.

In addition, nearly 1950 FBI documents, including notes from Special Agents released through the Freedom of Information Act, were used to expand or corroborate details in this book.

Articles

Black, Edwin. The Plot to Kill JFK in Chicago. Chicago, Illinois Chicago Independent November 1975

Chamblin, Tony. Jimmy the Greek. Niagara Falls, New York Gambling Quarterly Spring 1974

Derr, Jeanine. The Biggest Show on Earth: The Kefauver Crime Committee Hearings." Maryland Historian 17 (Fall/Winter 1986): 19-37.

Kerr, Robert. The Building of a Legend. Carson City, NV Nevada Magazine May/June 1985

Evans, Lance W. Rollin' With the River. Carson City, NV Nevada Magazine May/June 1991

Toll, David W. The House That Barney Built. Carson City, NV Nevada Magazine March/April 1981

Zauner, Phyllis King Karl. Carson City, NV Nevada Magazine December 1984

Richmond, Dean Reno's Brightest Corner. Reno, NV Gaming Collectors Quarterly 1994

Books

Berman, Susan. Easy Street. New York, NY The Dial Press 1981

ISBN:0-384-27185-9

Demaris, Ovid and Reid, Ed. The Green Felt Jungle. New York. Trident Press 1963

Demaris, Ovid. The Last Mafioso. New York, NY 1981

Dietrich, Noah and Thomas, Bob. Howard. The Amazing Mr. Hughes. Greenwich, CT. Fawcett 1972

Drosnin, Michael. Citizen Hughes. New York, NY Hold, Rinehart, and Winston. 1985 ISBN: 0-030041846-1

Dixon, Mead and Adams, Ken and King, R. T. Playing the cards that are dealt. Reno, NV University of Nevada Oral History Program 1992 ISBN: 1-56475-365-4

Elgas, Thomas C. Nevada Official Bicentennial Book. Las Vegas, NV Nevada Publications 1976

Fey, Marshall. Slot Machines. Las Vegas, NV Nevada Publications 1983 ISBN: 0913814-53-9

Garrison, Omar V. Howard Hughes in Las Vegas New York, NY Lyle Stuart, Inc. 1970

Giancana, Sam, and Chuck. Double Cross New York, NY Warner Books, Inc. 1992

Griffin, Dennis N. The Battle for Las Vegas Las Vegas, NV Huntington Press 2006

Jenkins, Don. Johnny Moss-poker's Finest Champion of Champions. Las Vegas, NV 1981

Kelley, Kitty. His Way. New York Bantam Books 1986 ISBN: 0-553-26515-6

Lacey, Robert. Little Man-Meyer Lansky And The Gangster Life. New York, NY Little Brown and Company 1991 ISBN: 0-316-51163-3

Laxalt, Robert. Nevada: a Bicentennial history. New York, NY W. W. Norton & Company, Inc. 1977 ISBN: 0-393005628-7

Mandel, Leon. William Fisk Harrah. Garden City, NY 1981 Doubleday & Company, Inc. ISBN: 0-385-15513-1

Moehring, Eugene P.   Resort City in the Sunbelt: Las Vegas.   Reno, NV   University of Nevada Press   ISBN: 0-87417-147-4

Moore, William Howard. The Kefauver Committee and the Politics of Crime, 1950-1952. Columbia, MO: University of Missouri Press, 1974.

Nelson, Warren with Adams, Ken, and King, R. T. plus Nelson, Gail K. Always Bet on the Butcher.   Reno, NV   University of Nevada Oral History Program   1994   ISBN: 1-56475-368-9

Smith, Harold S., Sr. with Noble, John Wesley.   I Want to Quit Winners. New York Prentice-Hall, Inc. 1961

Paher, Stanley W.   Las Vegas.   Las Vegas, NV   Nevada Publications 1971

Scott, Edward B.   The Saga of Lake Tahoe, Part II.   Crystal Bay, NV Sierra-Tahoe Publishing Co.   1973

Van Tassel, Bethel Holmes.   Wood Chips to Game Chips: Casinos and People at North Lake Tahoe.   1985

Wilson, Theodore. "The Kefauver Committee on Organized Crime, 1950-1951," in Bruns, Roger, David Hostetter, and Raymond Smock, eds. Congress Investigates A Critical and Documentary History. New York: Facts on File, 2011.

Licenses and dating from Harvey J. Fuller's Index of Nevada Gaming Establishments Harvey's Wagon Wheel, Inc. 1991

Thanks for reading *Vegas and the Chicago Outfit*. You might also like *Vegas and the Mob* or our Nevada Gaming History Website.

Printed in Great Britain
by Amazon

15490393R00159